WHAT PEOPLE ARE SAYING ABOUT JOANIE AND CAROL

"I have been fortunate enough to know Joanie and Carol and witness firsthand the love and devotion that they had for each other during Carol's earthly life. Their relationship makes me think of a famous passage from St. Paul's letter to the church in Galatia: '. . . the fruit of the Spirit is love, joy, peace, patience, kindness, generosity, faithfulness, gentleness, and self-control. There is no law against such things.' " (Chapter 5, verses 22-23)

— The Rev. Bernie Lindley, Vicar
St. Timothy's Episcopal Church, Brookings, Oregon

"I first met Carol and Joanie in 1993 . . . when I was 26 years old . . . I was immediately inspired by not only their sense of adventure, but that they were leading the adventurous life that so many of us just speak of. Every step of their adventures was wrapped in joy!

Individually they are powerful. Carol, inquisitive and caring, Joanie, curious and effervescent. Together they were continually unstoppable in their quest of adventure and their seeking of an understanding of the world at large and the people they met. A literal force of caring and curiosity!

Now, almost 30 years later, I recognize Carol and Joanie as not only dear friends, but my personal life heroes. Spiritually centered, open minded, with an unmatched capacity in their hearts for love. Their ability to deeply listen and care . . . for each other, for friends and family, and everyone they meet, is remarkable.

I have been so lucky to have them as role models in my life . . . and I am so excited that Joanie, guided by Carol, is able to share this in her writings. Her stories are uplifting and will provide a focus of joy . . . and adventure!"

— Daniel Perry Walkup, Founder
BookStayHop, Vacation Reservation Management

"Having had the privilege and pleasure of experiencing this relationship firsthand, I think everyone should read this book. Joanie and Carol's example of deep love and commitment will make you laugh, cry and inspire you to be a better person. How these two could get into (and out of) their life situations is unexplainable . . . unless you believe in a Higher Power who, having his or her hands full with these two, chuckled and just made the best of it."

— Peter and Kathleen Spratt

"*Nun Better: An AMAZING Love Story* is a heartwarming love story about trailblazing and allowing love to prevail against all odds. The stories shared in this book helped me overcome an internal conflict between my sexual orientation and faith—a source of great stress and personal insecurity in the past. The bravery and courage these two demonstrated through their love and commitments to each other is astounding. This is a remarkable story about leaping over societal, religious, and conventional hurdles, all in the name of love."

— Dalton Bradbury

"God has given us many beautiful things to enjoy in this life, but I feel the most beautiful of all is the love shared between two people. It was a blessing to be a friend of Carol and Joanie and feel the warmth of their love for each other."

— Doris W.

"Sometimes a friend is a gift in a surprise package. Carol and I were partnered together in developing an education/life skills program for welfare women. Instant partners, immediate friends. The circle began widening with my friend Dottie signing on to teach and Carol's partner Joanie adding smiles and sunshine... and kept growing to this day."

— Peggy Goergan

"Two people ~~ Carol & Joanie ~~ passing thru this lifetime
always smiling ~~ always joyful ~~ always full of adventure."
My friends. Love & Light.

— Fran

"When people used to ask me about Carol and Joanie—I would tell them, 'Carol and Joanie are the holiest people I know.' Your love for each other was very visible, and could be felt. It was constant, unwavering, unconditional and full of joy. Even when some part of life was causing struggles, you two always had the foundation of Christ in your life—and His unending love and joy."

— Terri Stewart

"When we think of the joyful happiness that Joanie and Carol have shared, we see their outstanding courage and their unwavering love for each other and for God."

With love and peace,
— Tom and Kathleen Lindenmeyer

"My husband and I have known Joanie and Carol for many years now. It was always wonderful to be around two people who showed so much joy and commitment not just to each other, but to family, friends and our entire community.

As ill as Carol was at the end, whenever I would go to visit, she would say, "Come and sit by me. Tell me a joke or funny story." She would laugh in delight, and for that brief period of time, she was well and happy, and so was I. She had those quiet gifts.

Joanie's gifts are compassion and honesty and an exuberant personality. Salt and pepper. Perfect seasoning. Friends who add flavor to your life."

— Pat Piper

"Carol's smile and Joanie's warm kindness. You are the most beneficent humans I have ever met in my lifetime. Your light and love guided me through rough waters at times. Friends forever."

Love, Rosemary

"Beginning in the novitiate, Carol was remarkably optimistic and upbeat. She couldn't be torn down. She was very close to God and trusted life and goodness, and she could identify beauty. She was JOYFUL. Thank you."

— Sister Frances Baker
The Congregation of the Sisters of St. Joseph of Carondelet

"Joanie and Carol were two very courageous women who loved each other deeply and trusted that together they could do anything. Watching these two courageous women holding hands while gliding through life's challenges was truly an inspiration to me.

My sister, my friend, my inspiration to live life fully. Thank you, Joanie, for your beautiful example of loving when it wasn't so easy."

— Gail Baker

"Joanie and Carol are the perfect example of love. Their care and concern for each other was constant and unselfish. Their love was undaunted by obstacles society put in their way. Their love extended not just to themselves, but to all they met on their path through life."

— Ronnie

"My friendship with Joanie has been filled with love, fun and laughter and I am grateful every day for her. Just like our friendship, I hope you find love, fun and laughter in this book. You'll be grateful that you read it."

— Jenny Leffler

"In December of 1986, Joanie and Carol fed me and healed me with compassion and a listening ear after my devastating divorce. As the years went on, it was just Joanie and Carol, not Joanie and her partner Carol. I'd call and ask for prayer and vice versa."

— Ruthie Murray

"When I think of Carol and Joanie, I think of how kind they always are. I think about how they spread love to everyone."

— Sue Griffin

"This book is the story of a brave adventure that became forty years of a quiet love story. Believe it!"

— Cousin Theodera Norton

You are a WINNER!

Nun Better...

Enjoy the book!! :)

Love, Joanie

An Amazing Love Story

JOANIE LINDENMEYER

With Carol Tierheimer

NUN BETTER: An Amazing Love Story

For information about this title or to order other books and/or electronic media, contact the publisher:

Atkins & Greenspan Publishing

TwoSistersWriting.com

18530 Mack Avenue, Suite 166

Grosse Pointe Farms, MI 48236

ISBN 978-1-956879-31-5 (Hardcover)

ISBN 978-1-956879-32-2 (Paperback)

ISBN 978-1-956879-33-9 (eBook)

Printed in the United States of America

All the stories in this work are true.

Cover and interior design: Illumination Graphics - cover illustration Tara Thelen, illustrator and Gail Baker.

Cami Schipke, age 7, painted the artwork on the back cover.

Author photos: The Lindenmeyer and Tierheimer Family Collections.

This Book is Dedicated to:

CAROL TIERHEIMER, THE LOVE OF MY LIFE.

AND TO GOD, WHO MAKES ALL THINGS POSSIBLE.

Contents

Acknowledgments

I wish to thank, from the top of my heart, the following people who made this book happen. Because of each of you, *Nun Better: An AMAZING Love Story* will be shared with the world. Each one of you are so very dear to me and I thank God for you everyday.

Gail Baker: creator and co-artist of the front cover and encourager.
Leah Bridgeman: co-editor.
Becca Bustamante: video production and social media organizer.
Tim Guzik: creator of title. *Nun Better.*
Carolyn House: typist and office file organizer.
Margaret Kish: reader, confidant and encourager.
Deborah Perdue: book designer and Tara Thelen: illustrator.
Megan Pucillo Slayton: Carol's biography writer and encourager.
Sally Roy: co-editor, organizer, computer guru and confidant.
Cami Schipke, age 7: back cover artist and her parents, Brad and Tina Schipke.
Terri Stewart: editor, picture organizer, reader and encourager.
Peter Spratt: attorney advisor.
Leslie Stokes: rose artist and photographer.
Daniel Perry Walkup: introducer to my publishers and encourager.
Ashley and Jared Wells: computer help.

Everyone who wrote a personal quote or an endorsement, and who encouraged, uplifted, talked, texted, and let me cry and laugh.
Everyone who prayed and sent happy thoughts!

Everyone who clarified stories, time and events!
You know who you are!

Extra special, special thanks, praise and yahoos to my new friends, phenomenal book coaches who listened, guided, always told me positive things, encouraged, laughed and cried with me many times. They were my grief counselors and my editors all in one. They are the best of the best with hearts pure and humble. They are smart, wise, fun and big visionaries. They are Two Sisters Writing and Publishing: Elizabeth Ann Atkins and Catherine Greenspan.

Most of all, I thank "the loves of my life": Carol Tierheimer and Jesus, co-authors and inspirers. Together we did it!

Thank you to each and every one of you!
I love you!
Hugs and kisses,
Joanie

Introduction

Welcome to our life in the form of written word, artwork and pictures as I remember it. I'm Joanie, a former Catholic sister who fell in love with a former Catholic nun, and, despite the world's and the church's disapproval of gay marriage, shared a lifetime of love with Carol.

Very important: sisters are apostolic, meaning they work with people. Nuns are cloistered, secluded and prayerful, and I will use the two **interchangeably** throughout the book.

Jesus and Carol were with me on this writing journey. Though Carol is in heaven now, her presence and spirit are still all around. I wrote this book with Carol in my heart to share our amazing 40-year story of love and how God worked in and through us. We called our Higher Power "God," "Jesus," and the "Holy Spirit." You may have another name for yours.

Our story shows how we blazed a trail for life and love in a world that showed us no path. Ours was a slow process over years of internal discovery within a harsh world where we were not free to love openly and could, in fact, have risked our safety, lives and careers by revealing our true relationship. Still, we carried on in a spirit of love and joy, guided by our love for God and Jesus, and created a beautiful life during four decades together.

Thank you for wanting to read and hear about us: our joys and struggles, challenges, truths, doubts, fears, secrets, never-ending hopes and dreams, humongous love for humankind, and our unwavering commitments of love to God and with each other.

When Carol and I started writing down our stories, our intention was to bring alive how we came closer to God and Jesus through our funny, serious, miraculous and amazing stories. Join us on our adventures and be ready to laugh and cry. Our honesty, love and faith will come alive and be contagious.

We hoped that by sharing our lives, we could give hope and courage to anyone seeking their truth. May you find faith, fortitude and inspiration to live every day to the max, out loud and in color, as we did!

My innermost thoughts will be shared with you *in italics* in our story. In a few instances, I have changed some people's names to protect their privacy.

We invite you to add your own creative pizzazz to turn *Nun Better: An AMAZING Love Story* into a colorful work of art, a coloring book. How fun is that? Carol and I have always loved flowers, rainbows and colors. Try using bright highlighters, crayons, pencils or pens to enhance each chapter's floribunda rose(s). A surprise awaits you at the final chapter. Oh, it's OK to color outside the lines! There are no mistakes: you are creating art!

Carol and I began every day together by exclaiming, "It's a brand new day" and "Never been lived before!" Each day ended with "Jesus hold you" and "God bless you."

Enjoy the read!
Love and hugs,
Joanie, Carol and Jesus

CHAPTER 1
In Love and in the Convent

Our Magnificent Love Story Celebrates Jesus at Its Core

Our love was forbidden by society, the Church and the vow of chastity required of Catholic nuns.

Yet our electrifying attraction was undeniable and soul-deep, and it pulsed through my 24-year-old mind and body when, by the grace of God, I was assigned to minister under Sister Carol at St. Stanislaus Parish in Lewiston, Idaho.

Carol Tierheimer was a nun, 15 years my senior, and I was a "novice" in training to become one, when I first looked into her joyous green eyes and felt the overwhelming love and peace of her spirit.

Carol was the Parish Sister, and she did everything, to put it bluntly, except say Mass. Then and even now, the Catholic Church prides itself on the male-only role of priesthood to celebrate Mass and consecrate the body and blood of Jesus in the form of Communion.

The magic moment of our meeting happened in 1983, a time when people could be beaten and killed for being gay; today's celebratory acceptance of LGBTQ freedoms, including same-sex marriage, were decades into the future. Plus, being in a convent required celibacy. We were the Brides of Christ, and loved Jesus so intensely, we were supposed to be nonsexual.

So I cherished, questioned and wondered about my secret love for Sister Carol inside my fluttering heart. My spirit soared with anticipation to see her every day as we engaged in our ministries and activities for the congregation of the Sisters of St. Joseph of Carondelet. Our intense and overwhelming, 24/7 commitments were rewarded by fun, inexpensive activities that included the outdoors, and for me, sports.

One day, after Carol introduced me to a star softball player from a local university, I played catch for an hour. After that, my shoulder was so excruciatingly painful, I was crying.

Seeking comfort and relief, I went to Carol's bedroom in the huge old brick, historical two-story house that had been converted into a convent where we lived with about 14 other sisters.

I did my typical "doorknock beat," which is the rhythm announcing Joanie's arrival to this day: "*Dunt-da-da-dunt-dunt, dunt-da!*"

"Come in," Sister Carol said.

"Carol," I cried, stepping into her room and closing the door. "Thanks for arranging for me to play softball catch, but do you have any ice packs and Icy Hot? I've really overdone it. Would you please rub me, Carol?"

"Yes, yes, yes, let me help you."

As a former college volleyball player who had infinite energy and award-winning skills, I laughed and said, "I'm getting old."

She laughed and giggled from her gut. "Sit here, Joanie."

Holding my shoulder, I plopped onto her twin bed, which was covered with a cushy quilt whose block design offered a kaleidoscope of blue and white polka dots, green plaid, turquoise flower petals, and pink and purple gingham all secured with little nobs of thread.

The Broadway musical *Joseph and The Technicolor Dreamcoat* theme song played in my head, as the vibrant pattern mirrored the joy in my heart because I was alone with Sister Carol. My romantic hormones were like jumping beans inside me, but I sat still.

I glanced up at the homemade burlap banner on her wall that said, "If love is meant to be, let it go and it will come back to you," amongst fluttering pink, blue and yellow butterflies. Gratitude overwhelmed me that the serendipitous circumstances of our lives had brought us together, here and now.

Then the magic moment happened—our first touch.

Carol's warm, soft, strong hands massaged and caressed my shoulder. Tension left me, and oh, the comfort and the pain relief was heavenly, as if she were touching and soothing the inside of my soul.

Warm and happy, I felt dazed by her compassion and unconditional love.

She enjoyed it as well, because she guided me in such a tender way that I collapsed onto her chest and laid my head on her heart. She cuddled me close, her large squishy breasts sending tickles all over my body. *Lub-dub, lub-dub,* our hearts were beating with the same rhythm!

Two hearts beating one beat.

This is EXTRAORDINARY!

This is INTIMATE!

This is REAL LOVE!

We just sat there. She rubbed me as a few tears streamed down my face. She wiped them with her gentle fingers and I cried even more. We laughed and held each other for a good while.

Time disappeared and life had changed.

Meeting Carol Leads to Commitment!

Sister Carol was my supervisor, leader, mentor and designated person alongside whom I'd minister during my three-month mission experience. This was during my first year of the novitiate and my second year of religious training that had begun at St. Anastasia convent in Los Angeles.

I arrived in Idaho as Sister Joanie, "the novice," bursting at the seams with energy and spunk to take on the world! I was excited to live in a real convent, with working women who were integrating their ministry with sisterhood life. I was far away from the structure of my novitiate, relishing the freedom to be me: a young woman, a Sister of St. Joseph.

It was "game on!"

Before joining the convent, I had been a passionate Physical Education teacher and athletic coach for a year at my alma mater, San Diego High School, after earning my California Teaching Credential and my Bachelor of Arts degree from San Diego State University.

Then and now, I was ready to give it my all and embrace each day as a playoff or championship game. How exciting to join a winning team with the Sisters of St. Joseph of Carondelet—whom I describe as the CSJs, sisters or nuns. I loved getting to know my teammates, the sisters. These were the real women I had heard stories about back in the novitiate in Los Angeles. They were bigger in life and I was on their turf.

The convent was one of three Catholic churches that supported the 27,000 residents of Lewiston, where cottonwood trees lined the streets of the small town set amongst rivers and wheat fields known as the prairies.

Awed and eager, I moved into the convent, which had once housed nurses who trained and worked at the hospital across the street. I was the youngest woman, followed by Sisters Carol and Frances who were 39, and the others over 60. Wow! These extremes could be bad, ugly or precious.

We shared Evening and Morning Prayers in our chapel or living room. Days began promptly at 7 a.m., followed by daily parish Mass at 8 a.m. A few sisters would rotate and lead the prayer times. Carol included progressive music such as Amy Grant, Sandi Patti, Praise Strings and Dan Schutte, along with poetry to enhance a scripture theme. It was fun, reflective and received well. I really liked her way of praying!

And I so appreciated her encouragement to build my confidence to lead prayer with the sisters:

"Just lead us closer to Jesus in your way."

"OK, I will."

Our daily work schedule began after Mass, followed by evening prayers around 5:30, dinner at 6 p.m., nighttime meetings and functions, then an hour of community time to watch the news, do puzzles, or have individual prayer time. We hit the sack around 10 p.m.

The good news was that we had a cook Monday through Friday for breakfast, lunch and dinner. I really liked that. I ate like a horse, loading my plate not just once, but twice because I burned a lot of calories and was never shy about digging in. I normally ate fast, but realized I needed to try to learn to slow down to build relationships with the elders.

Ask Questions to Get to Know Someone

The sisters asked me a lot of questions and it was actually fun.

"Sister Joanie, where did you grow up?"

"What Catholic school did you go to, Sister Joanie?"

"Who were the sisters that taught you?"

"Who's the novice director?"

"How many of you are in the novitiate?"

I would give short answers and gobble more food. A good thing because then it was like an Around the World Basketball Game where each sister told her own answers to the questions. It was a hoot! My pat response was always, "Oh, tell me more about it, Sister."

Sister Carol would look at me, smile big, and wink one time: she knew I was playing with them and they didn't get it. So she'd say: "C'mon, Sister Joanie, we need to go make a banner."

She rescued me more times than I can remember from the deluge of curiosity from the elderly sisters who listened attentively and were kind towards me.

Likewise, I really was inquisitive about these very interesting women, mostly retired, who had lots of stories of the Northwest Orphanage, Father Cataldo, cold harsh snowy winters with no heat, reliance on each other, and dedication to PRAYING their hearts out.

I was getting into a groove and it felt good to learn and live with diversity based on age and prior life experiences.

I felt connected. They were my sisters, but I didn't want to risk our budding relationships if I shared all my thoughts and opinions.

At dinner, I often wore my comfortable clothes: shorts and a t-shirt. One day I overheard one sister tell Sister Carol: "Tell her to change out of her shorts and not eat so much."

Carol kindly responded, "I think it would be better, Sister, if you talk to Sister Joanie yourself." The sister never did talk with me.

I compromised and often would throw a pair of sweats over my shorts as I walked down the hall, or I'd have my sweats hanging low so my shorts would show; I couldn't resist a little rebellion! The sweats protected me from further repercussions that could jeopardize my hopes of being a nun. It was instilled in me at an early age to stand up for who I am, so switching to slacks or a habit in my home was not an option.

I just had to be me. But who was I at 24? Who was I becoming? Was I the obedient, goody-two-shoes nun or the fun-loving Joanie nun? Or both?

Could I be the real true me and be a real nun?

How could I live my truth in true devotion to God amidst the amazing reality that I was falling in love with Sister Carol within an institution and a world that strictly forbid my passion and attraction for another woman?

My Life's Path Leading Me to Meet Carol

Carol was 15 years older than me, and we both grew up in solid, faithful and loving families that encouraged us to be and do everything our hearts desired. We both heard the "call" to serve God at an early age, and we believed that predestined us to unite here now.

So first, let me share how I became the young Sister Joanie whose heart and soul were swept away into the infinite ocean of love that I felt for Sister Carol.

I was born on July 5, 1957, to Lenore and Ralph Lindenmeyer. That year, my parents financed our stucco three-bedroom, one-bath home for $13,000 in San Diego's Normal Heights neighborhood. Along with my older sister Gail, younger sister

Terri and brother Tom, we and our neighborhood friends called it "Abnormal Heights" because our street did not show up on city maps; we thought being different was cool. Our home was in the middle of the block on the west side of New Jersey Street. It was directly across from the home of my grandparents, Alfred and Nellie.

Our home was full of love because our parents were deeply devoted to each other, showing us the beautiful blessings of love, monogamy, joy and faith. Mom and Dad were unified in cheering each other on, having fun, smiling, laughing and bringing out the best in each other.

Mom's Irish humor, laughable "Nut Charges" as we called them, kept our home happy, jubilant and healthy. She laughed so hard that tears streamed down her cheeks; we all inherited that special gift of the famous Lindenmeyer tears.

Laughter is healing. Laughter is contagious. And I only saw my mom cry one time from sadness. I was told that Mom cried at the funeral of her mother, Ruby Irene Moran; my middle name Irene is after my Grandma. I like that. Mom believed in resurrection and that death was conquered once and for all with Jesus. I agree that we will all meet in heaven someday.

Mom kept her smooth, worn brown rosary beads under her bed pillow, praying for all family members. She prayed extra Hail Marys for me, hoping to have a daughter as a nun.

Mom received 12 years of Catholic education while being raised in San Francisco. Her Irish father was a judge and her Irish and Native American mother enjoyed a career as head nurse at San Francisco General Hospital. My Dad converted to Catholicism once he married Mom.

Her motto was, "Never idle hands."

When I was in elementary school, in the evenings Mom sat in her sky-blue cloth chair under the living room light with her rosary box kit, then used wire, pliers and beads to make hundreds of rosaries every year. Her "altar society" ladies gave them away to God only knows. It was her prayer time as we kids sat on the floor and watched TV shows: *Leave it to Beaver, Bonanza with Little Joe and Hoss, The Brady Bunch* and Terri's favorite and my favorite, *The Flying Nun* with actor Sally Fields. I could picture myself flying, doing good and getting into many predicaments.

Mom was our angel, heroine, worker bee, homework helper, Irish musician and humor lady. Intelligent and quiet, Mom outdid Superman, Wonder Woman and the Hulk—the green giant superhero who could rip his shirt into shreds and save the world! Mom saved the world, too, with her gentleness and compassionate actions! When she spoke, similar to the TV commercial with E.F. Hutton, "Everyone listened."

She kept up with my dad's over-committed schedule of work, coaching and volunteering, and then becoming president of the Pearl Harbor Survivors Association of California.

Dad worked nights as a newspaper typesetter and had galactic energy. But when he was tired, his snores traveled through the open windows to our neighbors' homes. He had a crooked nose because it was broken during his youth sports days and it was never properly medically set back in place. They both dished out lots of hugs and told all of us how proud they were of us. We did chores together and Dad made it fun.

"Smile!" Dad always told us.

"Stand tall!" Mom loved to say.

We were raised Catholic, attended Catholic schools and Sunday Mass, prayed before every meal, and had priests and nuns at our house as friends. Dad had converted to Catholicism after he married Mom. We demolished home-cooked meals made by Mom, and I typically gestured the sign of the cross before our meals.

Once when I was four years old and a priest was dining with us, according to my family, I led the sign of the cross and said:

"In the name of the Father, and the Son and the HOLY COACH. Amen."

They laughed and patted me on my head and back, saying, "Good job, Joanie."

Since my father was the head coach at St. John's Elementary School, I truly thought we were praying for Dad at dinner when we gestured to the sign of the cross.

CHAPTER 1

Playing with our neighborhood friends on New Jersey Street included daily cruising on our blue and red fat-tire bicycles past about 25 Mediterranean and Mexican tile-roof, uniquely styled homes. The ocean breeze whooshed through the palm and hibiscus trees lining the street. We ate sweet purple Eugenia berries and yellow loquats picked from ours and our neighbors' yards. We always waved hello to everyone. Terri and I enjoyed helping our older and retired neighbors by putting up and taking down their Christmas lights every year as an act of service.

In the summer, where bloody toe stubs were common, we played hours of kickball under the streetlight until parents yelled for us to come home. We were a gang of friends, and nothing, even to this day, can separate us: the Fitz's and the Lindy's. We knew every neighbor and had nicknames for them.

Speaking of names, it's such a hoot that my childhood neighborhood became San Diego's super hip "gay area" known as Hillcrest. Back when I was growing up in the 1960s and 1970s, gay people were seen as "abnormal" and "queer." I despised that derogatory and hateful "Q-word" back in the day, as much as the "N-word." It surely did not accurately describe such kind and vivacious people who were beautiful and different from others.

Our public elementary school friends, the Helms, lived on the corner opposite our Catholic best friends, the Fitzmaurice family, at the top of New Jersey Street. We, Greg Fitzmaurice and I, walked the six blocks, sometimes catching moths that we put in the U.S. Postal mailbox on the way to Alice Burney Elementary School for Kindergarten. Then for first through eighth grade at St. John the Evangelist Elementary School, we either walked or rode our Schwinn bikes with a tandem on the back for our books and lunch bag or we walked. Often one of the Fitzies rode on our front handlebar. At school, guess who taught us? The best of the best, CSJ nuns.

Hearing God's Call and Knowing My Truth

Jesus' call came in many ways, beginning when I was a first grader, in the form of a warm and happy feeling that Jesus' love was all I ever needed. I so admired the nuns, my teachers whom I saw every day, for their joy, their prayerfulness, and their love of being with people, including me.

I'm going to be one of them. They are happy and in love with Jesus.

But my elementary Catholic religious education became a challenge. I almost failed second grade penance class. Yes, I could admit, say sorry and mean it! So why did I need to go into a box and say a memorized prayer? Oh well. I passed and received the sacrament of Penance/Reconciliation. I was a good kid and I never spoke badly or bullied anyone.

In fifth grade, I won a plaque in the school reading club. It said: "Be what you is, because if you be what you ain't, you ain't what you is."

This resonated deep in my heart, because when it came to boyfriend-girlfriend interaction, I was different. Very different.

The Healing Power of Love

When I was in fifth grade, I was struck with excruciating pain in my abdomen. My brother Tom drove me to the hospital, with my Dad still half asleep from working all night. Dad thought I was faking it to avoid taking a test at school, but I could barely stand.

Doctors rushed me into surgery, where my appendix burst as soon as the surgeon cut me open! The infection spread through my body and I was really sick.

When I woke up in the hospital bed, Mom clasped her sweaty hand around mine and Dad cried tears of relief.

"I'm hungry," I said.

They smiled really big.

My brother Tom, nine years older than me, is my hero. He came to the hospital with a deck of cards and for days I practiced shuffling them in a fancy way. Big Brother Tom holds a super special part of my heart with so many fun memories that light up my heart like a Christmas tree. He and his wife Kathleen have been married, happy and monogamous for more than 52 years. I am so proud of them for the crazy things they and their family have been through. Carol and I loved them so much and they always treated us as a couple.

When I was at Mercy Hospital in Hillcrest, two CSJ nuns who included my fifth-grade teacher, Sister Judy, visited and prayed with me. I felt really special when they arrived in my hospital room unannounced, wearing traditional, pre-Vatican II black and white penguin habits. Their smiles smashed against their white cardboard head pieces and the chest shields on their habits made me giggle. And it hurt to giggle.

(On a side note, Sister Judy was also one of the professed sisters I was privileged to live with during my first year of formation at St. Anastasia convent on West Manchester near Loyola Marymount Los Angeles.)

Soon after leaving the hospital, Mom took me to the doctor's office to have a syringe pump put inside of me to remove the pus from my infected wound. Only once did the stinky, nasty brown-yellow gunk shoot into the air. My mom gripped my hand and cried hysterically. The nurse escorted her into the hallway, where she kept crying. Thankfully, I recovered.

Loving Music & Sports

By seventh grade, I and my Catholic school classmates became leaders on the volleyball court and at Sunday Mass as the folk music group. My mom was thrilled that I wanted to learn how to play the guitar. A former high school trumpet player and child pianist, she always played music from her radio atop the stove in our kitchen.

Mom paid for my guitar lessons and took me to purchase my first guitar. I loved strumming and singing church folk songs. I played "Kumbaya" and "They'll Know We are Christians by Our Love" and other songs that used four simple chords: C, A minor, F, and G7.

From seventh to twelfth grade during the 1970's, my sister Terri, our friends and I were the parish musical liturgists at our local St. John the Evangelist Church in San Diego. Just teenagers, we were in charge of the 11 a.m. Sunday liturgy for seven years in a row. Three guitars, one tambourine and angelic voices. The CSJ nuns had taught us at St. John's School to be involved and to lead. Maybe that's why the song "Standing on Their Shoulders" means so much to me to this day.

I had been welcomed into their convent, their home, even though it was secluded from public view. I felt privileged to visit their TV room and kitchen. Terri and I would ride our bikes to their convent and wash their cars. Sister Ruth or Sister Mary Ellen would bring out a treat of cookies, fruit or juice for us. They were always so appreciative and kind with big smiles looking at us directly in the eye to show we were loved and cared for.

I was most enamored with Sister Mary Ellen, my eighth-grade teacher and principal at St. John the Evangelist Elementary School. She was a spitfire—a funny, dedicated, smart people-person who was in love with life. We were friends forever, beyond the student-teacher relationship.

Sister Mary Ellen was extraordinary. We stayed in contact and I affectionately called her "Mom." In today's terms, she'd be considered my mentor. I liked her as a fun, outgoing person who really cared about me, my family and my life. She and other CSJ sisters were living the life I needed to pursue.

Pushing for Sports Equality

I really wanted to play basketball, but our school only had teams for boys. This unfairness created an ugly feeling in the pit of my stomach. I wanted equality in sports!

"You know, Dad," I complained to my "Coach" in 1971, when sports were separate but not equal at our Catholic school, "me and the girls never get to play on the basketball court. We are always stuck on the volleyball court. It isn't fair!"

We had to put up with not being accepted, encouraged or allowed to show our athletic talent like guys did. As a result, from fifth through eighth grade, I only played volleyball. All year, every year, every lunch time, every recess. Boring! I must say, though, I became an excellent volleyball player.

Dad went to Sister Mary Ellen and expressed the heart-wrenching tale of his daughter Joanie's desires and resentment over injustice and discrimination. Together they worked out a "PE" schedule with Dad.

"YES!" he told her. "I'll take it."

Thank you, God! Thank you, Sister Mary Ellen and thanks Dad!

Dad led us sixth, seventh and eighth grade girls in basketball drills, games and fun times. He and us girls laughed, sweated and made plenty of bloopers along with miraculous scoring shots and terrible missed shots. These changes improved the spirit of our entire school.

The boys liked sitting on the benches and watching; our eighth grade class was connected at the hip, in the classroom and on the outdoor court. Happiness was being "good sports" and having the boys cheering us on! Absolutely amazing: my goose bumps were on top of my goose bumps. Alleluia!

Still, I wanted to play any sport I desired, and was itching to play football and baseball, just like the guys did.

This discrimination needed to end.

Seeking Equality for Female Athletes

Thankfully, while I attended San Diego High School in 1972, courts began to enforce a law known as Title IX, which was interconnected with civil rights and banned discrimination based on gender in education programs or activities that receive federal financial assistance.

I didn't understand the legalities. I only believed in true equality.

Female athletes were celebrating and still fighting for what the law had granted us. I'm grateful to tennis superstar Billie Jean King and many coaches, businesspeople, journalists, Olympic athletes and hundreds of thousands of female high school athletes who competed.

They led the way for me to play high school volleyball in the fall and softball in the spring. For fun, and to enhance my athleticism, I practiced with the coed badminton team after volleyball practices. But I was not allowed to compete in two sports in the same season, as the powers that be decided that as a female, I was too fragile. Focusing on and being the best team player possible was my biggest contribution!

Our parents always attended our high school and Amateur Athletic Union (AAU) games and sacrificed time, energy and money to support us. My mother made me a blue sports bag with colorful stitching that said, "YOU'RE THE GREATEST," with a female character bumping a volleyball. It was a precious, inspiring gift from my mother, who in high school had been a star tennis player who danced, sang, and played piano and trumpet.

My sister Ter competed in tennis, track and field, and softball. In 1977, she received a San Diego High Alumni scholarship and ran cross-country and track at the University of Redlands.

We've come a long way, baby!!

My heart was so full of joy for my little sister to be honored for her hard work in sports and academics. Our family legacy of sports greats—Grandpa Alfred, Aunt Evelyn, Mom and Dad, and my siblings Gail and Tom—all laid the foundation for myself and Ter! Thank you!

Receiving the Billie Jean King Award

I received the "athlete of the year award" during my senior year of high school, thanks to my volleyball and softball coaches, because they believed in me and in equality.

The certificate is signed by the greatest of all time (GOAT), Billie Jean King, who stood up for gay rights during homophobic eras. When I saw her on television, my heart leaped with joy.

Billie Jean proudly and openly articulated our voice throughout her lifetime—that women athletes who were once denied athletic scholarships, professional salaries, and accolades for their grand performances, should be respected and celebrated.

In her autobiography, *All In*, she described her years-long struggles with male domination in sports, her tenacity to beat Bobby Riggs in the "Battle of the Sexes" tennis match, her commitment to personal growth in "coming out" as a professional gay athlete, and her love relationships with CNN host Larry King and tennis pro Illano Kloss.

Billie Jean King taught me courage and inner strength.

Even today, tears well in my eyes as I rub my fingers over her signature on my high school award. I'm hopeful that my little sacrifices might have inspired a younger athlete, just as Billie Jean did for me.

She completely inspired me at age 17 and continues to feed my spirit today, at age 65, with more hopes in the next decade.

She may not know me personally, but I know her. I know of her love for EQUALITY and HONESTY as a gay woman.

Zero discrimination is the dream of my life!

Celebrating My Love for Jesus

I liked my choice to attend public San Diego High School, and chose to take Catholic Christian Doctrine education (CCD) every Monday night from Sister Pat and St. John the Evangelist Church. The class of four to eight high schoolers met in the rectory in a parlor with chairs, tables and sofas. Sister Pat—who had a scarred hand and a huge, beautiful, kind smile—instilled in us to pray, meditate, trust, thank and love Jesus.

A great storyteller, she was very passionate and could modernize Jesus' stories from the Bible, the living word of scripture. I loved our 15 minutes of guided meditation, eyes closed, sitting on a couch with the palms of my hands open and resting on my knees. Sister Pat's gentle voice transported us into Jesus' world as His disciple, walking in Jerusalem and strolling the shores of Galilee. My sandals gushed in the sand as I walked with Jesus.

As we discussed how the Bible passage was part of our current life, she helped us listen to each other and listen to God. That was the most amazing theology class I ever had. It was personal, and it was a God moment.

"I'm in Love!"

During my senior year, while my best friend Ruthie drove us through Hillcrest, I blurted, "I'm in Love!"

It felt fantastic to let the joy ring like bells on Santa's sleigh!

But it startled Ruthie. Our eyes met and we smiled.

"I'm in love with life!" I exclaimed. "I can't explain it, but it's big, Ruthie."

This was not about romance. I had none.

I was a late-bloomer about my sexuality and never had the urge to "go crazy" over a guy. I did not put the "gay" or "lesbian" label on it. Yes, I was attracted to women, but not in an ooey-gooey way. I was not "out" to my family or friends because I was not "out" to me. Being sexually different, opposite of The Norm, triggered lots of emotions for me: fear, joy, hate and love. People from Church, the neighborhood, school and work also made rude comments.

I despised when friends and family tried to "play match-maker" or set me up on a date with a guy. Feeling repulsed and awkward, I always said, "No, not interested." My deeper, harsher tone conveyed my desire for them to leave me alone. I did not want to be in any boyfriend or girlfriend courtship, yet I felt an underlying peer and family pressure.

So, music practice, church, school, sports and fun with groups of friends were a higher priority than being a boy's girlfriend. I chose not to go to dances or the prom because then I would have to be on a date with a guy. That just wasn't me. Repulsive.

Though my family never talked about gayness, my mom understood me. And she knew firsthand about diversity as the "norm" from being raised in San Francisco in the 1930s and 1940s, and personally about her "gay" nephew, her brother's son and my cousin. As pre-teens, if we used the word "queer," the demeaning and derogatory, hateful word used by some during the 1970s, she scolded:

"Don't you ever say that word. It hurts people!"

I just want to be me.

But I was coming of age during an era that was tough to be gay. In 1969, the six-day Stonewall riots erupted in New York City—where same-sex solicitation was *illegal*—after police raided a gay club; the protests sparked the gay rights movement. In 1978, gay San Francisco Supervisor Harvey Milk was killed. In the 1980s, the HIV/AIDS epidemic began a time of sickness, deaths, the AIDS quilt project, HIV testing, counseling and prevention, HIV/AIDS education mandates, fear, sadness and stigma. Churches lambasted "amoral" lifestyles, while violence, anti-gay hatred and "coming out" stories topped newscasts.

Meanwhile, legal protections were being sought for discriminations in jobs, housing, home sales and medical practices. Larger cities were making strides with national and state legislations advocating for legal help for gay people, and Pride Parades began.

Meanwhile, I was very happy all by myself, teetering between joyous and questioning:

Why don't I have the words or confidence to say to my friends and family, "I am attracted to women, not guys"?

What would happen if I said that?

Will I be scorned, judged, not loved, treated differently?

I was not willing to go there yet.

My Future Love Also Hears the Call

I didn't know that Carol Tierheimer existed when I was a high school senior, hearing Jesus speak to me in prayer, in everyday situations, and deep within myself. And I had no idea that in just a few years, I would learn that she, too, had heard this call as a teenager.

"The call" is a gut feeling that eventually needs action. It's like the phone ringing or a text message chiming, and it's God dialing your number to say:

"Hi, Carol!"

"Hi, Joanie!"

"Please answer and devote your life to serving me."

Later, we shared that we had wondered, *Is this really God calling us to do His will? Or is this my imagination?*

When I was only three years old in 1960, 18-year-old Carol officially answered her "call," a few months after graduation from St. Mary's Academy Catholic High School in Los Angeles.

Until we met, we lived parallel lives, just 111 miles apart, as she was raised in a similarly idyllic and faith-filled family in the Windsor Hills neighborhood of Los Angeles. Born on February 1, 1942 to Joseph and Elsie Tierheimer, Carol possessed a joyful, musical soul and held dance-a-thons in the family basement. Her Aunt Josephine and Uncle Buster, and cousins Shirley and Marylou, were a stone's throw away out her backyard, along with other family and friends on nearby streets.

She entered the convent and attended Mount Saint Mary's College on her path to becoming a sister of Saint Joseph of Carondelet, where our paths would meet and merge into one.

The profound part was that we didn't know each other even existed when Carol was choosing her life's path as a young adult. In fact, I was a toddler when Carol entered the convent. Imagine a three-year-old holy terror running and jumping around in the grass, collecting bugs, driving her older siblings and parents crazy with boundless energy and eating dirt while this young, talented and smart high school graduate was dedicating her life to the Catholic Church, to wear a penguin outfit called a religious habit and shake the world alive with joy?

Exploring/Discovering Myself and My Future in College

College life at San Diego State University (SDSU) introduced me to a diverse variety of people to know and trust without labeling them. I knew gay couples on my teams; I knew gay men; I knew straight men and straight women; I knew bisexual people. Friends shared about their sexual orientation and I loved them all. I never judged, nor did I think anyone else should.

Many of us, including me, were not "out" as gay and lesbian, and yet our secrecy was respected and honored within our "gay family." It was up to me when, where and how I wanted to share the intimate truth of my sexual orientation.

Coming from a racially diverse high school, I sat in the back of classes, not used to seeing so many white young people. I missed my Latino, Filipino and African American friends, back then known as my Brown, Oriental and Black friends. I was their white friend. I'm glad we use more appropriate and inclusive words today.

I was the first in my immediate family to enroll in and embark on a four-year university education. I first declared my major as Religious Studies, but after one year of completing the basic classes, I wondered, *What job will I do related to it? How many people are employed in the field related to their major?*

I wanted a major that was more broad and well-rounded. I considered becoming a surgeon, a firefighter and a professional athlete. I prayed and realized that I didn't want to be stuck inside a building or go to college for more than five years. So, I earned my Bachelor of Arts in Physical Education.

Pursuing Big Dreams Through Volleyball

I really went to college to play volleyball with hopes and dreams of joining the Olympic team. I played for two years and loved every minute of the competition, work ethic, comradery and fun of the sport. I gave every practice my all, every game my very best and I believed in the team approach. I lived in shorts, t-shirts with logos, white athletic socks that smelled like rotten eggs and worn-out tennis shoes, yet I saved my special volleyball indoor tennies for their designated purpose.

Along with my family and college friends, the Fitzmaurice family made up the loudest cheering section at my SDSU volleyball games. Nine of their 13 family members attended the games. I felt like I was performing for them as I used my God-given athletic talents. On my "stage," the Women's Gym during the first year and the Petersen Gymnasium volleyball court the second year, my sweat constantly dripped from my face as games progressed. I only heard voices from my coaches and teammates. I appreciated having such wonderful support from friends and family and looked forward to seeing them after every home game.

Once, during a four-hour match at the University of California, Los Angeles Pauley Pavilion against the University of California, Santa Barbara team, exhaustion was creeping in on everyone. I was normally a back row specialist only, being small at 5' 8" and not a sky-high jumper like some of my teammates. My skills were bumping or passing the volleyball, digging or running to save balls, and accurately serving. However, all the substitutions were used up, so I had to stay in the game and play the left front position. Exhausted and apprehensive, I was in a hitting or spiking position. Game point us, SDSU . . . the ball was set perfectly for me. The mega tall opposing players were ready to block me, so I jumped with all my might, soaring to the stars, cocking my arm, ready to let it rip with a spike.

I royally missed the ball. But the volleyball legally bumped off my forehead, over the attacking defensive block and landed in the court on the opposite side of the net.

We WON! The CELEBRATION was a fireworks extravaganza. Pure EXUBERANCE and JOY.

I couldn't believe it as my teammates hugged me and we laughed. What a show! The crowd of 4,000 people clapped and hollered or sighed and moaned. The opposing team's players and coach were stunned with the final play in defeat. My coach had his hands on his head in disbelief and relief. It was the Holy Spirit!! Woohoo! I knew it was a big God moment. It was my little 2% faith and 98% Jesus.

After two years of playing collegiate ball, I was cut from the team because I missed one practice to visit my grandmother in the hospital. I had notified my coach and had been approved to miss one practice for the first time in two years.

It was heart-breaking, unbelievable and shocking. My dreams were crushed, but in my heart, I had done the right thing—to go see Grandma. In that decision, Jesus taught me a bigger lesson: Life and love are more important than a game!

Jesus hold you.
God bless you.

CHAPTER 2
Answering the Call

Carol and I Were Sisters of St. Joseph of Carondelet

One of our favorite quotes by Yogi Berra was: "When you see a fork in the road, take it." This cute and powerful quote was true for both of us. Carol and I had an inner spiritual connection with our Lord and an outward connection to serve Jesus by unconditionally helping others.

So AN AMAZING LOVE STORY begins. A fairytale of sorts, destined by *Nun Better*: God, Jesus and the Holy Spirit.

Facing the Fork in the Road

I graduated from SDSU with my Bachelor of Arts degree, completed one year of post-graduate courses to earn my California State Teaching Credential in 1980, then became a teacher's assistant (more like a long-term substitute teacher), and the Junior Varsity basketball and softball coach at San Diego High School, my alma mater.

During that time, I lived at home with my parents. The three of us attended Sunday morning Mass at St. John's in Hillcrest. Mom, Dad and I also attended Saturday night Mass at the original adobe Immaculate Conception Catholic Church in Old Town San Diego. Built in 1851 and restored in 1917, its walls told historic stories in Mexican paintings and the rustic wood pews squeaked when we knelt.

After church in Old Town San Diego, we enjoyed a Mexican dinner of fresh homemade corn or flour tortillas, margaritas or cervezas (beer), chips, salsa, avocado and lime along with *fajitas especiales*. It was almost orgasmic.

Tormented by Inner Turmoil

At night, I tossed and turned, plagued by the scary and disorienting sensation I had felt while body surfing in the ocean: a wave flips you upside down and all around, you don't know which way is up, and you're trapped under the pressure and power of the water. Similarly, unrelenting waves of questions crashed over me:

Who am I? How did my all-loving and powerful God make me gay? Aren't I made in His image?

Still, I knew that Jesus would provide answers.

"Thank you Jesus for making me wonderful," I prayed. "Thank you for giving me a brain. Thank you for bringing me closer to you because I believe you have a plan for me."

But with only five of the eight hours of sleep I need, I awoke mentally and physically exhausted with dark circles and sacks under my eyes.

I was constantly filled with internal turmoil, crying at TV commercials, exercising more and taking my black lab, Sport, for walks at the dog beach in Ocean Beach, and letting the tears flow as I raised my face toward the sky. I basked in the sunshine, noticing my suntanned arms and legs had brown and white stripes from wearing ankle socks and tank tops. My health, joy in warm sunshine, and vibrancy of life reminded me that my body was a temple of goodness in God's eyes.

I am loving life!

Is God, Jesus, and the Holy Spirit really calling me to a vocation of religious life? Me? Why me? Who am I? As a gay woman, am I to spread Your word and love, Lord?

I lacked the courage or fortitude to talk in-depth about my bursts of emotions, my sexuality or my relationship with Jesus.

I could barely put it into words. I thought I could do it alone. It was a spiritual journey between me and Jesus.

Who would understand me . . . and this God thing?

I couldn't even understand it. In one hand was my deep personal secret wrapped around my self-esteem, future goals and sexuality. In the other hand was the joy and love for life that I shared every day.

In the privacy of my bedroom at my small wooden desk with a pen and lined paper, I wrote letters to Catholic women's religious groups. But I kept coming back to the Sisters of St. Joseph of Carondelet. I loved the joy and kindness they had lavished on me as my teachers and friends throughout grade school.

Why am I making this so difficult? It's right here and it's been right here. Wake up, Joanie. They were a group of ladies I could see myself with at work and in life together. I'm now a young woman. Could this be my call?

When I hit my lowest point, Jesus guided me with answers and action steps, and I slept for eight uninterrupted hours. It was like I had picked up the phone to answer God's call, and it felt as natural as breathing.

Europe, Here We Come!

Backtrack 18 months to the 1980 Christmas school break season, when my longtime friend Connie and I traveled to Europe to visit my sister Terri in Salzburg, Austria and to explore the continent.

While the three of us were in Rome, Italy, we visited the Vatican. Unfortunately, I slouched on the cold, cement steps, groaning with stomach pains from diarrhea caused by Montezuma's Revenge from drinking unclean water.

When I was feeling better, the Holy Spirit took over the words from my mouth and I blurted: "By the way, I'm going to be a nun! I'm joining the convent."

"Really?" Ter asked. "You'll probably be a good nun." (Today my sister recalls, "Joanie, you had mentioned being a nun before, so this was no biggie.")

Connie Fitz tried to smile with a swollen lip that she had busted open days before on a ski lift in the Alps.

Then we shared an enormous hug.

My nonchalant announcement regarding my career, my mission, my reason for being for the rest of my life, felt as natural as riding my bike on New Jersey Street. I was 23 and my future would be with Jesus. I was answering the call, whatever that meant.

I'm following my heart. I'm finally letting others know that God is alive and working for me at a deep, deep level. It feels good to let it out.

Going to the Convent

One beautiful sunny Saturday in the spring of 1981, I walked into our bright, sunny dinette where Dad was reading the paper and drinking coffee. Mom was in her chair at the table, near the yellow phone on the wall.

"Today is the day for me to take the next action step," I announced. "I'm on my way to OLP [Our Lady of the Peace convent] to talk about joining the convent. See you later. I'll fill you in when I get home."

They smiled and Dad said, "Good luck." I think Dad was wondering, "What is Joanie doing?"

Off I drove in my VW beige camper pop-up van to Our Lady of Peace High School convent to meet with a sister regarding my vocation call. I was super excited!

I put my foot on the clutch and slid the black knob gear shifter from first, second and third gear, cruising without a worry in my mind. The car felt like it was steering itself. It knew where to go: Our Lady of Peace convent.

During the 10-minute drive, my mind played a memory movie of all the moments that had lit the way toward this drive to the convent. I was 23 years old with blonde hair and hazel eyes; at 5'8" and 135 pounds, I was healthy, fit, energetic, talkative and happy.

Before I even turned off the key, set the brake and stepped outside of my vehicle, I surrendered EVERYTHING AND EVERYONE—my memories, my parents and now my future—to my Lord. It felt peaceful.

CHAPTER 2

Lord, thank you for literally steering me to this time and place. I'm yours.

A Miracle at Our Lady of Peace

I walked onto the gorgeous Our Lady of Peace landscaped grounds of sweet-scented roses, perfectly arranged like arms reaching to the Son/sun. Not a weed sprouting anywhere. A garden manicured for royalty.

Before I could ring the doorbell of the two story white stucco building marked Convent, a fast-moving sister with short brown hair approached from a walking path.

"I'll be right with you," she said, pointing west. "Please help yourself to the courtyard."

"OK."

The lush green crabgrass reminded me of lawn bowling, tennis or putt-putt golf. Past the lawn and roses was an Olympic sized swimming pool sparkling with hues of blue. Tempted to jump in, I caught my reflection—until I swished my hand in the warm water. The ripples tickling my fingertips and the gentle breeze moved me into a meditative state.

I am living my faith; not knowing what's ahead is OK.

Four-foot-tall statues of God's saintly messengers were looking at me, so I whispered, "Hi, Blessed Mary. Hi, St. Francis of Assisi. Hi, St. Joseph."

Gliding along the cement walking paths, I spotted Jesus in statue form: 15 feet tall, bearded with long flowing hair, barefoot in a long robe, with hands open with a "happy to see you" posture.

Was He inviting me for an embrace?

I stood for a moment, admiring his realness, then sat on a bench facing Him. I looked into His downcast eyes and—

They moved!

Yes, His eyes moved. Now they were looking forward, right at me. His eyes opened bigger, directly at and through me. I felt extra warm. It was like a sci-fi movie where a person enters the inside of your being. He was in the deepest part of my soul. I was stunned. Peacefully, I asked out loud, "What is happening?"

He gazed at me like . . . a lover? Way more than a friend. I had never had this intimate feeling before. I thought and felt something entirely new. I was the only person He was with at this very moment. It was profound.

Deep, warm happiness, peace and joy consumed me; it was 1,000 times better than my life's greatest moments.

I touched my face: the size of my smile had tripled; all my teeth were showing. My jaw and facial skin seemed to expand to my shoulders. I sat extremely still, returning my gaze onto Him.

His arms and hands, *oh wow of all wows.* Jesus reached out his arm to me, in a tender, kind, loving motion. He opened his large, soft hand, turning it up so that I could put my hand in His. And I heard His gentle voice:

"Come Joanie, take my hand. Follow me. All will be good!"

"OK. YES, I will."

My arm and palm reached for Him. We were together. Tears welled from my eyes, but did not stream. I sat there with Him: not thinking, not wondering, not upset, not startled, not anything.

Time—I had no idea where it went.

Finally, I heard birds and someone walking. I glanced past the bushes, then back at Jesus. He was in his sculpture mode again. His eyes, arms and hands were stationary—plaster, stone, concrete or clay. He was looking over the garden and the world, no longer at me. He had visited with me and he moved on.

Now it's up to me to do what I told Him I would do.

I promised to take His hand. I committed to following Him. Together we would be OK. I had accepted His personal invite.

Sister Carlotta, heels clicking on the paved sidewalk, quickly approached, in a black skirt, white blouse, nylons, black shoes, thick glasses and a big smile. Just over five feet tall she was 35 to 40 years young, with salt-and-pepper gray hair. Her last name sounded Italian and she had pretty brown eyes, and a slightly large nose.

I stood to greet her with a hug and she was surprised by my affection. I was probably wearing casual church clothes—jeans, polo shirt and nice brown flip flops.

"Oh, a hug." She let out a fun, fancy-free laugh. "Sorry you had to wait."

"It's OK, Sister."

My extroversion—as confirmed as an ENFP on the Myers Briggs personality test—kicked in: "Hi, Sister Carlotta? I'm Joanie. Thanks for meeting today. I am here to become a sister."

"Oh!"

"Yes! What do I need to do?"

"Oh, well. Umm. I'm from the San Diego connection, but you'll need to meet the L.A. Province Vocation Director, Sister Judy. She lives in Los Angeles."

"Ok," I said.

"Tell me a little about you, Joanie. Why do you want to become a sister?"

"Sure. Jesus wants me to. He's been talking with me for years and He just now asked me to follow Him."

"Oh!"

I told her about my life. "I've been thinking and feeling this for years. My vocation to God. **Today, Jesus talked to me and said, 'Take my hand.' I told him, 'YES.'"**

"Ohhh. Today?"

"Yes, right over there, while I was waiting for you."

"Tell me about it."

I described my miracle with Jesus.

"You are very special, Joanie."

"Thank you. It just happened."

"God works in all kinds of ways," she said. "I'm happy for you. I'll get a hold of Sister Judy. Let's get together again so we can get to know each other."

"Perfect. When?"

Carlotta said she needed a ride to see her mother, so I drove her. While she walked into the convent to retrieve her purse, I waited outside.

Thank you, Jesus, for seeing me today. She's nice. Thanks to her, too. You have a pretty garden here.

As I drove wearing my cool, black-rimmed sunglasses, she asked, "What's your favorite Scripture passage, Joanie?"

"I don't really know. I guess I know Bible stories, not sayings. Oh, I like the one where the laborers are few . . . "

She asked me to call her Carlotta and said, "One of my favorites is Hebrews 4:12: 'The Word of God is alive and active.'"

"Wow, that's powerful. What does that mean to you, Carlotta?"

She explained. My first-ever Spiritual Director had taken me under her wing.

"You're COOL, Carlotta."

"You, too, Joanie. I'll call you when you can meet Sister Judy."

"Thanks! Bye."

Jesus has His plan for me!

Some of my friends found life answers in marriage, the military, education and their careers.

My way was very different. I was a kite flying in the air: free, flying, moving, trusting and believing in HIS winds, directions and adventures with Him holding the string. Absolutely so COOL—*Nun Better* was destined. Proverbs says trust in the Lord with all your heart. YEP!

Thanks be to God, we all get to find our unique paths and ways to true happiness.

Jesus hold you.
God bless you.

CHAPTER 3
Join the Convent, See the World

Do you remember the military recruiting phrase, "Join the Army and see the world"? Well, that's what I thought when I was accepted into the Sisters of St. Joseph of Carondelet as an "associate." This was the first of a three- to six-year training program to determine whether it was a mutual fit between me and the sisters.

In August of 1981, I embarked on a journey that blessed me with four decades of bliss. First, I moved from my parents' home, my only home, to a convent near Los Angeles International Airport.

During the first year, I had opportunities on a daily and weekly basis to travel and attend classes and events as part of the expansive CSJ network in Los Angeles and other regions across the United States. One of my favorite events was going to "Nun Day" at an LA Dodgers baseball game. It was so much fun combining sports with nun-hood. I was in my element!

The next year, in 1982, I became a novice with the Sisters of St. Joseph of Carondelet in Pasadena, California. I lived with about eight young women novices, nuns in training, ranging in age from 20 to 26, and four professed sisters, ages 35 to 65, who were our role models, mentors and companions.

Our convent home was a two-story, brick building on Sierra Madre Boulevard, the path of the Rose Bowl Parade. Located on the grounds of a wealthy Catholic school and parish, it was surrounded by palm trees, landscaped yards with lawns mowed regularly by hired gardeners, and large homes with front porches and backyard pools.

My favorite part was the outdoor basketball court just steps from our back door. I even played ball with a young man, who lived with his wife behind our convent in the well-kept apartment buildings that housed young, professional working people.

The doorbell would ring and a young man would ask, "Can Sister Joanie come out and play basketball with us? We need a fourth person."

Delighted, I grabbed my tennis shoes, put on my shorts and t-shirt, passed through the gate to the court, and had a great workout with these young men in their mid-twenties. I laughed, sweat and enjoyed every minute of it. The sound of a bouncing basketball relieved stress and cultivated team spirit. I thought it was spiritual. I was in my yard, literally and figuratively.

Then out of the blue, at my weekly mentoring session, the Novice Director said, "Joanie, you need to stop playing basketball with the neighbors!"

What? Why?

"We are just playing ball," I protested. "There's nothing wrong with that. They are good people with good manners. His wife watches us, too. We have fun."

"No. No more playing basketball with the male neighbor."

Darn it!

I didn't understand why I was not allowed to play basketball. It was on my own time.

Was harm done? I don't think so. This is weird.

Though it irked me for a while, I applied my parents' wisdom: "Don't burn any bridges; you might need their help later."

OK, let it go, Joanie. If it's meant to be, it will come back.

Places to Go, People to Meet

Trips kept us nuns, young adults, from going stir crazy. A

big trip took us novices to St. Louis, Missouri in a large white passenger van with rows of bench seats for all nine of us. It was about learning, visiting and meeting other sisters along the way, soaking in the history of the roots of our congregation.

For our required "poverty experience," to learn how to maintain hope in challenging circumstances, we lived for a month with Navajo people in their nation in Klagetoh, Arizona. We slept in a rundown house where black, crusty cicadas and chirping crickets, by the hundreds, snuck under our old dilapidated wooden doors and crawled onto my bed. Every night, I would shake my bed cover and hear the cicadas crunch as they hit the wall. *Yucko!*

Because of the low water supply, we rotated taking showers every three or four days for about three minutes.

For food, our kind and generous hosts shared federally subsidized blocks of orange cheese, powdered milk and creamy peanut butter. We learned to help cook "fry bread"—a Native American specialty that is doughy, tasty and delicious.

Amidst this beautiful high desert's wildflowers, scrub bushes and dark, star-filled nights, I was seeing the world, opening my mind and heart, and experiencing new places in a spirit of belief, trust and obedience.

On this trip of a lifetime, my friend Maggie—who was from Manhattan Beach, California—and I played guitar for a Navajo couple's wedding who had lived together for 50 years and said it was about time they got married. YES, yippee!

Serendipity Sparkles on My Three-Month Mission Adventure

As novices, we would be "sent" on a three-month "Mission Experience" with the time and place determined by our Novice Director. The purpose was to orient us to living and working in a community of ministry and convent life.

Exuberant joy bounced around in me like a fish taking the bait and swimming crazily to avoid being reeled in. I was that daring fish, dreaming and anticipating so much more freedom, more service to others, less reading, less classes, and less introspective reflecting and studying. I was especially excited to enjoy freedoms that included no longer wearing dreaded nylons with my skirt.

Just two weeks before my departure, as I counted the days, our intellectual Novice Director called Maggie and me into her sun-filled office, which had a large glass tabletop desk and three chairs around a coffee table. Shelves holding religious books made me feel like I was in a room full of holy men and women who were scholars and authors.

Our Novice Director had arranged for Mag and me to go to Lewiston, Idaho for our three month "Mission Experience." I felt so blessed to go so far away from the hub of Los Angeles Sisterhood to serve the Lord.

Shazam! Holy Moly. It sounded like international travel to me. It's winter: it must be cold. Do they get snow? Do they really have spuds in Idaho?

We would be gone from the novitiate structure from January until March of 1983.

"Represent us well, enjoy getting to know the sisters and live out the Charisms," our Novice Director told us.

"YES, SISTER," we replied.

I was SO excited.

She explained, "You will work with and live in the convent with Sister Carol Tierheimer and Sister Frances. Sister Frances is the director of pastoral care or chaplaincy at the hospital. You will be ministering at the hospital two days a week, bringing holy communion to patients and families. Help Sister Frances as needed. You will work with Sister Carol, who is the Pastoral Assistant or Parish Sister, second in charge under the pastor priest, three days a week."

I responded and repeated back to her my new assignment: "Wow, a ministry! That means I get to 'work,' like a job, with other people. Thank you so much!" YAHOO!

I was even more excited because Maggie was also going to Lewiston.

"They are sending us out in twos," I told her. "How scripturally cool is that? Mag, we are going to the same place, the same parish, can you believe that?"

CHAPTER 3

Bring on the adventures! Let the journey blast forth and soon I will solidify my vows. How good you are, God . . .

A short time later, on Christmas Day, the surprise of a lifetime happened.

"Joanie, phone call from Idaho for you," a sister called from the hallway where the convent phone was located—a spot where everyone could hear your conversations. Back in the 1980s, only landline phones existed and long distance calls were expensive. No one had received calls from their new mission locations.

I eagerly took the phone and heard the most unique and joyous voice. It was Sister Carol, and she said, "Merry Christmas, Joanie."

I felt so darn special, my cheeks turned red, my eyes bulged, and even the air tasted sweet. *Sister Carol called ME to say, "Merry Christmas!"*

Sister Frances chimed in: "We are looking forward to seeing, meeting and working alongside you."

Then Sister Carol said, "I really am glad that you and I get to work together. I've heard that you are vibrant and energetic and a teacher. We wanted to wish you a Merry Christmas and welcome you to the Northwest. See you soon, and travel safely."

Never in my life had my insides done backflips and cartwheels after simply hearing a voice. Soft, slow, gentle and happy, her voice struck me as a shooting star from the heavens, eliciting calm yet incredible joy deep within me. It's still difficult to find words to describe the spirit of love circling me in that moment, lighting sparks that would later burst into flames.

Our less-than-two-minute call was exhilarating, out of the blue, and personally for ME. WOW, how special I felt. *What an honor! What a gift.*

After the call, Sister Carol's spunky, joyous tone reverberated through my entire being, awakening something in the deepest crevices of my heart. I didn't know what it was. It felt amazingly light, beautiful and holy, like guardian angels were looking over me. This blessed me with a permanent smile as her voice played over and over in my mind. And my heart said to trust in God with all your heart (Proverbs 3:5-6).

I believe that God had called me to religious life to meet Carol! I believe God orchestrated the serendipitous circumstances for us to fall in love.

Jesus hold you.
God bless you.

CHAPTER 4
Her Eyes Touch My Heart

Carol always asked newcomers, "How did you two meet?"

Let me turn that around to share how Carol and I began our amazing love story. Holy moly, it's over the top!

In January of 1983, Maggie and I flew from LAX to the Seattle-Tacoma International Airport in Washington, each with one bag, plus a purse/carry-on containing apples, nuts, a sandwich and water.

From the Seattle Greyhound station, we took a bus to Lewiston, Idaho. We were cautious of our surroundings since it had been awhile since we both had traveled by airplane or public transportation. We smelled the weed, watched the homeless, and waited like cattle in a corral before boarding our bus. Few travelers got on, so we sat near the front. Maggie and I greeted the driver and told him our destination.

We exuded happiness and hyperactivity, thrilled to venture into the world away from the strict novitiate, now free to live a purposeful mission. Being post-Vatican II, habits were not required in our religious order, so we wore coats, blue jeans, blouses, sweaters, warm socks and tennis shoes. We each had a snow hat and gloves, too. It was cold!

The driver informed us that a blizzard was causing detours and delays. If necessary, the Washington State Highway Patrol would escort the bus through the Snoqualmie Pass. After the other passengers disembarked, Maggie and I became great friends with the driver.

We were quiet through many sections so he could concentrate on the icy slopes on roads whose only markers were the tall snow-marker poles. The extraordinarily white, picturesque snow dwarfed the trees and mesmerized us with a *swish* sound under the tires.

After traveling more than 1,000 miles in two days, we neared Clarkston, Washington, driving over the Clearwater and Snake River confluence. Around 7:30 p.m., under a dark sky, we pulled into frigid Lewiston, where piles of dirty snow lined the roads.

"You shouldn't have your sisters drive downtown to the bus station," he said. "I'm taking you directly to your convent."

"Oh, golly, and thank you," Maggie said graciously.

"Super," I said. "That's awesome. Thank you! Here's the address." As our stomachs growled with hunger, I remembered the delightful phone call from Sisters Carol and Frances, and was pinching myself that we had arrived.

"Three months, Joanie," Maggie said.

"May our mission experience be awesome, Mag," I said.

Meandering through neighborhood streets, our chariot ride felt magical as we pulled up to the convent—a regular, two-story wooden family home with a front porch amidst other family homes. How awesome! It was not the big brick, sterile-looking monstrosity of a typical convent. The porch light was on! *Wahoo!*

When our driver double-parked the 40-foot bus at the entrance, a lady appeared in the front window. Her hands were in a prayer position and I thought she was thanking Jesus for our safe arrival, or was she in utter shock that a gigantic bus startled her neighbors and made the local news? Haha!

Within seconds, more sisters in black and white habits and veils peered out the living room window.

About 12 sisters bomb-blasted Mag and me with huge smiles as we dashed off the bus, jumping two steps at a time onto the porch and through the open front door.

The excited sisters embraced us in a hug-fest. We didn't even know their names, but they knew us: the novices from Los

Angeles, the future of their order. Maggie and I felt a freedom and release from the Pasadena novitiate rules and regulations upon our arrival in the Northwest. We hoped we would be on equal footing, coming to their turf, their neighborhood, their community and bonded sisterhood.

"Come in, Come in, Sisters."

As the sisters introduced themselves, Maggie and I beamed smiles. Some of them were in full habit, some in partial habit with black or blue skirts and veils; a few wore warm wool pants and sweaters—all symbolic of the post-Vatican II changes which afforded personal choice.

"Sister Joanie," one sister said, "Sister Carol is not here right now, but she'll be joining you soon. She had a parish meeting tonight."

"Thank you for telling me, Sister. It will be great to meet her."

Oh boy, the smells of homemade garlic bread and chicken with spices razzled my nostrils. The dining room table was large and covered with plates and bowls from the meal they had recently shared. They asked, "Sisters, are you hungry?"

"Yes, Sister, we are starving," Mag and I responded. I imagined three months of living, loving and working amongst these dedicated, prayerful, religious women who were great cooks.

This is the life.

They handed each of us a plate of home-cooked chicken and fresh, steamed veggies. To keep the sisters comfortable in the living room chairs, I sat on the carpeted floor, placing my meal—which looked yummy—onto the long antique coffee table. Mag joined me. We were within a few yards of the front door entrance. Alert and happy, the sisters gathered around us, watching us devour the meal.

One sister said, "They just sat on the floor!"

"Did they pray?" another asked.

We smiled and nodded in conversation as we vacuumed in our dinner.

"Thank you for this fantastic meal and compliments to the cooks," I said, happy to be with the sisters and even happier to soon meet "the voice" that had called me on Christmas day—the one and only Sister Carol.

Seeing Carol for the First Time

Within minutes, the front door opened with a burst of cold air, and two nuns with warm smiles entered.

Which one is Sister Carol, and which is the school principal, Sister Kathleen Mary?

Mag and I jumped to greet them as the one wearing a deep purple coat and blue and pink hat seemed to float through the door. She was 5'6", yet seemed taller than Washington's 14,000-foot Mount Rainier. With perfect posture, she was light on her feet, with a huge smile. Her facial skin had a healthy glow, framed by soft, medium-brown short hair; I guessed she was 10 to 12 years older than me.

And her big, gentle eyes were *dancing* as she looked into mine for the first time.

"I'm Sister Carol," she said.

Oh, that's the nice voice I heard on the phone . . .

Goosebumps and tingles tickled me from head to toe. I felt her aura and envisioned angels swirling around her. It was a very strange—yet so sweet!—feeling with this phenomenal woman.

Sister Carol and I shared a quick, cordial hug. Then she said: "Sit down, finish your meal. Do you like it?"

"Yes, fabulous!" I said. "Thank you very much."

The sisters shared the story of our grand arrival with the giant bus delivering us to the convent steps. Sister Carol beamed smiles, enjoying our pure youthful happiness as Maggie and I sat gobbling more food. The Idaho sisters would celebrate that "grand entrance" for a long time.

All the while, Carol stood close. Outwardly, she was calm, cool, and collected, wearing fashionably modern slacks and a colorful blouse and sweater that dazzled with designs and sparkles. Her coat draped over her arm. I later learned that she loved clothes, switched into three outfits daily, and preferred dresses, but her winter attire favored perfect-fitting blue or green stretch polyester slacks. As she listened to our travel adventures, she was like a graceful deer standing still and paying attention to everything.

Wow! What a sharply dressed, happy and confident person.

Carol was not the stereotypical old-school, boring, quiet and reserved nun. Her presence in the room was like a beam of sunshine flashing through dreary fog.

As she spoke to others, her mesmerizing hand gestures seemed to float, like she was directing a choir, her eyes sparkled with joy, and her big smile radiated warmth. She would give a little hand and finger wave and people would respond with happy smiles and energetic waves.

As she interacted with the sisters, I noticed we shared similar attributes: speaking with positive words, and being a light of hope, respect and kindness because we genuinely liked people.

Thank you God for the introductions of a new person in my life! A gift from only You.

As my delegated boss-co-worker-director-sister for the next three months, I had a wonderful feeling that Sister Carol would work out well for me and we'd get along fantastically.

"How did you two meet?" Carol asked me and Maggie as the sisters leaned in to hear our story.

As Sister Carol listened intently, her eyes twinkled while Mag and I told how we met at Saint Anastasia, the Associate House, as the newbies. We shared one story of our morning neighborhood jog, where meadowlark squawking birds dive-bombed our heads. When we changed course, their flock joined them. We laughed, considering this the start of our morning prayer. Carol and the sisters loved our story.

Oh golly, I was one happy, well-fed novice living a natural high. I prayed silently, "Let the remaining two months and 29 days unfold with glory, fun and love of our Lord."

My New Home

After dinner, Sisters Frances and Carol walked me to the hospital convent where I would live with 15 sisters, including them. They showed me to my bedroom and gave a rundown of bathrooms, the kitchen and the house layout, and they showed me where their bedrooms were.

"If you need anything," Sister Carol said, "just holler or knock. Let's meet tomorrow at 9 a.m. at my office in the basement of the parish rectory."

"Can't wait." My heart was beating joyously, my true self coming alive. And it felt so normal.

Sister Frances said, "Please join us at the parish Mass at 8 a.m. if you want. Breakfast is cafeteria-style at 7 a.m. Sleep well. Welcome again."

Carol added, "Do you need anything else? Ok, Good night, Joanie. God bless you."

I smiled. "Good night. Thank you for everything. See you in the morning."

Wow, this is my new life! With these kind, beautiful people for the next few months. It's all really happening. I'm in Idaho now. New beginnings. How good you are, God.

Happy music praising God coursed through my veins as He put me in the right place, at the right time, with the right people. I felt comforted and jubilant.

Much later, when Carol and I reflected on the night we met, she confessed that she had glanced at the two blond babes from Southern California beaches and thought, "I hope I get the short one."

I was seven inches taller than Maggie. So Sister Carol didn't get the short blond one . . . but she did get me!

Jesus hold you
God bless you.

CHAPTER 5
Carol Joins the Convent

So how did Carol get to Lewiston, Idaho where, by the grace of God, we would unite forever?

Well, imagine making a decision, and believing without a doubt in your heart that the Lord is asking you to be his bride. All at age 18, fresh out of high school.

That was the time and unwavering decision that Carol made in 1960.

Setting the stage . . . Carol grew up with devoted Catholic parents, aunts, uncles, cousins—one big family. A culture of honesty, truth, joy, faith, respect and quality time together that included yearly summer camping and fishing vacations to Virginia Lakes. With younger sister Elaine and brother Bobby, she was the eldest. She was confident, strong in character, loved to dance and music was in her soul. *Sing it, Carol!*

Her fantastic Catholic school education began with elementary schools, St. Bernadette and later Transfiguration, and then St. Mary's Academy High School in Englewood, graduating in the "blue tie class," the color of their uniform tie signifying Class of 1960.

During high school, her father remodeled the basement of their home so Carol could invite her friends and cousins over and play 45s records (singles) nonstop and dance their hearts out.

She also loved to sing, but was rejected from joining the high school choir. So she sang with great exuberance in church, in the car, in the kitchen and wherever else she felt inspired.

Carol told me she knew that joining the convent "was the right thing to do." She did not have any particular reason, struggle or questions. She just did it. It was no big deal to her.

Carol's close friend and cousin, Theodora, aka T, told me of Carol's casual announcement at their high school assembly where the graduating seniors crossed the stage and declared their next step in life. Proudly and calmly, Carol spoke into the microphone: "I'm going to Mount St. Mary's south." Meaning she was entering the CSJ's apostulate phase to become a sister. T said she was so surprised by Carol's announcement, having never heard of this before, that her mouth dropped open, but that she could see Carol as a nun.

At that time in the Catholic Church, many young women were entering the convent. This was the norm, and religious life in the Catholic Church was booming.

After high school graduation, Carol was ready to commit to becoming a sister of St. Joseph of Carondelet—a woman religious. Carol entered the postulancy in September of 1960, and entered the noviate on March 19th, 1961, where she took the name Sister Veronica Joseph. She made her temporary vows on March 20th, 1963 and her final vows, permanent profession, on August 6th, 1968 at age 26.

In September of 1960, her parents drove her to the Sisters of St. Joseph Mother House in Los Angeles on Chalon Road, where family contact was prohibited for awhile. After she started her ministry as a teacher, her belongings were stored and transferred from convent to convent in her brown, two-by-three-foot trunk secured with big metal latches. She kept that trunk for the rest of her life.

She wore a full, floor-length black and white habit with a veil covering her head and neck. A long cross hung around her neck, down to her white scapular chest cover. Her shoes were black and laced. Two years later, Vatican II modernized the Catholic Church and allowed blue or black modified nun habits. Carol then wore a skirt or dress shortened to show her legs, with a smaller veil that exposed some of her hair and neck. The Vatican's motivation was to make nuns more "relatable" to the public.

Carol was creative and talented in sewing and clothing alterations of her habit. When she described how she modified her "penguin" habit, feeling the joy of making something out of nothing, I thought of Maria in *The Sound of Music* making the children's outfits from curtains.

Carol was like Maria. It was like Carol's own movie-making transformations from old to new!

For four years, she lived at the Mother House in Los Angeles while earning a degree in Liberal Studies from Mount St. Mary's College. She lived among 50 teens who comprised her "reception"—each of the 18- and 19-year-old women had listened to their "call" and desired a lifestyle committed to Jesus and the Catholic Church. They weren't motivated by goals to land a future job. They were following orders to get through this "boot camp"—the novitiate—praying and offering oneself to the Lord in being led in His mission. It required powerful and spiritual discernment within themselves.

"I went through the novitiate on my knees," Carol told me several times. "I was always in trouble for something!"

As a result, she scrubbed and polished the marble floors more than once as penance for her outspokenness to her superiors. One task, over weeks and months, required sterilizing the kitchen and cooking equipment with bleach, which made her lose her sense of smell.

After she completed her training and earned her college degree and her California Teaching Credential, she made her pontifical (Pope approved) final vows as the Bride of Jesus.

So what did she wear for her final vows ceremonial Mass? It was customary for young ladies to wear a white wedding dress, as they were "The Bride of Christ." Cousin T was a seamstress extraordinaire and felt honored to be Carol's private seamstress. She wrote Carol's measurements on a match book cover while she and Carol's mother Elsie visited Sister Veronica Joseph, Carol, at the "Mount," the Mother house, in preparation for Carol making final vows. As a result, Cousin T designed and sewed a beautiful dress for Carol's ceremony.

For the next few years, T also sewed her heart out for Carol and many of Carol's reception friends by altering their three full habits: two for ministry and one reserved for their funeral. Both Carol and T modified them into the new, more relatable habit of a blue or black skirt made from the original black and white habit cloth.

"Never waste anything" was ingrained in the young women's minds and spiritually pure hearts. Even 25 years later, in 1986, T fulfilled cousin Carol's request for her jubilee dress. This time, T and Aunt Elsie went to Beverly Hills to select the gorgeous, mauve-colored Oriental silk fabric. Welcome to the nun world of fashion. (No wonder Carol loved her many outfits every day when she left community!)

After final vows, teaching or nursing became the next step for Carol and her friends. Carol's placement/mission was 12 years of elementary school teaching.

I bet her hundreds of students would say they were blessed to have had an amazing, happy teacher who would rather take you outside to think, be, draw, play and learn about God's glory. She believed in bringing out the best in everyone and encouraged all ages to know and love our God.

All of this brought her to CSJ in Lewiston, Idaho, where Carol was exactly like Whoopi Goldberg's character, Sister Mary Clarence, in the movie *Sister Act*. Please watch it. It's funny and entertaining with moral points throughout.

Carol was ahead of her time. Just like Sister Mary Clarence, Carol beat her own drum: confident, joy-filled, intelligent, passionate, talented, happy and standing up against the rude and righteous. She stood for the downtrodden, women, peace, civility, and "being the best person God designed you to be."

She personified Maxim #4: "Let your life be a continuous act of love," said founding Jesuit Frenchman Father Medaille, who developed 100 Maxims to help sisters grow in virtue, habits of heart and mind that were in Jesus Christ.

Jesus hold you.
God bless you.

CHAPTER 6
Eyes of Love

My First Day with Sister Carol

It was a cold crisp, sunny morning in January. Wearing a sweater, nice slacks, warm socks and shoes, I was thrilled to not wear nylons (as was required in the noviate in LA) as I joined the sisters for our cafeteria-style breakfast prepared by the kitchen staff.

I devoured eggs, sausage, toast and orange juice, often jumping up to get something for the sisters.

"More coffee, sister?" I asked. "Extra jam?" I was glad to serve them as they asked endless questions about me.

Oh boy, how fun.

"Thanks for breakfast," I told them. They smiled. Then I thanked the kitchen staff. The day was new and off to a fantastic start with sunshine, a full stomach and people who loved me.

Morning Mass: "Here's Sister Joanie!"

With a few sisters, I crossed the street to attend Mass; the cold air stung my face. We sat on the left in the first or second row of the pews. I felt welcome and at home. This was way more relaxed and natural than the church Mass march as novices back in Pasadena.

Sister Carol was flitting around doing pre-Mass things before joining our "nun section." After the service, she introduced me to: the priest, Father Morris; lay friends, Leah, Sharon, and Rusty; and people who worked at the hospital who were also parishioners.

Sister Carol's introduction was: "Let me introduce you to Sister Joanie, our novice from LA. She will be working with me for the next three months. It's great to have her with us, don't you think?"

People responded by saying, "Yes, happy to meet you, Sister Joanie. You'll fit right in. Sister Carol's the best. If you need anything, holler. Talk with you later. Have a great day."

Oh golly, what a warm welcome standing out in the cold. Everyone exuded warmth, love and respect by smiling and looking eye to eye.

"I like these people," I whispered aloud. "I think Sister Carol is really cool. She is really loved and taken care of. There is fun in the air."

Yet I was struck by an unusual foul, rancid, burnt, rotten eggs odor. *Yuck!*

"Carol, what's that smell?"

"Joanie, that's the Potlatch Mill. Gross, huh?"

It sure was. "Is that ugly smell here all the time?"

"Often. You'll get used to it."

I was excited to get used to how life had already changed: no longer Sister Carol, just Carol. It felt so natural, without pretense. Wonderfulness glowed in my heart and head.

Sister Carol's Office

Together Carol and I walked from Church to her "office," which was actually a multipurpose room in the basement of St. Stanislaus Church rectory. We entered through the back door, via the big parking lot, into a spacious room that evoked a good feeling. Bookshelves surrounded cold metal chairs scattered in a circle, and religious education posters pinned to the walls showed doves, probably the spirit of confirmation, a chalice with the communion host above it, and rainbows and butterflies with scripture quotes.

Later, Carol showed me the stairs from her office that connected to inside the rectory that led to Joan's secretarial office and the Jesuit priests' home.

"You'll be working with me for three days of each week," she said, "and then you'll be with Sister Frances working in the hospital as a Chaplain."

In her office, we went to her desk, where we sat facing each other. My chair was small and uncomfortable.

This lady is never at her desk. I bet she's out with people the whole time and that is miraculous: we are a match, both lovers of people.

She slid over a yellow pad of paper and said, "You'll need to write these three things down."

I had a pen ready for pages of notes. *Did she just say three things, that's it?*

"Monday you'll visit the shut-ins. Wednesday you'll help cook and serve meals for the poor, and Friday you'll be working with the youth."

All this took place in slow motion. Then she slid her car keys across the desk and said, "Here are the car keys for you. There is a full tank of gas and use it."

"What about you, Carol?"

"I'll let you know if I need it."

"OK."

I was flabbergasted that she had just met me and trusted me to do my jobs and have her car. This was more than what I had dreamed of. THANK YOU, JESUS! She was handing me the keys to the kingdom and I was screaming inside: "FREEDOM!"

"Joanie, today, Wednesday, you'll be helping out with the meals for the needy. Please see the work crew in the rectory kitchen right after our meeting."

"Cool, I love it." Pots and pans clanged up from the stairway. "Action time! I got this, Carol. Thank you!"

"Thank you, Joanie. You'll completely take over the visiting of our parish shut-ins."

Meeting Mildred

Meeting Mildred, the first shut-in I visited, was an eye-opener for how the elderly coped with living alone. Her gross living conditions have been in mind and prayers ever since. When I stepped through her front door, the warm house smelled like rotting garbage.

This underweight 80-year-old sat in a recliner with her feet up, wearing a long-sleeve nightgown and housecoat. Her long white hair looked unbrushed, and she wore thick socks with no slippers. Two cats sat on her lap.

Newspapers, unopened mail, and a wastebasket spilling over with used Kleenex sat near a plate of food covered in green-brown mold. *Ohhh, yucko.*

"Hi, Mildred, I'm Sister Joanie and Sister Carol asked if I'd come by and visit with you for a while. How are you doing?"

"I'm OK."

"That's good. Everyday can be OK. Can I sit here?"

"Yes," she flashed a huge smile and her glasses tilted slightly. "How is Sister Carol?"

"She's wonderful and said to tell you a big hi."

"She is so nice," Mildred said. "She comes and we talk about everything. She is really a good listener. I used to go to Mass every day. Sister Carol would always smile and talk with me. But I haven't been able to get out much."

"Ohhh," I said, "everyday Mass, you must be holier than God!"

"Hahaha. Not really."

"Do you have anyone helping you with things?"

"Yes, someone will be by later."

"That's good, but until then, can I at least put your plate in the kitchen and get you something to drink?"

"That would be nice, yes. A glass of water would be wonderful. Thank you."

I carried some things into the kitchen, where I tied up the stinky garbage bag, replaced the liner, washed my hands and found a clean glass for her water.

Mildred and I chatted for about 30 minutes; she was a really cool, nice lady just dealing with life alone, poor health, and needing more help than she realized. Then I remembered Carol saying, "in and out in one hour or less."

"I gotta run, Mildred. If it's OK with you, can I come back another day?"

"Of course, sweetie, that would be nice. Bring Sister Carol."

Oh boy, reflect on this, Joanie. This was only one on Carol's roster of shut-ins. Later, I told her about Mildred's conditions and Carol made phone calls to help Mildred. "Going the extra mile" for someone, I discovered, was one of many of Carol's qualities. She had courage, connections and was doing the CSJ charism "love the dear neighbor."

Next, on Carol's lengthy, handwritten roster were her elderly friends and I looked forward to meeting them all. This incredible lesson brought back memories of my family taking care of Grandma and Grandpa when they got elderly.

Who will take care of me in my old age or whatever happens? Will I be on a roster list someday?

I was startled with the shut-ins' enormous physical, emotional and mental needs. Mildred lit up with relief when I came to care for her. Ironically, I felt I was getting more out of our relationship than her. She captivated me, and I saw the meaning of HOLY.

It was Carol. Her ability to delegate and involve others to get things done was a fabulous gift because she did not see herself as the one and only savior. That inspired me to want to also go the extra mile to help people.

The 50-Foot Microphone Cord

Carol told me a story about a priest who presided at St. Stan's Parish in Lewiston, and how he gave her an amazing gift during the homily at a Sunday Mass.

"Sister Carol," he asked, "will you please come up here, front and center?"

He presented her with a 50-foot microphone cord and said, "Sister Carol, we love your musical talent and gifts. We love your singing prayer voice. We love your dancing. Now we want you to use this long cord and go up and down the main aisle of church, smiling and singing and helping everybody else to be joyful. Sister Carol, you are the joy of our Parish and this is our special gift to you."

The parishioners exploded with applause!

Carol responded, "Oh Father, really?"

"Yes, Sister Carol, we want to see you at every Mass leading us in song and prayer."

"Way to go, Sister Carol!" cheered the full congregation with more clapping. "We love you."

"Thank you, Father," Carol said. "This is an honor. This is a most special gift and I will do my very, very best to have all of you sing along with me. I do love singing for the Lord and I love praying together with each of you. Thank you so much."

I witnessed Carol in action with the microphone with the 50-foot cord, humming, harmonizing and spreading joy as she touched her ear to encourage others to sing louder.

Youth Ministry

Next she said I'd be helping her with youth ministry, which was exciting because I had taught all ages, from Kindergarten to twelfth grade, and coached in the past. *Yes! This will be a blast!*

Carol was superwoman, leading youth retreats, fun parish-wide activities, and adult Catholic education for those wishing to become Catholic (Rite of Christian Initiation of Adults, or RCIA), weekly Sunday liturgies, music, community morning and evening prayer services and council meetings. Carol must have had a secret closet of capes, flying powers, extra strong legs, arms and heart, intelligence surpassing Einstein, and the heart of a lion.

Wow, am I ever blessed . . . and for three months this is my life.

Nuns Respond to Crises

I felt like I was on call 24 hours a day. And sometimes I was! Being across the street from the hospital, calls came at any time from a hospital staffer saying:

"Good evening, there has been a terrible accident! Please send a sister over to console and sit with the family."

CHAPTER 6

I never went alone, but did accompany Sister Frances and Sister Carol twice. Scary stuff. It was heart-wrenching: sitting with family members during emergency surgeries or with people dying.

Once in the middle of the night, about 1 or 2 a.m., the knock came on my bedroom door: "Joanie, please come with me to the hospital."

After quickly brushing my hair, throwing on pants, blouse and my "Pastoral Care Sister Joan Irene" name tag on my gray blazer, I walked with hesitation into the Emergency Room waiting room. The wailing voice of a wounded animal came from a woman rocking back and forth, burying her face in her hands. Her agonized sobs and suffering were breaking my heart.

The ER nurse quietly said, "Thank you, sisters, for coming. Her child has been taken to emergency surgery. We will keep you posted."

We sat with her, her tears gushing like a waterfall. I also had Niagara Falls splashing down my cheeks.

We grasped hands and Sister Frances prayed the "Our Father." Despite my quivering voice, I joined the prayers. The mother began to calm down. I pressed her hand into mine. Then released it. I felt better and so did she. We emptied the Kleenex box while waiting for hours.

Sister Frances was absolutely amazing. How did she do this every day, working eight hours at her job, then being on call? She was a walking angel! Non-judgmental, strong and quiet, Sister Frances sat and gently patted and touched this woman. Her gestures brought tears to my eyes as I witnessed unconditional love.

Where does she get this strength of body, mind and spirit?

The next day, Sister Frances told me to go see the family from last night's harrowing event.

Oh God, me? OK, I can do this.

I arrived to find the dark-haired teenager recuperating from surgery in a sterile hospital room with a large window and view of gray sky. Their mother sat beside the teen, who was awake, sitting up with two fluffed pillows and a quirk of a smile as I flashed a huge one.

"Would each of you like to receive Eucharist or Holy Communion, the body of Christ?"

"Yes," the mother said and the teen nodded.

"Jesus is here for you," I prayed. "He will heal you from the tips of your toes to the hair on your head. The Body of Christ."

"Amen." I stood a little longer as the mother gazed on her child. "Have hope, God is Great," I said with conviction. "I'll check in with you later today, if that's OK."

They nodded; the young one's eyes closed to rest and the mother leaned back in her chair.

I entered the next hospital room smiling because I was carrying Jesus. It was a joy being the real me, saying "Good morning" to people and medical staff.

I carried my leather Jesus pouch around my neck, held close to my heart, sharing Him in communion with all who wanted Him. Sometimes patients were so weak, they had to muster the strength to have a tiny piece of the thin, sacred wafer. Other times it was me alone, quietly sitting on the side of the hospital bed, or praying aloud to the listening patient.

I said the universal "Our Father" prayer. Most of the time, I made up my own prayers as I talked with Jesus, asking for healing and thanking Him for a new day. I really liked praying with the nurses. They were super people!

Jesus, this is a new job, a new ministry for me. It's hard. But together we can do this. Holy Spirit be my words and actions.

The oncology floor, for cancer patients and family members, was extra special and difficult because it triggered memories of my father's cancer. I was empathetic and sympathetic, listened and listened more, trying to be 100% present and not rattle on about nothing. Often I sat with family members in the stark hallway or in a room. Sharing their pain and agony remains fresh in my heart. I was grateful to provide that support so they would not be alone.

As I was getting in the groove at the hospital as a pastoral care assistant, it was healing to share, along with Sisters Carol and Frances, reflections in our debriefing sessions. We gave it all to God. It really helped to vocalize my emotions triggered during these crises.

Likewise, Sister Carol was often called to help parishioners with problems, so I asked, "When needed, Carol, may I go with you?"

"Of course. You know you will need to sit in another room."

"Yes, I will stay out of your way."

"OK, great."

Speak and it shall happen. Seek and you will find.

Across the street from the convent in the two-story, red brick building that was the priest's rectory office, residence and parish offices, there was an upset and frightened person. I stayed in the parish office while Carol entered the conference room and closed the door.

"Oh, Sister Carol, you came," the upset person said (I could hear everything through the thin walls).

"Yes, I'm here for you," she said. "Why are you here?" Long, silent minutes passed. Patient beyond patient, Carol asked, "Would you like to talk about it? Maybe I can help you?"

"I think so," the woman sobbed. Fear and frustration sounded in her voice. "My husband hit my son! And he, my son, ran out of the house with a bloody nose. I can't find him. I'm so angry at my husband. So I came here and rang the doorbell. Father let me in and I asked him to call you."

I visualized Carol's relaxed body, hands gently resting on her lap, with her special smile and radiance of hope-filled green eyes, sitting next to this woman, attentively listening and watching her. With a soft, calm voice, Carol asked few questions and listened more. She exuded peace.

Wow, all of a sudden I was feeling really attracted to Carol. It was her voice! My hormones shot through my veins, capillaries and aorta like a dam that broke. My body flushed with warmth and tingles.

Wow, what's happening, Joanie? This feels so natural and great.

I pictured Carol leaning forward, being 100% there for this lady to plan her next move. Then Carol used a parish coupon to pay for the woman's taxi.

Carol and I silently walked in the cold darkness across the street to the convent, not saying a word. That was the ultimate respect and kindness in our relationship. If she wanted to talk, I would listen. If not, no worries. Our silence was magical.

I wanted to hold her hand forever. It took all my willpower to not reach out and touch her.

Is she feeling anything towards me? Or is this all my stuff? Oh God, my hormones are going ballistic.

We said good night and as we headed to our bedrooms in the long, wide hallway, I turned back and said, "Thanks, Carol, for letting me go with you. You're AMAZING! Thank you for helping that lady."

We smiled and our eyes connected like never before.

I look at Carol and see the face of Jesus.

Nuns at the Tavern

Carol encouraged her convent sisters to eat, drink and be merry at The Hideaway, a local tavern that served the best half-pound burgers, fried chicken, and thick-cut spuds with beer or soda pop. *Yummy!*

The sisters jumped on it! And of course, I was all in! The sisters frequented The Hideaway to enjoy each other away from the confines of our secluded, brick cave.

This "hole in the wall" was in a dark, decrepit, wooden building. The semi-dark interior's good, down-home atmosphere had blaring music, pool tables with clanging billiard balls, cigarette smoke, and old friends laughing and talking.

Carol and her sisters marched in like they owned the place, nodding to the bartender and staff as they greeted her: "Hi, Sister Carol."

"Hi," she replied, calling them each by name. "How's it going tonight?"

"Good, sister. You?"

"AMAZING. Thanks."

All eyes and smiles were on us as we went to the back room, our "designated area" with a long, thick wooden table and heavy wooden chairs with enough room for all of us. The locals watched us lovingly. The nuns were admired and respected. This was not a forbidden, unCatholic gathering, but a win-win human necessity to bring joy and the aliveness of Christ to the public.

Just like in the movies *The Godfather* or *Sister Act*, Carol (similar to Whoopi Goldberg) was the phenomenal leader of our "Mafia" of convent nuns.

Our ladies, some in modified habits with black veils, two in full-length habits and many of us dressed in jeans, slacks and bright-colored sweaters and coats, defied the nun stereotype. How fun and diverse was this?! We all were ready to dive into good food, good company and a place to let our hair down . . . or veil down. Oh, the laughter and the smiles, a natural stimulant.

This was totally awesome! Thank you, Carol for being our "boss."

Was going to a tavern allowed as a nun? Did nuns drink in public? How did they pay for this? What would the Los Angeles nuns think? Oh, how the novitiate rules and regulations jumped into my reflection and discernment mode.

Get rid of those thoughts, Joanie. Celebrate this day!

My first time at The Hideaway, about 10 of us sisters were seated comfortably with Carol at the head of the table and me at the other end. We could easily jump up and retrieve more napkins, drinks, etc. When a song blasted from the speakers, triggering my emotions of "life before the convent," I thought of my dear friends, Ruthie from high school and Diane from our close-knit softball team. I started to cry, missing my friends and humbly loving my new life.

"What's with Sister Joanie?" a sister asked Carol. "Is she OK?"

Carol replied, "She does that sometimes; she's fine!"

I laughed and cried more; Carol had just come to my rescue. Relieved that I didn't have to explain anything, I was oddly homesick and overjoyed to feel so at home here. *I believe it's a gift to let my emotions fly!*

Freedom to be Me in Private and in Public

My bedroom had a twin bed, a chair, a desk, a long counter, a small window facing the trees, and a white porcelain sink where I kept my washcloth and soap, toothpaste and purple toothbrush. It was nice, simple and super clean with everything wooden, even the floor.

We, the sisters on the second floor, enjoyed a college dormitory setting. We shared a communal bathroom with plenty of toilets, sinks and shower stalls. Poop smells, lavender lotions and jasmine-scented hair products placed near one of the sinks were in the air. *Oh, thanks be to God for the tampon boxes in the cupboard.* One kind sister had probably put them there for me.

I slept soundly and dreamed vividly of God's wonders, rainbows, mountains and flowering trees. My happiness overflowed like a bucket of honey.

I love it here. Prayers, food, helping people and sharing the Lord, all by just being me!

The freedom felt far healthier than the strict rules in LA.

Maggie, who was in a convent one block away, told me while writing this book: "I felt a freedom in Lewiston because we weren't treated as novices and we were not under a microscope. We were members of a community."

When Carol inquired about my good friend, I told her Maggie and I were excited to go out for huckleberry ice cream after her parents had sent her $5. Each engulfed in our ministries, we hadn't seen each other.

"We're both dealing with this," I told Carol, plugging my nose and saying in a nasal tone: "The ugly rotten egg, rancid burnt smell from the potlatch mill. The odor drifts all day long over the valley. Yucko!"

Carol's laughter indicated that she really did enjoy me, and when she invited Mag to play guitar with us at Mass, I knew Carol cared about my friendships with others as well.

Then Carol helped introduce me to the community by inviting me to explore the area.

"Would you like to go here and there with me?" Carol asked. "Errands and such."

"Absolutely, yes! Show me; take me; let's explore!"

Everywhere we went in her parish car, an old clunker, people lit up and said, "Hi, Sister Carol! How's your day going?"

She would stop, take a few minutes to socialize, and always

said: "Let me introduce you to my friend and Sister Joanie from Los Angeles via San Diego."

Her choice of words—friend, not novice—was so large and powerful to me. I felt absolutely whole!

Plus, the rapport, kindness and respect she enjoyed with people mesmerized me. She gave her undivided attention to everyone and anyone. Never in a hurry, never judgmental or critical. She could listen and talk to a stick, a beggar or a bishop. With all that sincere joy, and non-threatening presence about her, I felt extra special when she chose to have personal quality time with only me.

Romance Blooms: Our First Drive & Evening Jam Sessions

Our first drive was an outing to the scenic Dworshak Dam. Carol claimed that she only asked me three questions.

Voila! I spilled out my life history, my dreams included, in that two-hour trip that revealed her introvert side and my extrovert side.

I sat in the passenger seat, telling stories, waving my hands, and shifting like a person with ADHD. She gripped the steering wheel, gliding with the swerve of mountain road turns like a professional truck driver, slowing when needed and hardly ever putting her black-booted foot on the brake.

My novitiate status had kept me inside myself too long, top secret and too emotionally intense. With Carol, my thoughts, feelings and word expressions were flying free. Carol smiled, glanced over at me, shook her head, laughed and said, "Uh huh, Oh, really? That's AMAZING."

She was really interested in ME. I was really interested in HER. We had everything to share, nothing to hide. Absolutely wonderful.

Each evening, she invited me to her bedroom to play guitar, sing, laugh, harmonize and laugh more.

"Tell me about your family," Carol said, "your grandparents, your sports, your high school, your dreams, your . . . "

I jabbered away, excitement bursting out through my expressive hands, arms and face. My high, positive energy and booming voice delighted her as she listened intensely.

It was two-sided: I asked her thousands of questions as well. Slower in response, she figured things out or changed her mind as she talked. And Carol was amazing in remembering our conversations. I'm constantly working on becoming a better listener because of Carol's frequent reminder of my grandfather's words: "You have two ears and one mouth for a reason."

We had a blast sharing scissors to cut felt letters for banners; we talked about our families, interrupting one another with a cute story. And we threw around ideas: "What ifs" for retreats, youth activities, Sunday Mass, parish events and fun with our convent sisters. We loved feeding off each other's thoughts.

This woman is so open minded. I love her for that. Thank you, God.

We had fun jam sessions: playing Catholic hymns on guitar and singing, me off key, her on key, spontaneously creating and changing lyrics to make it more silly, personal and intimate expressions of our love.

Carol had a stack of music tapes, so we recorded our sing-alongs while she strummed and I played the chords on her guitar, a real dynamo duo, doing duets. Get it? *Haha! A real gay couple? I think so!*

Oh, did we even mention that topic? Gay vs. straight?

Let's not even talk about celibacy! Let's deal with who I am. Am I lesbian?

Plugged into the electric outlet was her prized JVC brown leather radio and cassette tape player. Her little machine—nine inches long and five inches tall—let in the world of artists, including Diana Ross, Neil Diamond and Michael Jackson of the Jackson 5.

As she swung me dancing the Boogie Woogie around her bedroom, she told stories about inviting friends and cousins to play 45s in the basement that her father had remodeled so they could dance their hearts out.

We were constantly laughing. Carol had the biggest of smiles. And the BEST HUGS. We loved holding hands, gazing into each other's eyes, engulfed, respecting boundaries yet with the passion of wanting more physical contact. We were so naturally comfortable together.

She loved her foot rubs and we played footsie, barefoot or with socks. I loved head and shoulder rubs. We interlocked our fingers and our eyes connected without words. We knew this was romance. Trusting in one another with our heart and soul, our friendship expanded as wide as the oceans. It was not infatuation. It was deep.

Is this real committed Love? Where is God leading us?

We were building a secret and forbidden romance in the stark crevices of convent walls. We were blossoming, the commitment of friendship to Jesus. And to each other.

"Oh golly, this is so much fun," I said.

"It sure is."

Living every day to the max with Carol in the convent was probably going against the norm—even bucking the conventional system of the Catholic Church and religious life. But it felt so natural. During my mission experience, as Carol and I fostered profound love for each other, it was a three-month mathematical formula: Jesus + friendship = something way deeper.

I questioned my heart and soul: "Is this LOVE for real? Is this for eternity? Am I putting too much into this? Or is this just good old fashioned friendship? Is this REAL LONG-TERM LOVE?"

Though we slept in our own bedrooms, we hugged closely to greet mornings and say goodnights. Every night I told Carol, "Jesus hold you" and she told me, "God bless you." It all felt normal, beautiful, sensual and blessed.

Wow, this is AMAZING! Love is AMAZING!

At night, as my head hit the pillow, my mind replayed the day's intimate moments.

Am I gay? Is she gay? Does it matter?

My prayerful reflections inspired the real question in my heart: *What is happening? I'm in a world of unknowns, help me, oh Lord!*

Snow Moguls

On a gloriously sunny but cold day, Carol took me up to a hillside playground where families and college students were gliding down a snowy 50-yard run on big black inner tubes.

Laughter punctuated the cold air along with boots crunching on the snow and tubes skidding on the ice, along with screams as the tubes flew over three mogul jumps, sometimes sending the person in another direction.

"I AM SO EXCITED! CAROL, I REALLY WANT TO DO THIS!"

I bee-lined to a nice family who allowed me to use their inner tube. Carol was all smiles.

Head first, laying on my belly, my gloved hands gripped the two handles on top of the large inner tube. With a small push from my new family, down the snow run I went. It was icier than the fluffy soft snow I had expected. I picked up speed really fast. I hit the first mogul, flew a few feet in the air and landed on the ice, still on the run with my tube.

"Wow, this is fast. Keep your chin up, Joanie; hang on!"

By the second mogul, I felt like a speeding bullet. What fun!

I hit the third mogul bump—fast, furious and hard.

The inner tube went one way as I flew about 20 feet and crash landed on my chest on the ice.

"UGH! That hurt!"

Carol screamed from up top: "Joa . . . nie!"

"Oohs" and "aahs" erupted from the crowd.

I laid flat on the cold, hard-as-bricks ice!

A man helped me stand; I was dazed—the wind knocked out of me, and maybe a head bump, too. The hill looked very steep; Carol clasped her hands at her chest. We exchanged nods to say, "I'm OK."

I thanked the people who helped me as a kid ran the inner tube up the hill. I walked very slowly up to Carol. She put her arm around my waist and said:

"I've been trying to figure out how I would tell your novice director that I killed you. Are you OK, love?"

She just called me "LOVE!" Oh boy, I think we have, with God's grace, just been made into an everlasting couple. Alleluia!

My mind spun: *Is this a formal courtship where we agree that we are girlfriend-girlfriend? Am I her everlasting "love?" I hope so? Only God knows and that's fine with me.*

I was alive and breathing! We hugged.

And even though my body really hurt, I said, "Wow, Carol, that was so exciting! I really want to go again. I can hold on better."

"NO, NO, NO! You are not going again!"

We laughed, which hurt my upper ribs.

"Let's head back home," she said.

Back at the convent's dinner table, we shared our great adventure, which inspired "oohs" and "aahs" from the nuns wearing black and white penguins habits.

Carol said to Sister Frances, with a wink to me, in her gorgeous green eye, "Next time, on soft snow, let's go cross country skiing."

Everyone laughed. Except me. Still hurting, I nodded and said:

"I've never done that before. That sounds awesome. I'm in!"

Later, my bedtime prayers included: "Thank you, God, that I am alive. It was a fun day with Carol. Thank you for her. Please heal my ribs and pulled muscles. Give Carol a gentle squeeze for me, please."

As my soul searched for answers, my heart jumped around doing back flips.

God, talk to me. Please. Carol's been a sister for 20 years, me just a few years. I really want to make the right decision. Should I take my time in figuring this out? We are both openly in love with each other.

I've never been this deep in a relationship before. I like it.

Did You plan this? It feels like a massive crisis!

What's next? Help me, Jesus!

God, this is complex. Where do Carol and I go from here?

What about my nun vows? What about the Catholic Church and gay stuff? What about her commitments?

Please, Jesus, what's next?

Take away my apprehensions and turn them into delight.

I believe in Commitment: to You and to love.

Lead me on, Lord.

Jesus hold you.

God bless you.

CHAPTER 7
Our First Kiss

One weekend, I remained at the convent while Carol led a retreat in a school gymnasium where 75 women slept on Army cots and held prayer circles in folding chairs. She arranged for home-cooked snacks and meals, and the kitchen crew worked tirelessly.

Decorations created a fun, festive feeling. On the wall were rainbow circles, while red heart mobiles hung from the ceiling and bright pink napkins adorned the tables.

This was Carol's largest retreat, titled Lumière (a French word for light), and her team included friends Nancy, Sharon and Lea, who were still breaking the boundaries of lay women being spiritual leaders; they were female prophets who enjoyed an incredible bond with Carol. For years, they had confided their innermost thoughts, marriages, life events, troubled childhoods and whatever else weighed on their hearts. They trusted and loved each other so much that they could spill their hearts out without fear. Their secrets would be forever honored. Their sacred, confidential, and powerful personal friendship was stronger than the Rock of Gibraltar.

It was not common for lay women to be spiritual leaders within their parishes. But they found the path and had a fearless leader in Sister Carol. These married women were reaching out to other wives, widows and singles, and were being called to spread the word of God to all women. This was no longer just the privilege of nuns and priests. Carol was not bucking the Catholic rules, but expanding them to include lay women by ignoring gender and other stereotypes. Carol knew we could all talk to and hear God.

After staying up all night counseling the women, on Sunday morning at 5 a.m., Carol returned to our convent. I was awakened by the sound of my doorknob turning and the door quietly opening. Carol entered and put my laundry on the desk.

"I have your folded laundry for you, Joanie. I'm on a break." She was filled with such excitement, buzzing into and around my bedroom.

I was groggy, forcing my eyes open. "Thank you," I said, feeling very cared for and loved by this simple act of kindness.

With radiant sparkling eyes, she floated over to my bedside, bent down and gave me a juicy, passionate kiss on my lips.

Then she said, "I told Nancy and the girls that I'm in love with you."

"WOW! I love you, Carol. And you folded my laundry."

"I need to go; I'll talk with you later." She joyously skipped out the door and quietly closed it.

I laid there thinking and thanking God for the miracle that this nun had openly admitted her romantic love for me—another nun.

She openly confessed this love to her closest friends, indicating her sincerity and trust in God. Wow, incredible! She had stepped out of her protected life as a bride of Christ. She must have felt the love of the Holy Spirit guiding her to our relationship. I felt the same, not ashamed at all, only blessed and filled with God's love in a human divine kind of way.

I was overwhelmed, with joyful tears welling in my eyes while smiling to the moon and back.

"Maybe this is why God sent me to Idaho on this mission experience." This magnificent moment confirmed that we shared a mutual love—not infatuation. This was the real thing.

I didn't go back to sleep. I laid there with an ever-beaming smile, thanking God for this incredible woman. Love was in the air!!!

Oh golly. Oh, God, how beautiful. Thank you, God.

Goodbye for Now

It was time to head back to the novitiate in Pasadena: my three-month mission experience had come to a close. Carol and I had our last guitar Mass with the parish together and were in the rectory, saying goodbye. All I could do was hold her in a close hug, then closer and closer in each other's arms as I sobbed! I mean, really sobbing! Uncontrollable sobbing for about 20 minutes, and loudly! What pain and joy overwhelmed me—the joy of having developed a remarkable friendship and love for Carol and vice versa, and the agony that we would be physically separated until who knew when or where. Throw in the questions, fears, unknowns from everything that had been my stable rock foundation beliefs.

Was this God, the Holy Spirit speaking to me again?

I did not want to leave her! I also didn't want to leave Lewiston!

I prayed that the priest wouldn't enter the room. Carol held me like never before. And my tears flowed like the 100-year great floods.

Here I was, 24 years young, experiencing LOVE for the first time. She was 39 with her own loving feelings toward me! We knew that being in love as nuns was not accepted, yet we were so happy in love. How could society's and the church's perception of gays and lesbians be contrary to our bliss?

God's Plan?

Oh my golly, what a storm of wild winds, heavy rains and smashing sleet with thunder and lightning was exploding inside us. However, I wasn't scared because I knew, and so did Carol, that after storms come beautiful blue skies, sunshine and even rainbows. That gorgeous vision was paramount in my mind and heart. This had to be God's plan. Oh how I totally put ALL my trust in the Lord about Carol, me and us.

Though we each questioned ourselves and each other, we remained confidential, secretive and hopeful. Were we blind to oppressions, trapped in boxes of rules or living in a sea of unknowns?

God only knows.

We had the courage, faith and fortitude to tackle our questions, to blaze our own trail and be true to ourselves. Love conquers all and our love for each other was strong and unbreakable. We both knew, deep, deep down in our guts and hearts, that God would take care of us.

What am I going to do? What is Carol going to do? Where and what will happen next?

God only knows and He'll let us know.

I left Carol!

I left the Lewiston convent and parish and returned to the novitiate for more prayer with a listening spirit. While I knew we would both miss each other terribly, I was confident that somehow, somewhere we would continue our budding relationship.

Jesus hold you.
God bless you.

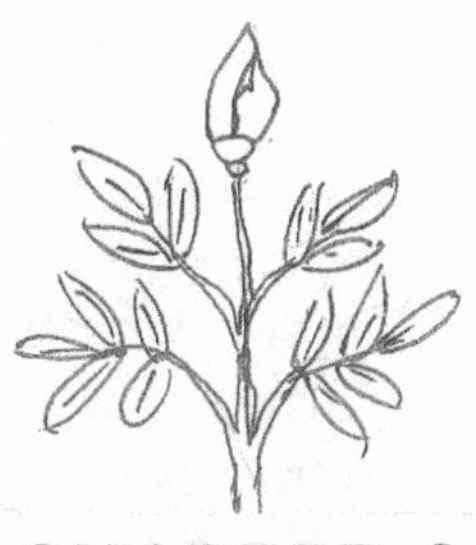

CHAPTER 8

God Orchestrates Our Path

Back in Pasadena—1,085 miles from Carol—I immersed into the novitiate routine, changed internally and out, but unable to vocalize it to others. My heart was doing back flips.

Carol remained at the awesome Lewiston parish pouring out her heart in her selfless love to her community, parish members and especially the RCIA and youth. Thanks to a CSJ sister, Carol was incorporating her Graphoanalysis (handwriting analysis) into her ministries of counseling and annulments, and she had been given permission, and was so excited, to spend summers earning her master's degree from Fairfield University in Connecticut in three areas: Psychology, Spirituality and Counseling.

We wrote letters and cards to each other. The 1980s did not have cell phones or texting for communicating. We wrote and drew pictures, sent copied-by-hand poems and told of our day's events, our funny quirky joke tales about ourselves, and our prayers and reflections with Jesus. We were not gossipers or complainers, so our letters were hope-filled and happy words about us, not other people.

We prayed for each other night and day, and we prayed for each other to get closer to Jesus. We relied on discernment powers within our hearts to guide and inspire us as our longing continued to grow in a special friendship—understanding and respect were paramount. We believed we could live, minister and be kindred souls. In retrospect, it would probably be best to have called this a long-distance courtship.

Our correspondence reminded me of my parents who wrote "getting-to-know-you love letters" back and forth while he was stationed at Pearl Harbor in the US Navy for World War II. Carol and her dad were also pen pals. A real thoughtful, heartfelt letter or card puts zillions of smiles on a face because it can be read over and over.

I Made Temporary Vows

I still had a deep desire and felt I was following the Lord with all my heart as I made my vows of poverty, chastity and obedience in front of my family and my new family of sisters of St. Joseph. I committed myself 100% to religious life. The studies, reflections, mentoring and spiritual directions all led up to the signing of vows and a universal celebration of Mass at the mother house in Los Angeles.

Standing at the colorful, flower-filled altar, signing my commitment document and speaking loudly with conviction to all in attendance, I read my paragraph of my pre-thought-out, prayed-over vows (which I believed in) typed on two white index cards secured with Scotch tape.

This was the most important day of my life!

Plus, Carol was one of the many sisters who stood and promised their love and support, too. *Yippee!*

At the reception following Mass, my colleagues, Maggie and Cathy, posed for pictures with family and friends; it was so cool that Cathy's father and my father were employed at the same business and knew each other.

Before making my temporary vows, Carol was allowed to visit me in Pasadena at the novitiate house. What joy sang in my heart as she came through the rear house door, all the way from Idaho. Everyone welcomed her as I kept myself from being a hyperactive volcano. No extra bedrooms were available in our convent; I received permission that Carol would sleep in my bed while I was in a sleeping bag on the floor. When sleep time came, I was enamored with her in her nightgown, and we gently kissed good night. I lay on the floor, reached up to grab her hand or touch her arm. We held hands until my arm tingled with numbness and we fell asleep.

Maggie, Cathy and I were accepted as Sisters of St. Joseph. I was so grateful for the wisdom of temporary vows. It was identical to a marriage engagement, giving time for myself and others while searching to see if it was really a mutual fit.

My favorite picture of Carol and me was taken that day—me kissing Carol on her cheek and her looking surprised and full of pure love and joy. Our courtship was secret, but I had a gut feeling that maybe others could see our true love bond.

I put my mind at rest and just BELIEVED that this was all God's plan, and by letting go and letting God do it His way, it would be perfect.

My First Mission Assignment

So began the next phase of ministry where I was placed as a Physical Education and Religion teacher in a Catholic school. I was to use this time, as long as I needed, to contemplate making my final vows. I had intense discernment about my love for Carol and my commitment to my congregational sisters.

Now, what are the chances . . . God opens the doors for me to minister and work at St. Patrick's school and parish in Pasco, Washington.

I was delighted to get back to my profession of teaching Physical Education. Known as Sister Joanie, I was one busy, happy person in love with life.

The best part was that Pasco was only a two-and-a-half-hour drive from Lewiston! I was thrilled to have the best of both worlds: Sister Joanie the teacher with dearest friend Sister Carol nearby. My convent residence was very comfortable with my bedroom on a second floor with sunset views and winds whipping around. The four seasons thrilled me. I worked, lived and loved our progressive Catholic church, an involved and engaged parish people, youthful nuns, elementary school enthusiasm and Mother Nature.

Once, sometimes twice, every month, I visited Carol to help her with youth classes and retreats, participate in an ecumenical volleyball tournament, play guitar with her at Masses, and feast at potluck meetings where all the Northwest sisters celebrated together. It was a blast! These talented, professional women made Catholic Church alive and joyful. They were a hoot to work and live with.

Carol Celebrates 25 Years as a Sister

We celebrated Sisters Frances' and Carol's 25th jubilee (25 years as a sister) on Saturday May 10th, 1986, in Lewiston with a lively celebration!! I played guitar along with Youth Minister Tom and Sister Rosie. Carol's brother Bob was the offertory reader and her parents brought forth the bread and wine as the offertory gifts. It was a joy-filled Mass and bountiful reception with lots of delicious food and extra baskets of loaves and fish at the end.

Carol and Frances were treated royally by the parishioners and other sisters. The banner draping the altar was covered with butterflies, flowers and their names dazzling with large font and gorgeous colors. Oh, happy day!!

All the Northwest sisters sat in a few front row pews, or were up front with the folk Mass ensemble. Carol had asked me to speak and share the homily. Wow! The priests were honored to have women of the cloth on the altar, although it was very unusual. I was so honored to be asked to do this at this very special occasion, rather than one of her sisters she had worked with for years.

I wore Carol's yellow and white polka-dotted hat while I gave the five-minute sermon from the wooden lectern normally reserved for priests only. Carol was all smiles sitting in the front row, confident I would do well and wondering what I would say. Such trust!

It was the beginning of meeting and getting to know her parents, being accepted by them and sharing hugs and kisses in the end. It was the start of a very special relationship for all of us. We felt like a bonded family; I was not just a friend of Carol's, but someone more important to her than a friend. I was not sure what that meant, but knew it would play out as we went along.

Is this another Miracle? God is SO AWESOME.

Our Friendship Deepens with Vulnerability and Honesty

During our first year of a closer- but still long-distance relationship, weekend times with Carol were fabulous: our letter writing was replaced with real hugs and kisses. Our courtship took on new intimacies that felt natural and free, private and secure. God was blessing us and preparing us for bigger things. We were not in a hurry and relished our alone times. No hanky panky, but oodles of tender loving care.

During our second year in Pasco and Lewiston, ministry and convent life were going fine for each of us. We were close, but had too many miles separating us, and wished for more in our friendship/relationship. Once, I was laying on her bed, gazing at her beautiful body. I was attracted to her body as much as her soul. Carol was the most amazing person I'd ever known. She was flustered under my gaze, so I said, "I'll close my eyes." She laid beside me—both fully clothed—and we talked and listened for hours about everything: family, travel, concerts, fishing, etc.

She inspired dreams and a future for herself, me and us.

I said something to the effect of, "Carol, I want you and I need you. I feel whole when we're together and I feel like something is missing when we're apart."

"You don't need me."

"Yes I do, Carol." More snuggles and kisses as words of affection spilled from deep within.

"No one has ever loved me like you do, Joanie."

"Me either, Carol."

Honest with each other forever! We were "one and only" soul mates, put together by God. God is Love! No labels, no boxes. Just Love. Monogamous in behavior and thoughts. Respectful of ourselves and each other. *Love is patient, love is kind . . .*

Our Weekend Visits Increase, Yahoo!!

I joined carpools to Lewiston or I was granted permission to take the car for the weekend. My inner joys were hyper and passionate, anticipating learning more about Carol and being so thankful to look deeply in her eyes and touch her soft hands.

Thank you God for placing me so close to Carol.

Friday night arrivals were like coming home, as Carol greeted me with delicious dinners that included her homemade, to-die-for clam chowder, made with cream cheese and rich milk, potatoes, clams and seasonings. So yummy and creamy, and, yes, I added extra pepper.

We sat in the kitchen or dining room, chatting with other nuns about our work week, happenings in our parishes and towns, and stories of the good old times.

Carol asked us in her calming voice: "What are you looking forward to?"

Oh, how stimulating this was. Personalities erupted, pondering and speaking before thinking, and it was fun hearing each other's dreams: from "I look forward to visiting my brother," to "a retreat in the desert," to "finishing a quilt," to "the Christmas tree bonfire event in the mountains," to "cross country skiing," and "going to my niece's wedding." I ate my chowder and hardly spoke.

God knows my true heart. To live with Carol forever!

In Carol's room, her double mattress was made up with sheets and a blanket on the floor, candles lit, with Neil Diamond, Amy Grant and John Denver on cassette tape in her mini stereo. We danced, talked and enjoyed our growing intimacy. I felt whole and so did she. We were united in all ways.

She visited me in Pasco as well, where we shared my twin bed. We went camping in a pup tent in an apple orchard and we drove to explore places, people and Mother Nature all while singing, telling stories and forming our forever bond.

We were a couple. Our growing love brought out the best in each other. The more we loved each other, the more love we spread to others. That was our personal mission and way of life during 40 years together—bringing Jesus to others by being the best couple possible.

We always included sisters or friends at meals, Mass attendance, prayer time and social gatherings. It was so fun seeing people enjoy themselves with us.

"You are the happiest couple at gatherings," people old us. We couldn't hide it; it just happened. *That's the joy of the Lord!! Alive in Christ Jesus.*

So, it's time to trust God to the max and believe in the new world ahead.

The Twin Bed

One day, Carol visited me in Pasco and to my delight attended a school event that I was overseeing. She saw me in action and I easily spotted her face in the large crowd. YES! She was there to support me.

That evening, after our sisters' community dinner in the convent, Carol stayed overnight in my bedroom, where I had prepared my sleeping bag on floor cushions. My room had a lovely window facing the green grass sports field, the running track and, way beyond, the barren hills of the high desert, all under a purple and black sky sparkling in the galaxy of a million stars.

We snuggled on the twin bed and remained there all night, wrapping our arms, legs and feet around each other. It was natural and warm.

God creates everything.

I felt so loved as she caressed me, whispering compliments, giggling, and tenderly kissing my cheeks and lips. We kissed for a long time before she said, "Let's get some sleep."

We gazed into each other's eyes for one final kiss goodnight. This was real love. Together we slept like babies.

I never worried about being interrupted by the other sisters, but I did lock the door just in case. Unfortunately, we were still secretly in love within the confines of convent life and society's disapproval of lesbians and gays.

Being Gay in the 1980s

In the 1980s, being gay was a sin in most churches and our innocence was probably a bonus. We had the protection of our convent walls, unlike many LGTBQ people who had neither family support nor safe living conditions.

Carol and I, along with most gay people and couples during the 1980s, were living in a time where we didn't talk openly about our sexual orientation for fear of being ostracized, ridiculed, hated and disowned. Though very unique due to our nun status, we were not yet free to talk about it; this was probably a disservice to us and to the community.

Why didn't we talk about it? The prejudicial attitudes triggered people to spew dehumanizing words like "queers" and "faggots." We were not willing to risk possible repercussions.

We believed that we would eventually figure out our relationship direction once we figured out Jesus' call for each of us. *Is our love wrong?* We were two consenting adults. It was a dilemma we both struggled with. Yet, our works in ministry were also dominant and we were better as a team than alone.

Carol Surprises Me: Lambrusco

During our weekend visits, Carol sometimes surprised me with my favorite foods, including an imitation crab dip on a sandwich of wonderful aromatic toasted sourdough bread with avocado slices.

I pigged out, enjoying each succulent bite, and she watched me drool and wipe my lips. In her room, her double mattress was on the floor with sheets and blankets neatly fitted. Two empty water glasses sat on her desk.

"What is this?" I asked.

"I got us Lambrusco, sweet wine. Let's see what it tastes like. It says it is 'sparkling' and hopefully celebratory."

"Oh, OK. I'm game. What are we celebrating?"

"Being together. I'm so glad you're here tonight. I think of you so much, Joanie. I miss you."

"Wow, oh, Carol, I miss you, too. I wish we were together all the time."

"Well, we have two nights together and until Sunday at 4pm."

We opened the twist-top wine bottle, and Carol poured the red-purple liquid into the glasses.

CHAPTER 8

"Here's to you, good looking!" I said to my sweetie. We clinked our glasses once, twice and three times.

"Yes, to us and to where God will lead us!" she said.

"YES!"

We drank half the bottle over a few hours. Yummy, sweet like a fruit drink. We giggled, talked, kissed and drank. And we answered Carol's favorite question of the day, "What are you really looking forward to?"

"To spend my life with you, forever," I told her.

"Oh wow! Joanie, I like it! Me, too!"

"I'm also looking forward to . . . I need to shower tonight, Carol. I stink from work and the drive over."

Softly she asked: "Joanie, would you like your back washed?"

"Oh, I'd love it. Thanks, Carol. Thanks, sweetie."

Oh, I'm calling her sweetie more often. This feels extremely special. I like it and so does she because she giggles and I know that means she is having big smiles, very natural and uncontrollable beautiful smiles. Pure joy.

She washed my back up and down, going to my neck, my shoulders and my rump with a soapy washcloth. This was intimate! How nice! I turned the water off. I did a full turn and there she was, staring at me with a towel in her hand. I reached for the towel, so soft, and so was her hand that I grazed in the process. Nice! I dried myself, stepped out of the shower stall.

She looked gorgeous in her light pink nightgown. Everything was all natural and comfortable. This was love. This was romance.

This could be our everlasting life. This is mutual and wonderful.

How precious I felt. She felt the same.

We laid on the floor mattress, wrapping our bodies together. Intimately holding and pressing into each other, stroking each other's hair around the ears, touching each other's faces, with smiles and gentle kisses.

We fell asleep around midnight. We were in our eternal time. I woke up, she stirred and I rolled over in the opposite direction, back to back. Carol said, "Sweetheart, please put your back into me so I know you are there. Let's go to sleep."

"You bet. You comfy?"

Later in the night, I reached over to touch her. My hand rubbed her arm; she did not move. She was sound asleep. How beautiful. I closed my eyes and drifted off.

I could feel that this was the start of another phase for us. Carol and I were needing and wanting each other to be complete: physically, mentally, spiritually and emotionally.

It was not just the passionate kisses; it was a deep, deep love that turned two hearts into one heart. It was adult and healthy, with no labels or gayness. Two people in love.

We believed the Holy Spirit was leading us into becoming a couple! Not separate entities in love, but one love, one entity: Carol and Joanie.

McCall Cabin

One weekend Carol and I went camping in an apple orchard. It was bliss to lay in our tent, talking and listening to the silence. We felt free, not enclosed in a bedroom or building with others around. It drizzled all night and we woke up cold and wet.

"Forget this!" we said. Back to the warm convent twin bed.

Another weekend, we went to McCall, Idaho, where Carol's friend offered a rustic cabin with electricity. We had really nice private, quality time. I sat on the long couch while Carol started the fire in the fireplace. I loved watching the white-hot flame, yellow and orange, then blue bursts, the crackling and smells of smoke and scented wood.

"Put your head on my lap, for a nap, Joanie."

"Awesome, I will." She stroked my hair until I fell asleep. Later, I awoke as she was reading a book. "Wow, I was out!"

"Yes, almost an hour, love. Must be a good sign we're meant for each other, don't you think?"

Becoming a Couple, But We Are Still Nuns

In the kitchen stocked with spices, we cooked a baked potato extraordinaire, loaded with yummy seasoned chicken and sauteed onions topped with orange cheese. Carol was a chef, a foodie and a pro in the kitchen. I was the sous chef, cutter and assistant.

CHAPTER 8

I can see us doing life together for many years to come.

The cabin windows were cold to the touch, offering views of tall Ponderosa pine trees. We shared toothpaste, blow dryers and Lambrusco.

During daylight, we drove to scenic sites and hiked pine needle trails, where the Ponderosa pine trees smelled like vanilla. We were careful on the slick ground; our tennis shoes were slipping and sliding, all the more reason to hold hands. The hike was about us, a couple finding our ways of creating a respectful and fulfilling life. It was fun and joyful, sincere, honest, void of fear and enriching. And hopefully to be shared with the world someday.

Being a couple, still nuns, the other's needs came first.

We visited Sister Rosie in Sedro Woolley, Washington. She introduced us as "Carol and Joanie" to her friends. That was cool!

We traveled twice to Spokane, two hours north of Lewiston. Once, we went to an incredible Neil Diamond concert where Carol knew every word to every song. I wondered if she should have had a microphone and been on center stage with Neil? We drove home late after the concert, still rocking and rolling from the extravagant show of lights, music and spunk. The dark skies and brilliant stars lit our path homeward as we held hands in the car.

Oh, golly, on our second Spokane trip, we couldn't wait to get into the hotel room. We threw our bags and purses onto the floor, undressing each other and kissing. Our bodies craved skin-to-skin touch. Slobbering wet kisses, our hot bodies melted together. There was no stopping our powerful yet surrendering love for each other. This passion was a miraculous gift—one in body and soul. We fell asleep, breast to breast, on the bed. It was an afternoon delight. This was a gift of humanity.

Ice Capades

Carol's cousin Shirley Costello was the choreographer for the Ice Capades, and Carol surprised me with tickets to enjoy the music, costumes and talented people! Wow!

After the show, we went backstage to meet the cast. Shirley introduced us as "cousin Carol and Joanie." We fit right in and felt accepted when they invited us to join them for dinner. It was wonderful being around our new gay friends, the stars of the show. Yes, we appeared to the outside as two nuns who were just friends, but this night there was the clear, unspoken acceptance of our gay love. For now, this was spectacular and we felt at home with them!

Everyone knew we were a loving couple, but the word "gay" was never used. From that time forward, all Christmas cards, letters, and phone calls were addressed to both of us.

Jesus hold you.
God bless you.

CHAPTER 9
The Power of Prayerful Discernment

When I received my letter about being missioned to Pasco, I was joyful to resume my teaching career and be so near Carol, while also starting my three-year, designated time period for the discernment of God's plans for me to make final vows.

Discernment is the process of prayer, contemplation and reflection that inspires inner guidance from God to know His will for my life.

Dear Lord, this will be my discernment process of your Will for me. I promise I will pray, live with joy, be an excellent nun in community convent living, teach and coach with all my might, and be honest with myself and Carol about our relationship.

In my heart of hearts, I was opening up to become whom the Lord made me to be. This exciting dream-come-true elicited a joyful, warm feeling that I was in the right place at the right time for the right reason. I could be the real me: wearing shorts and tennis shoes as an encourager, coach and nun.

In a variety of ways, powerful discernment happened for me. It was through the inquisitiveness and interaction with the K-6 school children that blessed me with humor and spirit-driven messages. They asked:

"Sister Joanie, do you pray for the other teams to miss their free throws?"

"Does God really talk to you, Sister Joanie?"

"What does He tell you?"

"Can you talk to Him for me?"

Oh my gosh and by golly, these young voices were the best spiritual advisors! It was amazing!

SO . . . what about the vows? Would I decide to make my FINAL vows? Or not?

The Importance of the Three Vows!

The vows were a big focal point for me and for the community as I listened and paid attention to the truth deep within my heart.

Now my most important questions in this different but good lifestyle of community living were: *Could I live the rest of my life in this community?* Some sisters went to bed at seven, and I was left by myself. *Was this community living? Were we "family"?* Filling my evenings with work was not fun or desirable! *How was I to relate to the nuns: as family, friends, or co-habitants?*

What about the vows? They were supposed to be about joy. And in my discernment, after five years, I did not find the vows to be joy-filled. The vows intertwined with this community living.

If I decide to make my vows, I will be choosing this religious community lifestyle.

Vow of Poverty

The Vow of Poverty meant a total surrender: totally letting go and letting God and the church be completely in charge. It was more than money or possessions. To understand poverty of spirit, poverty of selflessness was divine. It was more than being poor; it was relinquishing all control.

At times I struggled with totally embracing this concept. I wanted the freedom to make my own choices and be free to be me. I wanted my own car so I could go wherever and whenever I wanted to go. The Vow of Poverty meant I would never have my own car, but would have to ask for permission from the other sisters to use the community car. Asking for permission took the spontaneity and freedom out of my life.

Do you know that religious sisters don't keep their wages for themselves? Their wages go into the whole SISTERHOOD of the congregation, including your local convent or housing. Cool concept, huh?! Shared finances.

I found that many sisters had family inheritances or family monetary donations they personally used or gave to the congregation. Some sisters did not receive money from friends or family, but all sisters received a monthly stipend, such as $20, for their personal necessities. Special financial needs, such as my travel to Terri's wedding, would be approved by the sisters in the convent. These discrepancies didn't seem right to me at first, but the generosity of all sisters was valued and instilled. Sharing was a way of living, to be generous and kind.

I struggled with the Vow of Poverty as I realized that I preferred to be in control and in charge of my own life. I had difficulty surrendering to the congregation.

I also witnessed the reality of "the haves" and the "have nots" within the church. Early on, as a religious sister in the Los Angeles convent, I went to deposit a check at our local bank. I was 24, and when I went to the bank before joining the convent, I would ask for our convent's current balance. So I asked the teller to provide our balance.

"Sister Joanie," she said, "please sit and wait over here and I'll get your balance for you."

A half hour later, she handed me a just-printed, two-inch-thick financial report and said, "Here you go, Sister."

It was a complete list of the Sisters of St. Joseph's Los Angeles Province's assets: numerous hospitals, hundreds of schools, properties, convent and facilities. It was our big non-profit business. I was stunned!

"Thank you so much," I told the teller. "You've outdone yourself. Would you please write down what our little local convent balance is?"

"Oh yes, Sister." She provided a single piece of paper showing we had a few hundred dollars, enough for Sister Claire to buy our groceries.

What a hoot! The "haves" and the "have nots"—an issue since Jesus' time.

Vow of Obedience

We also took a Vow of Obedience: a submission to the will of church superiors who stand in the place of God, Jesus and the Holy Spirit.

For me this was the toughest of the three vows. I tried with all my heart to follow rules, guidance and the way of life of the obedient, but my heart wasn't in it. I did not want to follow all the rules and regulations, but wanted to have my own game with my own rules. I was a strong, independent woman my whole life and had made good decisions, so why should I surrender that to the church now?

I loved prayer in the morning and in the evening with my sisters when I was rested. However, I didn't like early morning prayer when I had worked until 10 p.m. with the youth group and until 11 p.m. with the staff team. I was tired and needed more sleep, but I would feel guilty not supporting the other sisters at prayer if I didn't go. The congregation rule was to go, but I wasn't respecting myself and my needs when I did.

The Vows of Poverty and Obedience overlapped in my mind.

Vow of Chastity

The Vow of Chastity is becoming the Bride of Christ: celibate and nonsexual. It was not clear to me if it included intimate thoughts or feelings for others.

What should I do? I fell in love with Carol. What about my vows? Could we have a life forged as a couple?

Lord, my biggest question in my deepest heart discernment is: can I love You and Carol at the same time?

Attraction to women . . . oh, so many questions. Help me Lord.

Discernment is a Work in Progress

When I fell in love with Carol, and she fell in love with me, it was mutual and mature. We were in each other's thoughts and felt as one.

Letter writing expressed my feelings, as well as journal entries of hopes and dreams with our future together. I played guitar and sang with her in my mind, remembering the depth and quality of our friendship talks and walks, planning our next fun times, and wanting more time with her. All of this was the sign that the Vow of Chastity was being heaved out the window.

When apart, we missed each other's presence: physically, mentally, emotionally and spiritually. We discovered that we wanted and needed each other in those identical magnetizing ways.

Oh yeah, this Chastity vow is in the way of us being the best people for God.

For a few years, I was hoping to find a way where I could love Jesus and love Carol in the same way at the same time. I always wanted to be in two places at once.

So why can't I/we do both?

My big heart and active mind worked simultaneously during prayer to understand if what I wanted was also what Jesus had in His heart and mind for me.

So What Did I Discover About Obeying Vows?

After five years of learning about me, community life and God, the lightbulb went on with LED brilliance. A lifetime brightness from and with Jesus.

For me, I wanted and needed to live in a loving monogamous gay woman-to-woman relationship centered on honesty and faith with someone who was also willing to commit to Jesus and to me in a reciprocal way. I could not do this and be a nun.

God took care of that for me! YES. He did!

A blessing beyond my wildest imagination and fantasy.

Thank you, God, for my sweet Carol!

"My one and only," she said and I said.

We brought out the very best in each other and in You, oh Lord.

My questions about obeying the Vow of Chastity were about more about thoughts than sexual acts. Thinking of another person, wanting to be more for them and with them. That was love.

Two hearts becoming one. That was not chaste.

How do I reconcile the Vow of Chastity with an intimate relationship? I can't.

Carol and I were surrounded by caring, loving and lovable people. We ministered to "God and company," her exact words when she listed her last employer on a job application.

We lived the truth.

Being Honest with Myself & Listening to Jesus and God

After five years of convent living, incorporating temporary vows, I realized that I wasn't being me. Through lots of praying, hoping, believing and being honest with my true self, I felt another distinct call from God. He had never left and had carried me through every question I ever had. This time, He told me: **"Leave the convent, Joanie. I need you to be more in the world for Me!"**

"YES! OK, I will, Jesus."

I understood Him, and His will for me: to think bigger than Church—being open to a wide variety of experiences and He would be with me. His message, strong and bold, was: **"I am always with you."**

My heart was wide open and vulnerable! It felt wonderful and I had no fear or concerns.

What's ahead? I don't know, but it will be great. I just feel it.

My deepest thoughts engulfed me: *freedom to be the real true me and to love and be loved. To be with one incredible soul mate, and that will bring me all the joy in the world, so I can share more kindness with people everywhere. Oh, that sounds absolutely the best.*

I felt an enormous amount of peace and contentment with this call to freedom. I had made an informed decision within my heart of hearts, my soul and my entire being.

This is right, this is the exact same thing that led me to join the convent. Wow, God, you are funny and amazing. I'm doing it your way.

I had learned so much with the Sisters of Saint Joseph: regarding them as sisters, learning the power of prayer, and experiencing the value of community.

With all my being, the answer to my main question of

"Who am I?" surfaced like a school of dolphins ready to play, flip and swim fast as they leapt through the air, diving into a new life. That was me, discovering that I was amazingly filled with unique talents and personality while young, beautiful, loved and gay. I was a lamp, as one of my favorite Scriptures goes, no longer hidden under a bushel, but dancing on the table of the entire world.

Sharing My Decision with Carol

I drove alone to Lewiston in our Pasco convent car through a surprise snow flurry to tell her my decision. With confidence, happiness and trust in her bedroom, I exclaimed:

"Carol, I'm leaving the convent! It's time! My deepest desire is to live with you, Carol."

She was extremely happy for me, shown by her immediate beaming smiles, a big, long bear squeeze and soft, gentle kisses on my cheeks.

"I'm so happy for you that you arrived at your decision. Joanie, I would like to live with you, too."

Wow, what a response! She wants to live with me, too. Shazam!

I did not expect that. It was all fantastically great and would all work out. I had faith! Carol and I were more joyous than sad, overwhelmed with indescribable FREEDOM!!! Peace!!

I decided to leave the convent on my birthday, July 5th. 1986, after five years of personal growth and service to God and community. It would be a real Freedom Day, a New Birth.

I needed to love Carol with all my being and to receive Carol's outlandish love for me—without being a nun.

My blessed years as a St. Joseph of Carondelet sister were the most impactful of my life. They brought out the best in me and brought me closer to Jesus.

Jesus had and has me . . . Jesus had and has us. ALWAYS! Let go, let God.

Back in Pasco, I set up a meeting in person, with Sister Clair Marie in her school office. I said, "I got to go."

"OK. Where do you need to go? Do you need the car?"

"No, Claire, I have to leave the convent."

With tears in her eyes, she said, "Oh, Joanie. All the good people are leaving."

We hugged. For once, I didn't have tears: I was not one bit sad.

I called Carol, who didn't know when my appointment was with Sister Claire Marie.

"Carol, I've spoken with Claire about me leaving the convent. And I am so happy! Here's how it went down. Oh, I love you Carol."

"Good for you, Joanie. Thanks for calling me. I love you."

"Carol, let me call my parents and then it can be public knowledge."

"Joanie, that's a good idea."

I called my parents and my dad said, "It's about time." Smiles of affirmation burst onto my face.

Mothers know their children well. I was blessed with my spiritually strong loving mom, who said, "Good for you, sweet Joanie. We will see and be with you soon."

There is a season and a time for every purpose. *God is calling . . . time for me to move on and embrace a new life of love with no limits.* The only security I needed was knowing that God, Jesus and the Holy Spirit were always with me. *The end result will be in heaven.*

"Keep doing all the things I taught you," Jesus said. "I give you free will, forgiveness and peace."

When I "left Community," that was a turning point to reach out to more and more people, for God. That was His plan all along. AMAZING!

Carol's Discernment and Decision

Carol's discernment timing and heart-moving moments were unique as she was. She was a deeply prayerful, reflective, uncomplicated person. In many ways she was naive and unassuming, whose soul was filled with so much joy from having a personal relationship with Jesus and more so with the Holy Spirit.

Carol believed in an all-encompassing, loving God. Her God was bigger than religious life, bigger than one church and bigger than humanity. Carol lived and danced with one foot in heaven and one on earth. To her, they were the same place! She was a walking rainbow of joy, yet had doubts about future progress in community and in the church. She shared her deepest dreams and "wanted people to be happy." She was miles ahead and beat to a different drum. Her prayers and her openness gave way to her heart bursting with newness almost every day.

I Surrendered Carol to God

"If love is meant to be, let it go and it will come back."

That quote was on a butterfly burlap banner in Carol's bedroom wall in Lewiston with the words and imagery stuck to my heart's delight ever since I had been invited into her bedroom.

Never had I believed more in that saying than when I left Pasco and returned home for a month to my parents in San Diego while I completed the process of leaving the convent. With my new freedom found, I completely surrendered Carol back to our loving God.

I figured she'd have to find her own way and timing. I was 100% at peace that whatever decision she would make, I would honor and support her. Carol had an amazing personal relationship with God, a direct line. She was in good hands and would know her answers to her own questions.

The crazy thing was, Carol initiated more calls and letters to me during my first month "out" as she craved to help me transition from being a nun to a single woman; in turn by helping me, she helped herself.

During my month at home in San Diego with my parents, I had an abundance of courage and a belief to follow God's new plan without a congregation or convent behind me. Could I ever do that? The answer was, I was doing it! I felt fabulous! The Holy Spirit brought back my spunk for living, my creative juices abounded as Mom and I painted their dinette room in gorgeous yellow and we watered and gardened together in the backyard; big-time hopes and dreams, fortitude and faith were alive and kicking.

During this extra special month, Mom and I really connected at a deeper level. We shared a lot of historical events from our lives. She sat in her comfortable powder-blue chair and I sat on the couch by the living room window with my feet up on the table. To be closer to her, I'd sit in Dad's brown recliner so I could see her Irish hazel eyes that held the faith of our family. She was wonderful, never pressing me, just accepting and loving me as she always had. I was no different to her and being gay didn't matter.

"My brother, your uncle, has a gay son," she said with no judgment.

This was news to me. No wonder she felt so comfortable with me being gay. I don't remember actually saying, "I'm gay," but she knew.

"I'm going to the Pride Parade in Hillcrest today," I told her, referencing San Diego's gay neighborhood. "I want to be with my other family."

I had so much fun there, feeling so proud and free. Color everywhere: rainbow flags, rainbow floats, rainbow t-shirts and hats. Gay and lesbian couples holding hands, standing with arms around each other and smooching in public view. A total delight I witnessed and felt at home with.

I wish Carol were here with me holding hands and walking in such freedom.

In my neighborhood, where I once walked and rode my bicycle, was the enormous, happy, gay pride parade. Like Dorothy in *The Wizard of Oz*, I clicked my bright red tennis shoes and gave thanks for being at home.

Happy inside and out, I shopped in gay-owned businesses. I saw and purchased a sterling silver necklace with a large marble-sized silver ball with a 3D sun and moon design. Perfecto mundo for Carol, my sweetie! We loved to sing and laugh under the full moon.

I showed Mom my purchase, and that started my coming out to myself and my parents. Mom intuitively knew at that point.

"That's beautiful, Joanie. Carol will love it!"

That was my "coming out" to my mom.

When I showed Dad the necklace, he thought it was nice. He didn't have a clue about me being gay and what this necklace meant.

As I laid in bed or drove around my old neighborhood, both

my silent prayer and talking aloud confession were:

"Oh, God, I love Carol so much! I give her back to you. I want to be with her forever, Lord. But in the end, it is totally up to You!"

I repeated this prayer like a mantra, my own version of the rosary. Tears flowed, then peace and quiet gently surrounded me and hugged my heart like warm sun rays caressing your skin.

It was short-lived, just one summer month, because Spirit can work quicker than the speed of light; unbeknownst to each other, we had both applied for jobs in western Washington.

God's Miracles

Carol didn't believe the convent was progressive enough, and she wanted to move out of convent living and into a new place. In a phone call to my parents' home, as I sat in the yellow-painted dinette, she said, "I want to live with you, Joanie."

Yahoo!! OUTSTANDING!! Things were falling into place better than I had imagined.

Less than two hours from where we would live, Bishop Hunthausen of the Seattle Archdiocese was promoting a unified, more open Catholic Church based on an increase of laity involvement and less priestly hierarchy. This was identical to Carol's vision of the church.

Carol had declined church positions offered in Washington and Montana. I had declined a youth ministry position in western Washington.

I really wanted out of church ministry to instead follow God's words in being more worldly. I was a risk taker and trusted I would have a job that would pay for my lodging and put food in my mouth. I was not worried one bit.

Carol had said yes to a parish sister position in remote western Washington, in Aberdeen. She informed me of her happy decision the same day that I had scheduled a job interview in Hoquiam, Washington, the city next to Aberdeen.

Catching our breath, we were surprised and excited that maybe our love miraculously was going to continue in unexpected, God-only ways. Our dreams of living together, working in the same city and having life as a couple was meant to be. YIPPEE!! Now that was the phone call of all calls!

The process of letting go is gut-wrenching, but it really works. We did not plan on it, but we had hoped for it. We had let God do His thing in His time. God knows what's best. He's in charge, no matter how much we think we are.

Wow, this is unbelievable. Can I believe it? YES!

The love of my life, Carol, was part of this new plan. YAHOO, Alleluia, Yippee, oh YES.

I, the love of her life, and she, the love of my life, will be in each other's arms everyday forever!

Jesus hold you.
God bless you.

CHAPTER 10
This is Bliss

Our Life Together in Aberdeen

Just two months after leaving the convent, I was stepping into heaven on earth by searching for a home to share with my beloved Carol. Yipee!

This happened in August of 1986. While staying in a cheap rundown hotel, we met with a realtor to find a rental house. She wore designer glasses, gold and silver necklaces and bracelets, and dressed in a professional business suit with high heels. Her perfume was elegant.

The realtor said, "Perfect timing, ladies, my mother-in-law recently passed away and her house is available for rent." She gave us the address to go look.

As we exited the parking lot with a map in hand, Carol flamboyantly said, "Look, a rainbow!"

To me, that was a sign of gay pride; Carol didn't have a clue that rainbows and gay went together. It wasn't the end of our rainbow. Just the beginning.

We followed the directions, which took us straight toward the rainbow. Both led to our new home on Ho Hum Lane in a manufactured home complex—literally at the end of the rainbow.

Carol was scheduled to start her job in a few days as a parish sister at the Catholic Church. I had a job interview with a non-profit agency that supported teens and their health issues, including teen pregnancy—the top health concern in Grays Harbor County and the state of Washington.

Although Aberdeen is known for immense rainfall, 84 inches a year, there was no rain the day of my interview. I was praying for a huge sunburst!

I was offered the position of Youth Case Manager in the Teenage Pregnant and Parenting (TAPP) grant-funded program with a salary of "22."

"Yes," I said, "I'd like the job, but... oh no, I can't do 22 because I've barely been living off of 25. I really need at least the same amount."

All eight interviewers nodded and motioned toward the CEO. I figured that meant, "Yes, OK."

The CEO said, "Yes, we can do 25."

My positive vibes triggered my eyes to get wider and bigger. This was exciting!

"All right, 25 it is. Welcome, Joanie."

I signed papers immediately, not really reading them, and said, "I am hired! Yahoo, my first job NOT as a nun! Thank you so much. I will be an asset to you and for the youth. I promise."

I focused on the official paper contract everyone had signed. The numbers looked huge and bold, flashing my new salary. I cocked my head in amazement.

The CEO looked inquisitively at me, "Are you OK?"

"Yes, I thought it was just $25 not $2,500 a month. Wow!"

Everyone laughed.

"I have been living in the convent with my monthly 25 dollars to buy my personal hygiene items and a treat of an ice cream cone once in a while."

They seemed stunned—smiling, showing thumbs up signals and chuckling. I bet they were thinking, "What planet has she been on?"

"Oh golly," I said. "I have a lot to learn! I've been cloistered, shut in, away from the world of money. Again, thank you for believing in me."

I can't wait to tell Carol!

My drive home was quick and fun in my red, convertible VW Beetle—a gift from Terri and brother-in-law Billy when I left the convent. It felt like the race car Herbie from *The Love Bug* Disney movie. As I daydreamed about our future, Herbie came skidding to a stop under the carport. There were gray skies, a few sprinkles and then, a big double rainbow.

I leapt two steps at a time into the front door and yelled, "Carol!! I got the job! Come look at the double rainbow!"

We twirled and danced.

"I'm so proud of you, Joanie! This is all meant to be."

Our furnishings in this, our first home together, came from the "dead lady's house," a parishioner who had willed her house to the parish. Pastor, Carol's new friend and associate, took us to the house and offered us anything we wanted. Since we had nothing, literally, but the clothes on our backs, we were thankful for furniture, kitchen supplies and her double bed with linens.

Shopping for Commitment Rings

Living together, and sharing every single moment in time and space, was bliss.

Through our work, we met new friends and began a new lifestyle. We were known as Sister Carol and Joanie—two very good friends. Only we knew of our lifetime commitment and profound love for each other. We talked about wearing "love rings," but during the 1980s, we couldn't get married because gay marriage was not legal, we were not "out" and Carol was still a nun. A perfect trifecta. Or the perfect trinity.

"In God's timing" was our core belief. *That will be the DAY!*

Patience is trust.

So, with burning desire, we went to the Wishkah Shopping Mall to buy rings in honor of our love and commitment to each other. How fun, standing in the J.C. Penney jewelry section, with envelopes of saved money stuffed in our purses. We huddled together eyeing the diamonds, emeralds, gems and bands.

"Look, Black Hills Gold," Carol said. "Let's try them on!"

They were wonderful, simple and pure.

"I like them, Carol. They're light, they don't stick up and, wow, it looks good on you."

"It looks great on you, too, Joanie."

We both selected a unique Black Hills Gold band, each ring slightly different, beautifully designed with hearts, vines and leaves. This was amazing!

In our jubilance, we slid a ring on each other, our left hands, third finger. While our hearts throbbed and burst with love, our smiles radiated beams of light through the store, then imaginary rainbows appeared in my mind.

The sales lady was casually watching us. For once, we didn't know her and she did not know us. That was funny because normally we knew everyone and they knew us.

Sized to perfection, the circle of oneness, our gorgeous gold rings symbolized our eternal love and life together. For richer or poorer, in sickness and in health, we stood proud, blessed and highly favored.

Our emotions burst out as we left the store, arm in arm. Before driving away, I wiped joyful tears as we each kissed each other's hands and rings.

At home in our private sanctuary, we shared more passionate hugs and kisses while admiring each other's rings. It felt so fantastic! Yet we kept this special moment confidential; we were uncertain with whom, when or where we would share our couple status. There was a real-world fear that we could be harmed, as other gay couples had experienced.

Carol was still a nun; I had left the convent three months ago. We felt jubilance yet apprehension. I was glad that Carol still wore her "nun ring"—a silver band engraved with a cross and dove, on her right hand, third finger. She was committed to both Jesus and me. I trusted that her continued discernment would provide her answer.

Our commitment rings were our second big financial purchase. Our first was a king-size waterbed.

Living Together Was Beautiful Bliss

Carol and I celebrated morning, noon and night. Our intimacy sprouted like a field of wildflowers.

CHAPTER 10

While incorporating nun life with non-nun life, we continued prayer times on our own schedule; music and dancing happened spontaneously. When needing quiet times, we asked, honored and respected each other. After work and on weekends, we snuck into tennis rallies in the nearby recreational park, laughing and chasing tennis balls.

In early December, we acquired a permit to tramp through the forest to cut our own Christmas tree. Soon after, we planted bulbs sent from Carol's dad, Joe, who worked for years with David's and Royston Bulb Company. Springtime included road trips to visit sister friends near Seattle, and a trip to the gorgeous Skagit Valley tulip fields. One day we received a gift box containing hundreds of two-inch diameter gladiola bulbs and we had a ball planting them. Silly me, I planted hundreds of them upside down! We stood in the yard and laughed our heads off.

We loved "exploring the countryside," making U-turns as we spotted new things to check out.

"Where does this road go?"

"I don't know. Take it, try it."

We held hands, wore our shades and enjoyed gorgeous views of the Northwest.

Our road trips took us to places like the fishing village of Westport. At the Lighthouse Restaurant, we scarfed up the best beer-batter fish & chips, drinking our signature root beer drink with two straws.

Then we beach-walked, kicking sand over hundreds of miles of beaches, leaving our sunken footprints. We dodged waves, and collected white shells, tiny and large, 20-year old Saint James scallop shells and baskets of sand dollars.

"How fun," I exclaimed daily to Carol's delight.

We gave shells to family and friends, telling them stories of our adventures. Even today on our bookshelf in the prayer corner by the big window, is an assortment of those sand dollars.

We held hands on secluded beaches and loved cheek pecks, saving lip-to-lip kisses for when we ducked under tall grasses near the high tide line.

Someday, we believed, *we and others like us won't have to live in secret love.*

With laughter and zillions of conversations, "our routine" life was outrageously fun.

Life was bliss! I loved my life! She loved her life! We loved our new life!

My True Self Emerges

Through my work commitments, I was privileged to receive community health and sexuality education training. More importantly, it provided the opportunity to grow, understand, love and accept my true self. All my years of questions were being answered and the puzzle pieces were fitting together perfectly. I became comfortable in saying aloud that I was gay, but was very selective about who I told.

However, because of Carol's discernment process, I respected her privacy and confidentiality. In our small town and in her church position, our love remained our secret. We didn't want people finding out about us as a couple and we were guarded in public. We were not ashamed nor did we feel we were lying. I was not going to "out" her just so I could be "out."

For two years, we patiently waited for Carol to be released from her religious vows so she could get on with her new life with me.

Carol Makes Her Decision

Carol decided to leave the convent after we had lived together, grown inseparable and complemented each other with the style and grace of a destined love couple.

God called her into the convent and God told her to leave. She was on that direct line with Jesus loud and clear.

Carol met regularly by phone and visitations with her regional superiors regarding her exclaustration: the official process of leaving the convent and vacating her vows of poverty, chastity and obedience.

This was as big as a married couple's divorce. Maybe bigger. This process would take several years, including her personal times of discernment, hearty prayers and conversations with the CSJs.

She talked with her mentors and regional superiors about what that all meant. She trusted in God. Compassionate and loving sisters visited her and us in our home. Carol was honest about her life, her choices and how we lived as a faithful couple.

Carol wrote a personal letter to the CSJ General Superior requesting to leave the convent.

She wrote: "Since 1986, I have been discerning my call to religious life. I have looked deep into my heart. At this time, I would like to request an indult of secularization. I am asking to leave religious life because I feel that it is right and good for me to do so. I have believed for years that God calls some of us to religious life for different lengths of time. My heart has chosen a different road and I am at peace with my God. I no longer feel the commitment to community or my vows. I have prayed, talked for hours, listened to others, and discerned with myself, God and spiritual directors to help me come to a peaceful yet exciting call. The Sisters of Saint Joseph will always be in my heart. Lovingly, Carol Tierheimer."

One day, as I walked in the front door, she smiled wider than the Grand Canyon, jumping up to give me a huge hug. Her heart was free and she said, "It's time. It's you and I, Joanie . . . and with Jesus." Carol's CSJ discernment mentor was sitting there, also smiling big, for Carol had signed her official paperwork to leave religious life. The finalized paperwork was on the big coffee table. Her mentor jumped up and hugged me. I had tears in my eyes and Carol was like a dancing feather!

God had a plan the whole time!

He does for you, too!

God never leaves you! You are His one and only.

Answer your call.

Carol would eventually receive her final dispensation from her vows and approval from the Papal office in Rome. When all was said and done, she was officially a sister for 32 years.

Our hearts were one! We knew, deep down, that God was calling us to become and be a loving couple for Him.

We were spiritually and profoundly surrounded by rainbow-promises that life was here for us to share.

Family and Friends Visit Us

We were thrilled that our families were 100% supportive! They planned thousand-mile trips and we were overjoyed that they were coming to visit us.

By phone and letters to her parents, Carol joyfully exclaimed, "We have a guest room for you and we will have so much fun together."

We looked forward to sharing whom we'd become and our life together as a couple. Our families were just as thrilled.

Mi casa es su casa is Spanish for "my house is your house." Carol and I believed in sharing what we had as well as who we were.

"Don't be selfish," and "Remember to share and take turns" were constant phrases spoken in our families as we grew up.

So Carol and I incorporated this into our home life on Ho Hum Lane—a funny name because we were definitely not "ho hum"!

Carol's Beloved Parents Visit First

I had met Carol's wonderful, delightfully kind parents—Joe and Elsie Tierheimer—in Paradise, California, twice and at Carol's 25-year jubilee celebration as a nun.

So when Carol and I invited them to Aberdeen, we were beyond excited when they jumped on the chance to visit us. Carol's excitement electrified her joyful dancing and singing.

Joe had already told us by phone how to clean and cook crab, but he wanted to go catch, clean, cook and eat crab with his eldest and most special daughter.

Dad and Carol were lifelong fishing buddies, letter writing friends, traveling companions and confidential counselors. They had a unique father-daughter adult friendship bond. On many occasions, Carol asked him for advice and insight, as did extended family members. People respected her dad's opinions, intelligence and savvy business mind. He was a people person, a man of integrity for whom a handshake sealed a commitment.

Her mom, Elsie, was quiet and gentle—a behind-the-scenes

wonder woman, wife and mother who complemented her husband in an equitable relationship. She instilled confidence and happiness in her husband and children. Her family knew her as the "little submarine" for her acrobatic performances on water skis. Carol even wrote a short story called "The Little Submarine."

I loved them both very much and they knew of my great love for Carol. They totally supported us as a couple: two women in love and forever committed to each other.

Her father even wrote me a personal letter thanking me for being his daughter's partner for the rest of her/our life. I opened the letter not knowing what to expect. He wrote, "Joan, you understand Carol. I know you will take great care of her."

Absolutely, Joe, it is my pleasure! And Joe, we take care of each other.

Carol told me one time that she didn't need to tell her parents anything about us being gay. It didn't matter because it was about love. They could see the ways we looked at each other, affirmed each other with truth and honesty, and brought out the best in each other with compliments and selflessness.

Elsie said it was wonderful to hear the kind and delicate words that we used as we talked to each other. Elsie said we would last "forever."

Her parents slept in the guest bedroom while we retreated to our sloshy waterbed. We treated them royally and they treated us royally. We shared hugs and always said "please" and "thank you." We graciously accepted her parents' insistence to pay when we ate out, but we paid the tips. We had lots of fun days crabbing, beach walking, playing card games at night, talking, singing and driving here and there.

"Remember when . . . " Joe and Elsie started countless stories about Carol that were all news to me.

"Tell me more!" I said. "You did that, Carol?"

Once they were in Yellowstone National Park and as a toddler Carol chased a big black bear. Her daddy had to run to scoop her up and save her. Carol's nickname became "Bear." Her family's annual summer fishing and camping trips were at Virginia

Lakes, California for two weeks. I could smell the trees, fresh air and visualize a campfire with s'mores, and how the kids' faces became smeared with slobbered chocolate and marshmallows. We called those "angels with dirty faces"!

More Joy When My Family Visits

My parents, Ralph and Lenore, came to Washington a few times, driving 1,200 miles from San Diego. I loved having my parents vacation with us and I loved sharing Carol with them. They treated us as special daughters. It was total acceptance, never mentioning gay or lesbian. It didn't matter.

My loving siblings, along with nephews Brad and Steve, visited us during the summer. They had a blast crabbing with their "aunts," Carol and Joanie. Brad watched every detail of those crabs, especially how their pinchers gripped the bait in the crab ring, from which they escaped onto the dock. There was laughter and fear as he jumped back. *How fun!*

Jesus hold you.
God bless you.

CHAPTER 11
Nuns in Love and Loving Life

Crabbing in the Rain

We bought our first crab trap and supplies at Lookie Lou's Hardware Store, then learned to crab off the piers in Westport, Grayland and Tokeland, Washington. We baited each trap with dead, ugly, smelly fish carcasses that were free at the fish-cleaning stations.

We tossed the crab star trap into the water from the dock, and within 20 minutes, pulled up several fresh Dungeness crabs. It sounds simple, but it was really an art. This was the life.

Carol and I were such crabbing addicts, we braved pouring rain and gusty winds. In green rain slickers and purple and black OR (Outdoor Recreation) waterproof hats and crabbing gloves with exposed fingertips, we bounded down the old wooden pier, each carrying a crab trap, tossing them into the blue-black water 20 feet below. We tied yellow ropes around the wooden railings to prevent losing our traps in Mother Nature's currents. Then we hurried back to our Honda Accord and warmed up inside.

"Your turn to pull up the crab ring," Carol said. "It's been 20 minutes since we heaved up the last trap of crabs."

"OK, I got it." I jogged down the dock, using all my strength to pull up the rope. The trap usually contained about 10 crabs as I hoisted it over the rail. I threw back the females, then used an orange plastic crab measurer to select seven male "keepers."

Oh golly, look at those pinchers! That will be a hunk of sweet meat. Yummy.

Carol and I took turns braving the elements to harvest the crabs.

"I love you, Joanie. This is a great day. It is another amazing adventure!"

"How fun!! It sure is, sweetie!"

Our 20-minute drive home to Ho Hum dried us off, yet when I kissed her hand, it still tasted like the ocean salt water.

"How do we cook these, Carol?"

"I don't know. Let me call my dad."

Joe Tierheimer, outdoor hunting and fishing expert, told us to put rock salt in boiling water.

"Carol, what's rock salt?"

"I don't know."

"Let's zip to the market and find it."

At home, we dumped the bag of enormous Dungeness into the two-sided, chrome kitchen sink. The crabs crawled, pinched and pulled on each other trying to escape.

"Joanie, the two large pots of water are boiling. YOU put them in."

"OK, but they look scary." I had learned to grab them without getting mauled by their hefty pinchers. Carefully, without splashing boiling water on us, I dropped one crab at a time into the red soup pot. No deathly scream, only the vibrant color of red marked their demise. Their entire bodies, backs and claws succumbed.

"We are doing this, Carol!"

Oh the fishy, nasty smells of the cooked crab permeated the house. Carol quickly opened the front door and kitchen window for fresh air to blow out the smell.

"Let them cool in the sink, under running water," she said. "Remember to unpeel the back exposing the inside guts and rip it away from the fresh white meat."

"Oh, like this," I said, peeling it off and showing it to Carol like a trophy.

"Yes! Great!" She smiled and her eyes twinkled.

Side-by-side at the sink, we leaned over to "clean" all the crabs while the stereo radio music played.

This was another marvelous, fun day with my sweetie.

"Joanie, we need to trash that crab gunk!"

"Yes, I'll take it all to the outside garbage can when we are done, OK?"

"Good. Thanks, love."

"Is it dinnertime?" I exclaimed as my stomach gurgled.

"Almost."

Oh golly, a baked potato, fresh salad and a crab for each of us. It took awhile to pry the crab meat from the shell. We had lots of time to talk, laugh and replay the catch of the day. We so enjoyed each other's company—all the time.

"Carol, next time, let's have the crab already shelled and in the warm butter. This is way too much work when I'm famished to eat dinner. What do you think?"

"Good idea, Joanie. We can do that, sweetheart."

Carol was the pro at gently cracking the claws with nutcracker pliers and picking away the shell to access the sweet, well-packed meat. Her hands worked like magic, fast and accurate. She could pick three crabs for my one. Her strong hands and coordinated fingers were another love-joy moment for me. I loved watching her, especially when she had no idea that I was watching. I blew kisses to her saying, "I love you, sweetie."

Easter Morning Mass? Or Razor Clamming?

It was Easter weekend of our second year living together as Sister Carol and Joanie. Carol had been working long hours for months with the Rite of the Christian Initiation of Adults (RCIA) religious education program, readying them to become baptized and receive the sacraments as New Catholics on the Saturday night Vigil of Easter. This enormous, festive Mass happened on a decorated altar of white Easter lilies and pastel banners draping the lecterns. The Alleluia music resounded and attendees rattled their keys during the Gloria, Sister Carol's rendition of "ringing the bells," as Sister Carol involved individuals and families in this two-hour spectacular liturgy. It was a welcoming celebration!

The next day at 7 a.m., we were up and at 'em, on the road, and ready for another adventure. After hearing of "razor clamming" as a local endeavor, we purchased two metal-scooped clam shovels. I wore my old beach tennis shoes, gray sweatpants and a blue sweatshirt. Carol wore her warm red stretch pants with rainbow leggings as well as green and blue tennis shoes. She chose her cutesy flowered hat and I had my favorite purple and black fishing hat.

We awoke early to drive north through Hoquiam to Pacific Beach, a flat, mile-after-mile sand beach. We assumed that it would be quiet, not crowded, while people were sleeping in, doing egg hunts with the kids or attending an Easter sunrise service.

Wrong!

We joined a long line of cars with headlights on, all heading to the Pacific Ocean, and driving on the hard-packed sand! *Oh golly, this is my first time driving on beach sand!*

We parked and grabbed our gear. People were bending, shoveling and using tube things to dig up sand and eventually clams. The morning was calm and windless, with soft orange sunlight glowing through the mist.

Carol's radiant smile and colorful outfit attracted three older gentlemen—or were they the Three Wise Men? They were about 75 to 80 years old. One had a scraggly beard; one was clean shaven; and the third did all the talking. They wore black rubber boots and fisherman's slicker bibs with long-sleeved flannel shirts rolled up past their elbows. Each wore an old baseball cap. Under their bibs were jeans with the brown cloth clam bags hooked on their belt loops. Their heavy catches weighed down the bags.

"Can we help you ladies? Have you ever been razor clamming?"

"Uhh, no, but we'd like some lessons. How do you dig for them?"

"Watch us, this is how you do it. Stay between the high tide line and the breaking water. Do not dig in the water. Look for a tiny hole in the sand, like a doughnut or a dimple. Dig fast, because the clam will burrow down and then the shovel angle will stop the clam from going down further in the sand. The larger the hole, the larger the clam. But you have to dig fast or you might chop the clam in half. Reach into the hole as quickly as you can and search for the clam shell with your fingers. You might end up going deeper than your elbow. Grab a hold of the clam who is still burrowing, and pull it up."

"Wow! This is cool!"

These old guys made it look so simple, quick and easy. Our Wise Men disappeared down the sandy beach, leaving only their boot prints.

"OK, Joanie, we can do this!"

What she meant was, she would find the hole, I would dig and stick my arm down the hole, and she would hold the bag. Haha.

For the first one, I didn't do well. My hand was down in the hole up to my shoulder. I messed up. Cold, wet sand granules jabbed under my fingernails, and my sweatshirt was wet and cold from laying on the sand.

Next one, I dug faster, reached in and pulled it up, but the shovel broke the clam shell.

Third try. Carol found a big doughnut hole. "Joanie, let's get this one!"

I dug even faster, scooped and scooped, and finally pulled it out of the hole with my hand raised in the air, like the Statue of Liberty.

"I got one!" It was about five inches long.

"Nice. Way to go, Joanie!"

Wow, I was elated. Carol was cheering me on. We took turns spotting and digging. Carol was also successful pulling up clams.

"Congrats, Carol, way to go!"

One time two of my clams fell out of my bag while I was digging. Carol screamed, "Joanie, they're loose! You have two clams that are loose!" She picked them up and put them in her bag as I kept digging.

Carol was our eagle eye in spotting the dimple or doughnut hole. She found the wider the hole, the bigger the clam.

Teamwork made the dream work!

We each carried our own heavy bag of clams; Carol properly, like a fancy purse, and me, casually, with the plastic bag handle tied to my shorts' belt loop.

Yes, that's us.

It only took about an hour of hard work to reach our limits. We had a blast!

Thanks to our dear friend and coworker, Cathy, who provided us with the delicious, mouthwatering family recipe for fried razor clams: "Fry in butter-flavored Crisco or oil. Make sure the oil is hot! Turn the clams when golden brown. Then enjoy!"

Absolutely scrumptious!

Next Adventure: The World's Fair

Our next adventure led us to the World's Fair, called Expo 86, in Vancouver, Canada.

Carol had arranged for our lodging in an upstairs bedroom and bathroom at a couple's home in Vancouver. She knew someone who knew someone who knew someone. We spent two nights and three days there.

It was fantastic being around people from all over the world; the exhibits were visionary and educational. It was an outdoor-indoor playground of dreams, knowledge and inventions. I really loved the "Bodyworks" ride where we sat in a car, a "blood cell," and we traveled through the entire body's internal organs. Carol closed her eyes and held my hand.

The most memorable adventure was getting "take out" food in Chinatown, second in the world to San Francisco's Chinatown. It was 9 p.m. when I drove through this hustling and bustling city with dark, narrow, crowded streets. Our car doors were locked. Police were on every corner amidst car traffic and the chaos of pedestrians zig-zagging along the sidewalks and streets.

We were the only "non-Asian" females around. Carol spotted a restaurant with an older Chinese man sitting on a stool in front of the store's huge glass window, stirring a four-foot-tall cast iron cauldron.

"Stop, Joanie, let me out. I'll go get us something to eat and we can take it back to the room."

"Be careful, I'll drive around the block as many times as needed and you wait inside until you see me."

"OK, bye."

Carol entered a room of about 15 people at five tables, with only Chinese writing on the wall with a few pictures of food. At the counter, she pointed to food on someone's plate at their table. Families and couples were laughing, having fun and eating lots of noodles, vegetables, soups and garnished platters.

An older man nodded and gestured for her to sit at a small table with one chair. He brought a small glass of hot tea to her table and smiled. Carol pointed to the cars on the street, conveying that it was a to-go order.

I circled the block. No Carol. And the police wouldn't let me double park. I circled a longer route. Still no sign of Carol. My doors were still locked. But I peered in and saw her drinking from a tall, thin glass. *OK, she's good.* I took another longer route around the congested streets and returned.

She was at the front door with a big brown bag of food. Yea! She slid into the car, and off we went.

"Carol, what did you get for us?" It was aromatic!

"I was in China, Joanie. I was the only Anglo English-speaking person. I drank hot tea served in a glass. They were so nice. Oh, I ordered potstickers." I had never heard of that.

"They will be awesome. Thank you, Carol."

We arrived at our room at almost 10 p.m. We had had a fun and very busy day.

"Do you want to shower before we eat, Joanie?"

"Great idea. I'll go fast."

Carol relaxed on the queen bed and I took a quick shower.

Next was her turn for the shower.

Our guest room was in a dimly-lit loft of a private residential home located just a few miles from the Expo and Chinatown. It had a queen bed with a soft, luxurious down comforter. It faced a bookshelf and had a small TV on a wooden counter, with a small microwave, mini refrigerator, tea bags and mugs.

I sat on the cushy queen bed, the brown bag of food staring at me from the counter. It was still closed tightly. I got up and peered inside the warm bag, savoring aromas of ginger and onions. I grabbed a hand towel and opened the bag.

Oh, what's this sauce? Black and reddish? Looks fabulous, oh I'll just have one of these things. OMG these are great!

Each fresh, doughy dumpling was palm-sized, lightly seared and crispy on the outside. The soft meat-and-veggies filling melted in my mouth with an amazing combination of spices and flavors that I had never tasted.

"Hurry up, Carol, dinner is here!"

"Just a minute."

"OK."

I whispered, "I'll just have one more, then she'll be out here. OMG the pork, veggies, shrimp, too. Oh, so delicious."

I wrapped up the bag before I vacuumed them all.

"Carol, this is the best Chinese food ever! Wait till you taste it."

"You started without me? I waited for you!"

Feeling so bad, she was right; I wasn't kind. My puppy dog eyes welled up because I had been selfish. I was upset with myself.

Joanie, you nincompoop. That was totally uncalled for. Where was my patience and self-control? Gone.

"Ohhh, Carol. I'm so sorry, sweetie. That was not nice of me. I'm so sorry. Please forgive me."

"OK."

She opened the bag, "How many did you eat?"

"Two."

"Two? Or too many?" she said with a twinkle in her eye.

"Oh boy, did I eat more than two? I'm so sorry."

"Doesn't matter. There are still plenty for us!"

She smiled!

Thank God.

I smiled and she has forever kidded me about potstickers.

We pigged out, trying to control our giggles and laughter, to not disturb our hosts. We ate them all, sitting on the bed together in Vancouver, Canada. They were so good!

"Night, night. Love you," we said, cuddling in our plush bed.

The next day, we returned to the same restaurant. We each had a glass of hot tea, awaiting our double to-go order of potstickers. The nice old man frequently bowed as we drank our hot tea. In return, we smiled and bowed back to him.

CHAPTER 11

More Chinese Food Inspires Friendships

I met Brad at a fun Chinese restaurant with our HIV/AIDS support group comprised of two counselors and people living with HIV/AIDS. We were friends who leaned on each other's shoulders during a time of prejudice, hate, misunderstanding and longing for acceptance, compassion and deep friendship.

We shared appetizers, dipping them in a single hot mustard container in the center of the table. Brad flashed a huge smile and said, "Joanie, my new friend, you now have AIDS!"

I was stunned. I looked at the hot mustard that we were all sharing, knowing as an HIV/AIDS prevention educator, that I couldn't become infected from food. No way! The virus was only transmissible through semen, vaginal fluid, blood and breast milk, but I doubted it for a second.

I am scared spitless.

"I have AIDS," Brad blurted, reaching across the table to pat my hand. My brain re-engaged in the truth, and while his humor hit my funny bone, this was a teaching moment; I saw him as a person, not a disease. This began our long, beautiful friendship. I love how God works in mysterious ways.

Brad was 6'4" and 150 pounds of laughter and joy. His glasses-covered, brown, intense, loving eyes and his commanding and powerful voice was like a circus lion trainer. Brad was the first person I ever met who had "full-blown AIDS" with a T-cell count of 145-180.

He and the rest of the people at the table laughed their hearts out and said, "Welcome to our world, Joanie."

"Thanks Brad," I said, "have some more hot mustard."

"Don't mind if I do. I like this stuff."

"Me, too, new friend."

During the 1980s and 90s, gay people were blamed for creating and spreading the HIV/AIDS disease. My heart ached for my gay friends who were bloody and bruised after severe beatings—with lips swollen from being punched, blood caked around their noses, and bruises on their arms, knees and faces. At support group meetings, I heard stories about members' friends who were murdered.

It was demoralizing to see graffiti and even newspaper articles that said: "Go back to Africa" and "Get your own island" and "You deserve this from God" and "Our government shouldn't use our taxpayers' dollars to help you" and "You are a disgrace in the eyes of God."

One night, I was giving an educational presentation at a school district parent meeting. People threw tomatoes at me! They refused to accept HIV/AIDS as a communicable health issue. My heart cried, but my legs stood steady and tall, for I was the one to protect, defend and speak for my new friend Brad and others. Relieved that none of them were there that night, I felt like Joan of Arc in battle defending love, empathy and compassion.

If it is to be, it's up to me. Tonight. Oh lord, help me.

As tomatoes struck my head and blazer, hate boiled in the eyes of the throwers. Yet I was not mad at these people. As a bodyguard escorted me to safety, I felt calm, envisioning peace and happiness.

Eventually they will get it. Someday they will understand.

This inspired our team to create an HIV/AIDS panel that toured the county. People living with HIV/AIDS, family members, friends, nurses, doctors and support staff spoke about their experiences. Those telling stories about living with HIV/AIDS inspired significant positive acceptance in the county.

Our support group later found peace while gathering to make squares for the AIDS Memorial Quilt Project for friends who had succumbed to this epidemic. Our unity soothed our grief. Each of these warm, soft quilt squares expressed our love, honor and remembrance for our friends.

This was the era of young Ryan White, who had contracted HIV from a blood transfusion. Many parents opposed Ryan's ability to attend school, fearing for their children's safety. However, Ryan helped reduce the stigma around the HIV/AIDS disease. He put a new face on AIDS: this was a disease that anyone could catch. People were learning that it was only transmitted by bodily fluids and that it could not be caught from a desk, lunch bag or a shared pencil. It was OK to hug people with AIDS. Understanding and knowledge were replacing fear.

When Brad died of pneumonia, my heart heard the theme song from the Broadway musical, *Rent*.

I was only 31 years young, yet death surrounded me. As a gay woman, I remained silent, protecting and honoring my lover's wishes because Carol was still a nun. For five years, I protected the rights and integrity for Brad and other people living with AIDS. Abundant joy and love of life filled me in the middle of this storm. This was my ministry, my life, sent by God.

Olympic U.S. Figure Skating Championships

As adventures and surprises were our middle names and Carol loved ice skating and ice performances, I surprised Carol in 1987 with a trip to attend the USA National Olympic Preliminaries in Tacoma, Washington.

Carol broke into dance moves when I showed her our room reservations and tickets for two days and two nights. Our time at the venues was like taking a child on their first boat or airplane ride. Carol's eyes were as big as two fried eggs.

She was so excited, she took more clothes than she wore. Thank goodness we had been graciously warned to wear warm clothing, including her pink and black gloves and my gray mittens in the cold arena.

The second day, we carried a blanket into the ice dome, laying it on our laps and holding hands underneath. What a fun and exciting event it was, watching Brian Boitano and Jill Trenary, along with other talented individuals and skating pairs.

I did it! I planned a romantic couple's weekend and Carol loved it!

Jesus hold you.
God bless you.

CHAPTER 12
Adventures, Giggles and Laughter

Carol and I had favorite sayings and songs that injected joy into every word or action. She loved to belt out the lyrics to "That's Amore," but my rendition was all wrong, and made her laugh so hard, she almost peed.

"How does it really go?" I asked.

She would sing slowly and say, "repeat after me." We would end up hugging and laughing while swinging in circles of delight under the stars and the full moon. We laughed and giggled and laughed some more when I snorted strange noises.

"Carol, one day I'll get it!"

"You will, Joanie."

Natural Beauty and Fresh Fish

Carol had an eagle eye in beautiful nature; she could spot whale spouts far out in the ocean or ospreys flying miles away. From our kitchen table, she could spot monarch butterflies on a verbena bush in our yard.

"Joanie, can't you see it? It's right there!"

We logged miles, not by footprints or hours, but by our smiles. Total joy!

"JOY, JOY, JOY!" Carol would sing and do a happy dance.

Surrounded by natural beauty, Carol and I would "eye love" each other—silent eye contact expressing our shared appreciation of Mother Nature and our deep love. It was romantic, passionate and eternal. It tickled our insides and brought alive our love for each other to share nature.

Carol invented "love moments" or "love breaks" when we would think and feel the other, then experience that love once again while physically together or apart. This was her idea of a coffee break without the coffee. She would sit and ponder how much she loved and thought of me or someone. It was a "God, thank you" prayer. Such fun times, leaving notes in the bathroom sink or in her books. I tried leaving a note in the shower one time, but it got waterlogged. Oh, golly.

Look Forward

While walking sandy beaches, Carol focused 30 to 60 feet ahead, spotting sand dollars in the sand or at the brink of the tide level. She taught me to look outwardly, to look further up the beach. So many times, I was bending my neck, looking down at my feet and getting dizzy.

My neck hurts. This isn't very fun.

"Look forward, Joanie, scan the horizon. Look at the bigger picture."

I was so focused on finding sand dollars, shells or colorful agate that I was missing the whole adventure right in front of me. Silly me. It worked. On the beach and in life!

"Look forward, not straight." A gay answer, of course. In the gay world, we never say, "Drive straight." We always say, "Drive forward." Wink, wink.

Travels and Fun Times in Hawaii

Carol planned a surprise trip to Hawaii, the island of Kauai, for my 50th birthday in 2007, in a condo just 12 steps from the warm Pacific water.

I had never been to Hawaii. We had dreamed of it and Carol wanted us to have a really special time, just the two of us on a rare trip where "visiting others" was not the top priority.

CHAPTER 12

On Kauai, we went to a fun luau where native Hawaiian dancers (athletic, hunky, strong, agile, gorgeous bods) in grass skirts twirled rings of fire at a fancy, five-star hotel. We ate fresh ahi at a sugar mill plantation, and found the local kapaa breakfast place where the pineapple syrup is served fresh, hot, and in a pewter carafe and recommended by the friendly police officers.

We shared a coconut milk drink, sipping through two straws that squirted onto our tank tops; we drove to Princeville and snorkeled in the surf. We watched young men carry a wild boar on a trail, then put it into their truck. They were so excited about their wild beast catch and shared that this would be the family dinner to celebrate a wedding anniversary.

We strolled under tall, waving palm trees, holding hands, sitting close together, arms and legs touching. We rocked and rolled with the waves on a boat trip up the Nepali Coast.

"Oh!" we yelled at schools of dolphins who performed leaps and twists so close to the boat that the saltwater spray tickled our faces. We were blown away with the vastness and dryness of Waimea Canyon State Park, the "Grand Canyon" of Kauai. We only hiked about 15 minutes in the heat of the day.

The island offered incredible views in every direction; we kept thanking God for being the master artist. Carol and I shopped for hibiscus flowered dresses for her and shorts and tank tops for me at roadside boutiques and in small communities. We met and talked with beautiful people, the true highlight of our tropical travels.

At the Catholic Mass we attended at St. Catherine's (I think), we sat beside the eight-member choir with their instruments of guitars, ukuleles and flutes. Fun, upbeat, spiritual, prayerful music was welcoming and we belted out exuberance praise for our Lord.

Before this trip, Carol and I practiced snorkeling in Oregon. We would grab our water shoes, snorkels and masks during 80 degree summertime weather and drive inland along the curvy road through tall evergreens amidst fresh, clean northwest air, then immersed into the wild and scenic Chetco River as our "practice pool." The gently flowing river is clear with a rock bottom, though more deep and swift in some areas than I preferred. It was so much fun!

We learned to put on and take off our masks without complications. We gurgled and laughed, filling our mouths with fresh water before spitting it out. We eventually learned to not laugh with open mouths underwater, but to be calm and peaceful, enjoying the moment. We got comfortable wearing equipment on our faces, practiced calm breathing skills and learned to keep an eye on each other.

This prepared us for two rock-enclosed lagoons in Kauai's Lydgate Beach Park. Carol wore her purple swimsuit and I covered my black and white polka dot suit with a shirt to prevent sunburn. With masks on our heads and snorkels in hand, we walked down the grass in our tight-fitting water shoes with rubber bottoms for traction. The sand was as fine as powdered sugar and the breeze light. We waded into the warm, reef-protected water on this beautiful day with the blue-green ocean, palm trees on the shore and sunshine tickling the tops of my ears in this perfect place for snorkeling beginners. The water was warm, still and soft—very different from the Chetco River's chilly depths and incessant flow.

With her mask and snorkel in place, Carol floated face-down in a water-world of colors and wonders. She was having a great time! Carol was part fish, always a water lover since childhood. Today was her day! She was in her element. What a joy to watch her without her knowing I was watching her. A lover's delight!

We were astonished by the bright yellow, red-orange, black-striped and black polka-dotted fish, as small as a pinky finger, as large as half an arm's length. They were magnificent! Never had I seen anything like this in its natural habitat. An aquarium, no matter what size, does not compare. These fish were in their neighborhood. We were the guests.

I spotted Carol to my right and thought, *I'm going to swim where she is.* Wow, I couldn't believe what I saw. *Joanie, don't laugh, don't smile, just follow Carol's exotic purple shoes. Remain calm.*

Following Carol was an amazing, single line of 30 beautiful yellow, turquoise and black-nosed fish. They wove and flowed in unison as Carol leisurely swam through the warm, crystal-clear waters of the Pacific Ocean. Unbelievable! What a sight! She was oblivious as the fish continued to follow exactly whichever direction Carol veered.

This is a miracle. All of these fish think that she's their leader, maybe their mama. This is also the kind of leader and person Carol is in life.

I swam up to Carol and tapped her shoulder for her to surface. We removed our black, rented snorkels and neon-green masks. I told her what happened. She was flabbergasted.

"Really, I had no idea they were doing that. Why were they doing that?"

"I don't know, but maybe it's because you're wearing wonderful purple shoes and a purple bathing suit. They are simply attracted to you. Could you feel them behind you?"

"Nope, but cool! Later, Joanie, I want to see more."

We swam hours more, witnessing beautiful and unique God-made fishes. We later learned their clever names and descriptions from a picture brochure of the tropical creatures: rainbow fish whose bodies were splashed with color; Picasso trigger fish with a cute small nose, bright white fins and blue-red teal body; the raccoon butterfly fish with black eyes and a yellow body. It seemed like a hundred more varieties of sizes and shapes. Some fish looked rectangular, or round as a cantaloupe, or slender like the orange-reddish wrasse.

I was most amazed by the 30 fish following Carol single-file. A miracle! Certain people are followed in life no matter where they go because they have a love for all. They are unselfish, humble and thankful.

People followed Carol. Carol had a direct line with God. Just as the fish had a direct line with Carol. And you know what? Carol was always a purple shoe leader, standing out in style and in spirit, attracting people and even fish to follow her Godly path.

This Hawaiian snorkel day reminded me of our beginnings as a couple. We followed, led, trusted, and were colorful to each other, day in and day out—monogamously, sacredly, and delightfully. Twenty-six years into our love-life commitment, here we were together, snorkeling in Hawaii.

How good you are, God. I am so thankful! Thank you God for the colorful rainbow in the skies and in the tropical waters of Hawaii. Thank you, Jesus, for my sweetie. We'll keep following you Lord, purple shoes or no shoes.

New York City Arrival

Just you and me, babe. More adventures, living the dream while loving and laughing more.

Our evening arrival into New York City in July of 2002 was spectacular—glimpsing the blinking city lights from the airplane.

We pulled our rolling red luggage—tied with Christmas ribbon to distinguish them from the others at baggage claim—and joined the sea of people in the shuttle area. It felt like we were among more people than the total population of our hometown in Oregon. The huge crowd had off-the-charts noise amidst body odor, perfumes and colognes from weary travelers.

We were all smiles as we bumped shoulders, holding our luggage tightly, excited and pinching ourselves that "we are here" in the "Big Apple"—a first time for me and second time for Carol. New York City's population was seven million plus. Oh golly! Terrifying and exhilarating all at once.

All around us, people spoke German, Spanish and French. They wore jeans, shorts, bright-colored smocks, head pieces, glasses glittering with bling, sandals and tennis shoes, and men and ladies in suits, ties, and fancy leather shoes.

I purchased our hotel shuttle tickets from a kiosk attendant who needed some people-skills training. Or maybe that was the New York way: "Hurry up! Next!"

We were told to wait for our names to be called. Carol, not a patient waiter, and me wanting to get out of the stuffy crowded space, clung to each other and leaned against a wall. After 30 minutes, our names were not called. People who had bought tickets after us had already left.

So I asked the men who organized people into shuttles, "What about Tierheimer and Lindenmeyer?"

In a language difficult to understand and harshly spoken, I was told, "Wait, just wait."

"OK," I kindly responded. Another 30 minutes, nothing. So frustrating! It was getting darker outside. Then we thought we heard our names, and it was still difficult to understand the accents, but Carol and I agreed.

"That's us." So we boarded the shuttle and squeezed into a van with smelly people; the wind tossed loose trash and papers around.

Carol said, "Look at all the lights. Wow, what a city."

After about 15 minutes of us riding, jerking and eyeing this huge city from the back row of the 12-passenger van, our driver barked over the loud radio in heated communication with another van driver. "Do you have Tierheimer? Lindenmeyer?"

He yelled to the back of the van, "Is Tierglimer and Lindenheimer here?"

Oh golly, our names were just mutilated.

"Yes, that's us," I yelled, crunched with Carol in a row with others who also wanted to get to their destinations..

"You on the wrong shuttle lady!" the driver said. "We have to move you. NOW!"

On a four-lane highway, he pulled to the fast lane shoulder, the far-left emergency lane. We are told to get off, put our rumps on the cement divider and lift our legs over it and transfer to the van parked the opposite direction on the shoulder of the highway.

You gotta be kidding!

"Carol, I'll help grab our bags. Wait by the wall for me."

"Oh, my," she said as cars, trucks, vans, and limos all zipped by at 45 miles per hour. The driver and I grabbed our luggage from the rear of the long van and he handed them over the cement barricade to the other van driver.

"You're supposed to be with me, not him," the other van driver angrily yelled at us.

"Alright," I said. "No problem."

Off we went, two hours later, our penalty for screwing up. We were the only remaining passengers. Carol and I really made the most of it: we had our own private tour of the Big Apple. We arrived safely at the Radio City Apartments where a nice gentleman welcomed us to the city and assisted us with luggage. He escorted us to the front desk to check in. He had a distinct accent, but his smile, demeanor and joy spoke loudly and clearly.

Subway Adventures

Carol's niece was living in New York City and completing a chef internship with Daniel Bould. We were so proud of her and we carried big love from her mother, Elaine, Carol's sister in Oregon.

She taught us valuable skills, like how to get on and off the subway.

Every day in NYC held hilarious events like our grand shuttle entrance. As explorers, I wore a red backpack with our water bottles, jackets, maps, etc., stashed inside. Carol was in charge of loading it and unloading it while it was on my back. We kept our hands free for safety and for the magic of touch we shared so often.

New York City was a place of LGTBQ people expressing their love and affections. We did the same. It felt so freeing and beautiful. We loved it. For a week, our love was not confined to our bedroom.

Our first subway ride was a thrill. We walked down the cement steps, used cash and got a ticket from a machine, went through the turnstiles like on TV, and waited in the correct section. We hoped it was an express one. Whatever that meant.

The platform and train were crowded with nowhere to sit, so we stood. I held the top bar and Carol held onto a pole extending from floor to ceiling. The subway jolted forward and she literally swirled around one complete turn! My mouth dropped wide open in this surprise athletic event. Definitely the best pole dancing I'd ever seen. Score, a ten, as I raised both my hands to Carol. She smiled like she was on a wild Space Mountain ride at Disneyland. Her feet finally touched the floor.

I looked at her and we laughed. I said to the people sitting around us, "We've never been here before."

In a chorus of happy voices, the subway car crowd said, "We

know!" We all laughed and two people offered their seats to us. We were thankful and talkative. Then they gave us helpful advice about their city and subways: "Sit versus standing if you can. Move to the right if people are walking fast past you."

I almost hugged them goodbye. They were so kind and glad we were visiting.

Freedom . . . Ferry Ride to Ellis Island

We got off the subway at Battery Park, the southern tip of Manhattan, planning to go to Liberty Island. Then we took a gorgeous ferry ride, cruising and looking at the sites of New York City, bridges, and gargantuan buildings higher than the helicopters flying around. The shipping boats, sailboats and wave runners were around us in the sparkling water. Permanent gawkers we were. I had a camera around my neck. Sunglasses protected us from the wind and glare. I wore my red shorts with lots of pockets and Carol was in her multicolored dress. We stood out like a vivacious couple.

Someone said, "You must be mother and daughter."

We laughed and said, "Good guess, but we are best friends for life!" Sometimes we would say, "We are domestic partners." We kidded with each other on who they thought was the mother. Carol and I were 15 years different in age, but we looked and acted younger, too.

As our boat toured around the Statue of Liberty, we were amazed by this iconic, sculptured woman—300+ feet tall and built around 1886 in her gorgeous blue-green copper attire. We docked minutes later at Ellis Island, pretending we were the Tierheimer immigrants, landing in the place of "FREEDOM for ALL." The hairs on our arms stood up as we disembarked and toured the historical museum. We saw with our own eyes under a glass case a book of the signatures of people who arrived at Ellis Island.

Carol screamed, "Look Joanie, my grandfather's name—Frank Tierheimer!"

Clear as could be! That was it. Then we saw his name displayed on a piece of brick where he had carved his name into the rock. The ranger heard us talking and came over to us. After Carol told him the story of her grandfather, he escorted us to a specialized archive room. Carol, shaking like a leaf with pride, proceeded to document her family history for the National Park archives. It was momentous and emotional. Tears streamed down my face and Carol was over-the-top, so proud to be a United States citizen once coming from the land of Egypt. It reminded me of the song "Standing on the Shoulders."

Pretty cool, huh?!

Ground Zero

We visited the Ground Zero site of the 9/11 attack, one year earlier, and saw the twisted metal ruins of a configuration that formed a cross. Unbelievable!

We slowly walked, with our heads down, around the chain-linked fence, the exposed and once-deadly grave of innocent people. We cried and prayed in silence. It was one of the few times I ever saw Carol cry in public.

We heard other people crying, and a few local pastors were preaching for love not hate, for God's saving grace and for remembering the souls lost. Extreme emotions. It was still recent grief.

Philadelphia Freedom

When Carol and I ventured to Philadelphia, we stood together as two gay women in the room, the exact location of the signing of the 1776 Declaration of Independence at Independence Hall.

Back then, people had faith and hope in each other and in goodness, and were willing to break free of the old ways and ties to the rule of England and its king. Likewise, Carol and I had broken away from the bondage of church and law. We were freedom-seekers. With free will and choice, we decided to follow Jesus' all-encompassing path and create our own union.

We lived 40 years together united in faith, hope and goodness. No regrets.

I love the last line of the famous Declaration document. It states, I paraphrase, that we've relied on the protection of the divine, we've pledged our lives, our fortunes and our sacred honor to each other and to a country that was founded on EQUALITY for all.

YES! YES!

Which brings to mind questions that are essential for growth, meditation and contemplation. Please consider them in your life.

Who am I to be?
What else can I do?
Where does God lead me?
When is it my time to be free?
Why do we stand up for others?
How can I make sure that "I am my brother's/sister's keeper?"

The Phillies Baseball Game

To top this vacation off with my dream-come-true, we had a blast at a Major League Phillies baseball game. Carol had another dream come true and ate a real Philly steak sandwich. We actually shared it.

I wore black shorts, a red Phillies game shirt and a red baseball hat. Carol was decked out wonderfully stylish in her wild and bright dress, her wide white-brim hat and her Oregon Ducks green and yellow sunglasses. We were seated in the section between third base and right field, Carol in the aisle seat and me beside her. We sat with the sun to our back and a super view of the gorgeous green ballfield park with restaurant row behind and to our right. We were relaxed and enjoying the game in these excellent seats that I bought online, a first, back in Oregon before our trip.

A young man tapped Carol on her shoulder and asked, "Can I take your picture, ma'am?"

Carol's smile exploded. "Yes, of course."

"In just a minute, I'll have a camera person here and would you be willing to pose like a circus body builder and flex your biceps like this?" He showed her his clenched fists, arms up in the air and elbows out, like a strong Rocky boxer.

"OK." She imitated him perfectly.

"Perfect," he said. "You'll be fantastic."

A few minutes elapsed and he waited, sitting on the concrete steps in the aisle and chit-chatting with Carol. "OK," he said, and two cameramen with lenses bigger than a dinner platter were staring in her face, maybe 10 inches away.

He said, "Now!"

She reacted quickly with her big hat and colorful dress—as if she were attending the Kentucky Derby—and posed with her gorgeous, contagious and beautiful smile, her strong arms showing off her large bicep muscles.

I had my camera in my hands, ready to capture "the moment" and I snapped a picture of her with the stadium jumbotron screen in the background. There was Carol on that huge stadium monitor, big as life!

The stadium fans went absolutely wild, yelling and clapping for her! Thousands of people were cheering with her! She kept posing and smiling, rocking her head back and forth and side to side with total joy! The louder the crowd, the larger her smile. Carol was AMAZING! It was 30 seconds of pure, wild, frenzy fun. OMG!

The people nearest us were saying, "Who is this famous person?"

The young man motioned his hand to stop the live action camera. He leaned over to her and said, "Thank you so much! You were just on national TV for a Motrin commercial."

She looked at me, and we laughed and laughed and laughed. People in our section were saying, "Way to go. You did great." A few came over and shook her hand. She was famous!

How fun!! Carol the TV personality of the day. *Miracles and joys in our adventures of life are never ending. Thank you, God.*

Driving Through Life

Our adventures continued on a trip to Sun City, Arizona, where we attended a leadership conference.

"Wow, Carol, this is amazing," I said as we held hands, touring our rented beautiful, three-bedroom house in an adult retirement living community in a desert landscape. "It's bigger than our house and sure better than a hotel room. Thanks, sweetie, a whole bunch!"

"I'm impressed too, Joanie. You are most welcome, love. Wahoo!" Carol shouted, swinging me around in a twirl of happiness. "Let's wander around."

"Let's see where this goes." I opened a door, which revealed a golf cart in a huge garage.

I hopped into the driver's seat while Carol took the passenger seat. I turned the key, but nothing happened. I gently tapped the accelerator—no movement.

So Carol bent over the dashboard, reading directions on how to drive the golf cart.

Oh, what's this? N for neutral? R for reverse?

Voilà . . . shazam! I put the shifter into R and pushed the gas pedal to the floor. The golf cart took off, backwards! Carol's entire body jolted. She grabbed the safety bar.

At the top of her lungs, surely waking the coyotes, she screamed, "Stop! Joanie, Stop!"

"How?"

"Stop, stop, stop! Joanie!!"

We traveled at the speed of light down the curb, across the street and up the other curb.

Finally, I slammed on the brakes—avoiding an imminent crash into our neighbor's garage door.

We just sat there, laughing hysterically, about ready to pee our pants.

"That was close!"

"Oh yes, so close!"

With my foot firmly on the brake, we roared in laughter again.

"Can you believe this? Do you think anyone saw us?"

"Maybe they heard our death screams?"

"Are you OK, Carol? You jerked like there was no tomorrow!"

"Yes, I'm fine. Drive, Joanie, drive. Let's go. Let's get out of their driveway."

"I think D is for drive." I slid the shifter to D and gently touched the gas pedal. Off we went, slowly, carefully and methodically, down the curb and onto the brightly-lit street.

We cruised for nearly an hour on well-lit streets in the moonbeams and warmth of the still night. We never saw a coyote, but the folks in the security check-in gate smiled as we waved.

Adventures, ex-nuns and love. What a life!

There could be *Nun Better* for us.

Jesus hold you.
God bless you.

CHAPTER 13

It's All About Love and Jesus

Starting Our Day Off with Gusto

Carol and I were "doing life" with gusto, living our mantra, "Everyday is a new day. Never been lived before."

We were both happily employed on the Southern Oregon and Northern California coast where our Monday through Friday routine of rise and shine was joy filled. We awoke back-to-back, a preselected CD as our musical alarm clock. I opened the blinds to see the pink cherry blossom tree and the large cypress trees against the sky.

For work, I wore athletic Adidas or Nike warmups with shorts under the pants and my Physical Education logo polo shirt. Choosing the tennis shoes of the day was my big thing: red, black, white, leather or mesh with pink laces. My short blond hair was easy to brush, and I was ready to go in less than 10 minutes.

Carol had brown, shiny, silky-soft hair with a flare of wave brushed backwards to show off her gorgeous green eyes, which popped with wonder. She patiently admired her choice of fun, beautiful clothes, smiling, dancing and rocking as she chose her outfit for the day. Her choices were colorful, solid, flowered or printed patterns in cotton, nylon, spandex and wool blends for dresses, skirts, pants, blouses and sweaters. Next was jewelry: her watch, earrings and always the necklace I bought at the San Diego Pride Festival in 1986: a sterling silver sun and crescent moon. Her shoes and sandals, snazzy and bright—Imelda Marcos, watch out!

Carol left her boutique and stepped into the kitchen. Voilà! Hollywood Carol had arrived, looking sharp, beautiful and radiant.

My attire was boring compared to Carol's unique, trend-setting styles. Every morning was a fashion show on the red carpet. I loved it and so did she. This routine was better than any caffeine drink. We didn't even need any coffee!

We kissed and hugged goodbye each morning and when we returned home. I remember my parents smacking a quick kiss to each other when they said goodbye and hello. I guess it rubbed off on me.

I was a comedian quite often, with my lifelong silly streak. On several occasions, out of the blue, I would kiss her as a quick goodbye, go retrieve the mail or the garbage cans, and return to share another kiss. In and out of the front or back door in two minutes.

"Did you miss me, Carol?"

Her answer, "ALWAYS."

We'd laugh and laugh.

Around 4:30 or 5 p.m., we met back home. The feeling of coming home was not monotonous at all. When I left the school parking lot, I would touch and turn my ear with my right hand. A gesture that signified that I'm in "our" mode, not work mode. Like turning the channels on a TV station.

Carol was my most important part of life and I was her most important part of life.

We were equals at home and in our household duties and chores. It felt good and right to share responsibilities, finances and the day-to-day stuff of "living to the max" as we called it. We constantly discussed and shared ideas. We did not take life for granted or think things were set in stone and couldn't change.

She took charge of the laundry, I folded, she cooked, I cut and prepared the food and I did the dishes. Together we set the table. She did the grocery shopping; I mowed the lawn. It was teamwork or more like team play.

Here's a funny story. I was out in the yard, in front of the kitchen/back porch, when the weed eater suddenly made an odd sound. I looked down; the drawstring on my shorts was stuck in the weed eater. We were attached and I didn't know how to get out of it! Fortunately, the weed eater turned itself off. I yelled for Carol, who was in the kitchen, "Come help me, Carol!"

She recognized my emergency voice and high-tailed it outside.

"Joanie, what did you do?"

"I don't know. My shorts just started moving, and got eaten up by the machine."

We laughed hysterically.

But I couldn't get free of this extra yellow and black appendage. She tried to pull the shorts cord out of the machine, but it was a no-go. I asked her, "Please call Curry Equipment Company and ask for help."

I heard her voice explain to them, "Joanie has her shorts cord stuck in the weed eater."

She had the phone on speaker mode and I heard, "Is it still running?"

Oh golly, I laughed even louder and harder, like a clan of hyenas.

"No, of course not, but what do we do?" Carol was so sincere and worried for me. So cute of her.

Finally, a big sigh, then Carol and the person on the phone line started laughing, too. A huge nut charge.

Life was one big adventure.

"Cut the cord on her shorts," they said. "We'd be glad to take a look at the weed eater."

Healdsburg Getaway and Another Step Forward

Carol surprised me with a romantic getaway to Healdsburg, California, to soak and relax in a mineral spa. Yippee! I loved her surprises. They made me tingle.

Our rustic hotel cabin was only 20 paces to the spa facility. So nice, stretched out inside the wide and deep enameled bathtubs, spaced close enough that we were within arm's reach of each other, able to touch hands and blow kisses while regulating our own amount and desired temperature of bath water.

This was the life for kings and queens. We were the queens!

I think her Egyptian heritage longed for this moment. We twisted and turned the sparkling metal faucet knobs enthusiastically as she and I added more warm water from the silver, neck-shaped faucet. I glanced over at Carol. She had begun to sink, melt and travel to the pyramids in her mind. I could imagine plates of fresh fruit presented by Cleopatra's female staff, palm branches being waved and bizarre music echoing off the catacomb walls.

Total delight!

Curtains were drawn around our own private and blessed pools. It was symbolic of our private, and probably secret, love life.

Maybe people could see through the façade that we were just friends, and knew we were lovers. The staff certainly could tell by how we acted that we were lovers by our eye contact and tender touching. Or maybe some people felt more comfortable ignoring it or were blind to it. *Ehh,* it didn't matter to us.

Carol had chosen a different kind of adventure for us this weekend. I liked this non-hurried atmosphere. I relished the moment of solitude and reverence with my sweetie pie. I saw her naked and unafraid and I felt the same way. Her face lit with peace and tranquility of our trusting relationship. I felt so happy and so thankful for so much.

Few words were spoken as we, each individually yet together, cleansed ourselves with the smell and taste of fresh spring mineral water coming forth from a different spout, filling and refilling into tiny paper cups. A sip here and a sip there.

From the inside of my heart and soul, this feels so fantastic, actually difficult to put it into words.

Could it be just a simple grateful prayer to my Lord saying, "Thank you for the gift of Carol. She truly is a treasure with a giant colorful bow on it." That was my visualization.

Thank you, God. Thank you, Carol, for loving me so much.

CHAPTER 13

It was like being baptized in the Jordan River or sitting in a warm spot in the Chetco River back home in Brookings.

Barely able to walk to our cabin, my legs felt like floppy spaghetti noodles with zero control of where they go, Gumby style. Falling on the bed, we took a short nap. This was bliss. Relaxation turned to sleep.

We went to dinner at a local pizza place in downtown Healdsburg. The room was filled, but not overly crowded. We were enjoying each other, chit-chatting, and feeling awesome about this "splurge, mini-romantic getaway."

Smelling fresh pizza dough, exotic cheese, olives and meats, we ordered a large pizza.

"Carol, I'm starving. How about we add some sundried tomatoes and artichoke hearts to the pizza, too?"

"Salad, sweetie?"

"Let's share one."

"Good idea."'

A tall stein of local beer came for me and for Carol, a soda glass filled with cubed ice and a paper straw in her fizzing Pepsi.

How fun to celebrate a wonderful weekend away from our Monday through Friday work schedule, where we both were always inundated with serving and helping people.

This was taking care of us, just us.

No phones. No visitors. No "have to's."

Quiet time as a couple.

So wonderful!

"Carol, this is the best! Thank you, lover dover. Are you having fun?"

"Absolutely, Joanie," she said with her huge smile. Her skin looked refreshed and plumped with happy cells singing *alleluia.*

Suddenly she said, "Joanie, that man is staring at me. What should I do?"

"Ah, ignore him. It'll pass."

"No, he's really eyeing me. Now he is walking over to me—"

"You don't remember me," he said.

Carol blurted, "Steve Dix!" She jumped up and he hugged her like an old lost friend.

"Hi, Sister Carol," he said. "I'd recognize you anywhere. How are you?"

She gestured for him to sit with us and he quickly motioned for his lady friend to come to our table. Carol's eyes and Steve's eyes stuck like glue, connected in a beautiful way. Introductions were made and the old stories from the deep magna of the earth bubbled up with excitement.

Great vibes were bouncing between Roz, Steve's companion, and myself as well.

Carol, shaking like a leaf in the autumn winds, told the story of the Dix family in Sonoma where she, as a nun, taught at the Catholic elementary school. Carol taught Steve's brother to play the guitar and approved them to play a particular song at their graduation.

Steve chimed in, "Stairway to Heaven." He shared updates about his parents and family while Carol listened intently, her greatest of all gifts. We exchanged contact info and they said, "Please come see our house tomorrow on your way home."

"Of course! We'd love to."

"Oh, this is so amazing, running into you, Sister Carol. I am going to go call my brother. I just knew it was you by your smile."

"Call me Carol."

"OK, Carol," he said in a sweet voice like he was a kid again. "A big hug before we leave you two alone."

Carol and Steve winked or sent their last look of the night at each other as a sign of their forever friendship dating from his childhood days with his beloved former nun teacher.

The next day, we were thrilled to see their gorgeous house and property, and were welcomed with even more warmth.

Steve said, "I hardly slept last night, Carol. I can't believe it that we have been reunited."

Roz and I were loving watching these two for whom 25 years had been timeless. Like rainbows that never lose their glow of colors and brightness. Steve and Carol.

We shared Christmas cards and occasional emails for years with them in the Eugene, Oregon, area and us on the southernmost coast of Oregon. It was wonderful when they came and visited us, too. Neat people!!

Our blooming friendship with Roz and Steve was fun. We talked about anything and everything from gardening flowers and veggies, wildlife, birds and the great Oregon outdoors to golf, baseball, and church, the past, the present and the future, recipes and yummy eats.

Connecting with them in the pizzeria was extremely affirming, because we were accepted as a couple!

From the past, the old ways, the Phoenix has risen into a new beginning. Wow!

Jesus hold you.
God bless you.

Joanie and Carol, August 1983

Joanie, SDSU Volleyball 1976

Carol in Idaho

Carol

Carol & Joanie, Lewiston bedroom, 1983

Sisters Frances, Joanie, Carol 1986

Sr. Veronica Joseph (Carol Tierheimer) 1962

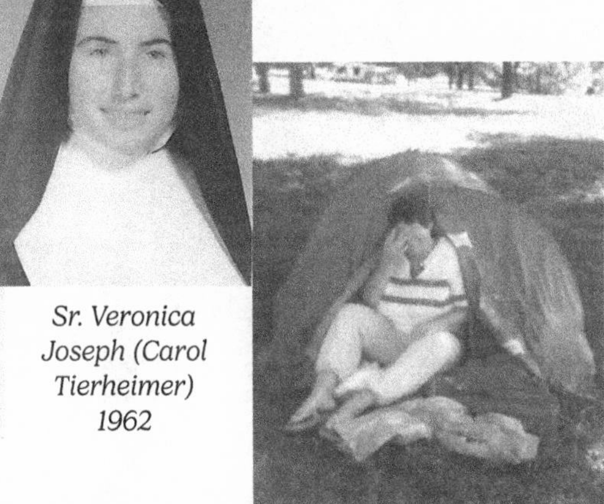

Carol camping in the apple orchard, Pasco area 1985

Joanie as a novice, Lewiston, 1982

A drive to Dworshak Dam, 1982

Joanie & Carol, bedroom in Pasco, 1986

Playtime in Lewiston. Our courtship, 1986

Carol cooking in Idaho

Carol, Lewiston rainbow, 1986

Carol, convent house in Idaho

Carol's family at her 25th Jubilee

Joanie gave the homily at Carol's 25th Jubilee at St. Stanislaus, Lewiston, 1986

Off to work, Sister Carol, Aberdeen, 1988

Joanie's family

Carol razor clamming, 1987

Carol & Joanie in Aberdeen

Joanie & Carol, Hawaii, 2007

Carol & Joanie's used mini RV

The very first LGBTQ gathering in Brookings, 1993

Joanie & Carol, 2005

Traveling to Alaska on a cruise ship

Our typical faces, Brookings 1986

Our first and only house

Getting our kicks on Route 66

Carol & Joanie on a picnic on the Rogue River, 2006

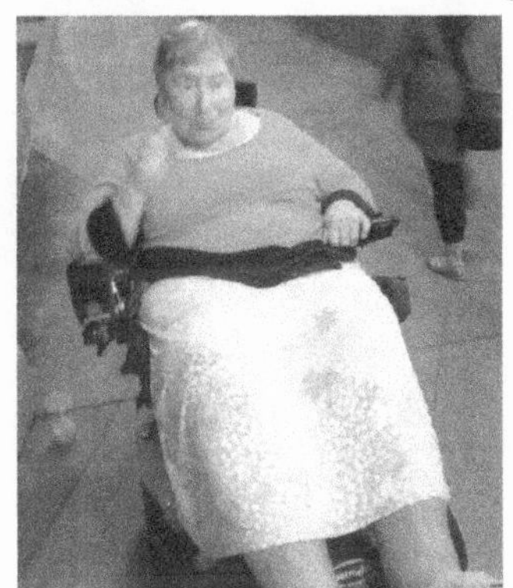

Carol dancing to the music, Oceanside, CA

Carol on the megatron, Phillies baseball game

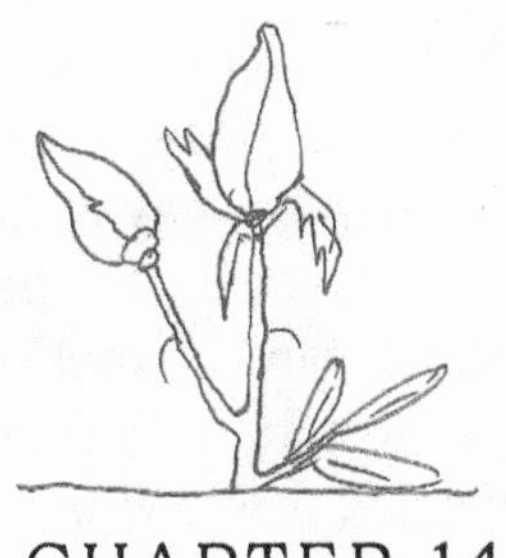

CHAPTER 14
Our New Life Together in Brookingss

Finding Our Forever Home

Carol and I loved looking at homes for sale, to fire up our dream juices. *What if? Can you imagine us living here? Oh golly, look at this location. Why not us?*

We cultivated an attitude of hope and wonder, even when people stared at us, a realtor avoided us, and we were "outbid" on a house. Was it discrimination by the seller?

Our dream house would be where the trees meet the ocean on the Oregon coast. In Brookings-Harbor, we discovered a red cottage-style house on flat ground, with lots of grass, natural bushes, a creek on the side and ¾ of an acre of land. Its grass yard for golf and badminton, and a bathtub, met my two requirements. Its 1,000 square feet had lots of light from south and west windows, a huge kitchen and huge living room—Carol's requirements. Yippee, yahoo! And the price was decent. Coming from nun life, any home price felt like reaching into outer space.

In February of 1992, we bought the little red house on Oceanview Drive. As first-time homebuyers, we were proud to make this house our home.

We are homeowners and this is our life!

During winter, we had a peek of the Pacific Ocean through the barren trees. We loved to close our eyes and listen to the changing tides and the roar of waves breaking on the shore about 200 yards away. The low tide smelled like rotten eggs.

We also loved the small birds tweeting and flitting around the bubbling creek. We also had 15-foot-tall overgrown wild blackberry bushes, and thick wild fuchsia bushes with pink and white blossoms. Woodpeckers pounded the alder and cypress trees, and lots of fresh green grass grew year-round.

We painted rooms in vibrant colors: greens, purples, aquas and all the rainbow colors in the song about Joseph's Coat of Many Colors. We were ready to take on the responsibilities of upkeep, taxes, etc., and meet new neighbors as friends.

"Let's always keep sharing what we have," Carol said. That was how we did life. Thanks to Carol's sharp mind for numbers, she monitored our finances, including our joint savings and checking accounts. We even held weekly financial meetings. Our biggest question was, "Hey sweetie, do we have enough money to go out to eat this week?"

At the same time, we dreamed of our California family and friends, as well as the CSJ sisters, visiting in the summer months, spreading out sleeping bags on the living room floor for the kids. The only drawback was the one bathroom.

I am 35 years old and Carol is 50 years young. This will be our fresh start of our brand-new life as fun-loving women ready to take on the world. A gay couple free from vows and religious life, we were adventurous risk-takers, prayerful and Jesus-centered, while loving life and each other with vim and vigor.

Abu the Juggler Blesses Us with Intuition & Courage

Carol and I inherited furniture, house wares, artifacts, jewelry, bowls, plates, and more, and we owned cherished photos of our grandparents, parents, and siblings.

Carol said, "OK, we have four households of furniture here. This is exciting. My mom and dad's buffet, tables and chairs, your grandmother Ruby's china cabinet, credenza, table and chairs, your sofa, my bed: now it's all OURS!!"

I beamed as she continued: “Let’s hang and display our family pictures up on our walls and on our cabinets and shelves. My favorite and most precious memorable portrait of all is my grandfather, Frank Salih. Also known as Abu Salih, my mother’s father.”

Carol’s father, Joe Tierheimer, was German and her mother, Elsie, whose maiden name Salih, was Egyptian.

The Egyptian side of the family started with Frank, known by his stage name, Abu Salih. Very popular and famous, Abu was a juggler who traveled with his acting partner from Egypt and Syria for exhibition shows in New York City, Atlantic City and San Francisco. Abu juggled machetes, swords and rifles, while integrating Egyptian artifacts into his props. The picture on our kitchen wall shows Abu Salih surrounded by his entertainment props and a painted background depicting Egypt and its culture.

Carol inherited a fantastic quality from Abu: “intuition.”

When Abu and his show partner were in San Francisco, Abu had a vivid nighttime dream of raging fires, billowing smoke and death by the hundreds. He knew that he and his partner needed to leave the city. So they did, after packing in the middle of the night, they left town.

The next day, the 1906 San Francisco earthquake—one of the worst in U.S. history—registered 7.9 on the Richter scale, killed more than 3,000 people, sparked fires and destroyed 80% of the city.

“I have the same gift as my grandfather Abu,” Carol said. “I see things before they happen. It’s not always good, but I just KNOW. I can’t explain it to you or anyone, Joanie, I just KNOW.”

I nodded. “I totally believe you, Carol. You bear and hold this great gift for a reason.” I always encouraged her that together we would rely on this remarkable, unexplainable gift of intuition.

Another time, Abu returned to Egypt in the early 1900s to bring his wife to “America,” the land of the FREE.

They had tickets and they were ready to board the ship to cross the Atlantic Ocean to their new home. Just before the giant ship left port, he walked around it. Then he told his wife: “Honey, I’ve just sold the tickets. We’re not going on this ship. We’ll go on the next one.”

She said, "OK, that's fine with me. Whatever you think is best." She believed 100% in her husband and his premonitions and intuition.

"That ship was the Titanic," Carol said.

Oh, my gosh, this story gives me goose bumps on top of goose bumps!

When Carol and I talked about writing our stories, she insisted that we include her grandfather Abu.

Carol believed with all her heart and soul that Jeremiah, Abu, her family lineage, herself, and me were lives orchestrated by God. One of her most beloved Bible passages was Jeremiah 29:11-14:

"I alone know the plans I have for you, says the Lord . . . plans to bring about prosperity and not disaster, plans to bring about the future you hope for. Then you will call to me. You will come and pray to me and I will answer you."

The Night We Almost Died

Carol's intuition calmed me during a terrifying flight from San Francisco to Crescent City, California.

We boarded the small plane amidst battering rain and 75 mile-per-hour winds. When we took off in the dark, our seat belts were tighter than strapping your Christmas tree to the roof of your car. The 24 passengers and I were very nervous, but Carol was calm.

"We will be OK, Joanie."

"Really? This is pretty bad, dangerous actually."

"Yes. Just hold my hand, and we will be OK."

Carol and I held hands under the blanket we had requested from the flight attendant. In public, we were smart, proactive and cautious. It was the 1980s and 1990s, when anyone different than the heterosexual norm was regarded as disgraced, sick, mentally ill, possessed or even contagious with HIV/AIDS. Verbal and physical attacks on gay people happened everywhere.

No resources such as Parents and Families of Lesbian and Gay (PFLAG) existed to help families of gays and lesbians learn how to support their family member, and for gay and lesbian individuals in how to communicate their sexuality to their friends and family.

Carol had a super aura around her that shielded her from harm. Her guardian angel protected her naive, beautiful soul. I was more street-wise and could sense evil. But goodness has always been more powerful.

It was also the beginning of standing up for and with each other. Carol and I didn't like the label or box called Lesbian. We liked being called Carol and Joanie.

We "came out" to some friends and family and told them about our love together as a couple. But we also had friends and acquaintances who had rude manners and cruel attitudes, and used homophobic talk. They were selfish and set in their own bigotry, not open to anyone different than themselves, so we chose NOT to share or hang out with them.

Very simple in our minds.

Be the best US and let God do the rest.

We knew our love was unbreakable.

We were also smart and aware of the many voices of hatred and attitudes of discrimination against "gay people" and people of color. We prayed for peace and harmony every day!

As a loving couple during the 1980s and 1990s, we chose to not "rock the boat" in public places. We could not go to Lover's Lane or crowded beaches to watch the sunset. Yes, we wanted to hold hands, walk arm in arm, stand with arms around each other, and kiss each other in public, but we chose not to. Instead, we gazed lovingly into each other's eyes and saved our intimacy for behind closed doors in our home or car, or on a secluded beach or a trail. At weddings and celebrations, we danced together, but never a slow dance. We prayed for that culture of prejudices and homophobic attitudes to change someday.

So, in public we were "undercover," as with the airplane blanket. The pilot announced an unexpected detour landing in Redding, California—a four-hour drive over a mountain range to our home!

As the plane swerved up and down, our heads bobbed, babies cried, and passengers prayed aloud: "Oh God, help us all. God I don't want to die!"

I prayed harder and harder in my heart. Tears streamed down my cheeks. Air drops, more air drops, I smell vomit.

I think this is going to be the end.

Carol was not scared. She knew something bigger.

We landed safely in Redding. While our plane sat on the tarmac for 20 minutes, one man tried to use the exit, but a flight attendant stopped him.

When the plane took off, Carol said, "Joanie, we're going to be OK. It's all right. I just know it; I just know it."

"OK, sweetie, if you say so."

The 45-minute flight to Arcata was ROUGH! The seatbelts couldn't keep our butts down; our whole bodies were coming off the seat. My head even hit the ceiling.

Luggage spilled from the top bins. Suitcases crashed onto the floor, sliding in all directions.

"Oh God, I don't want to die!" people screamed. "Please God, please God!"

The flight attendant and pilot were silent.

I said to Carol, "I see lights."

She leaned over me to look out the tiny window. "Yes, lots of them."

As we approached the Arcata airport on the ground, it was lit up with blinking, roving, emergency flashing lights: rows of fire trucks (at least 10), ambulances, military people standing on the ground in rain gear, helmets and boots, and police cars. They were ready for us to crash!!

As we passengers were bounced around, Carol calmly whispered, "Joanie, it's going to be OK."

"It is?"

"I told you we are going to be OK." She lightly squeezed my hand, tenderly with dry palms.

Carol's intuition and faith in her God were at work; I felt lighter, believing.

We landed hard!

Someone asked, "Is everyone OK?"

"YES!" I said. "Thank you, God. We didn't die."

As we disembarked amidst flashing red, blue and green lights, we all clapped, crying with joy and exclaiming, "Thank you, pilot," and "You saved us," and "We made it!" The man who tried to get off kissed the ground.

Carol clasped my hand between hers. "I told you we would be OK, Joanie."

"Yes, you sure did and you are so right."

With a huge smile, she added, "You and I have more work to do for God. It's not our time yet." This reminded me of the scripture: "Trust in God with all your heart." (Proverbs 3: 5-6)

As passengers raced for the bathrooms and hugged family members and lovers, Carol and I embraced and kissed in public. It was a safe, secure and loving place!! Better than the happiest place on earth—Disneyland.

Still an hour and a half south of Crescent City, a passenger and her father offered us a ride in his van to Crescent City.

"I'm here to drive you all home," he said, carefully navigating the wind and the rain on coastal Highway 101 to Crescent City.

Carol and I said, "Thank you so much for picking us up and including us in your family."

He said, "We are all family tonight."

In our car, Carol and I drove 25 minutes to Brookings-Harbor to our home. Inside, we embraced in the kitchen, looking at the picture of Abu in his juggling performance outfit.

"Carol, I'm so glad that you've been given the gift of intuition, just like your grandfather Abu."

"Joanie, thank you, love. You trusted and believed in me, in my intuition and in my faith. That to me is the best gift of all. I love you, honey."

"I love you, sweetie."

Our New Parish

As we settled into our beautiful life together, we registered at Star of the Sea Catholic Church, participating in weekly Mass and making many Catholic friends. We engaged in church events but did not volunteer for any specific roles; it was relaxing and peaceful to attend and not be a leader. We were known as Carol and Joanie, two friends.

One Saturday night during Mass, Carol and I were honored to be asked to walk down the middle aisle carrying the offertory gifts to the altar. Later we held hands during the Our Father prayer. Holding hands with Carol was automatic and natural.

After the Our Father prayer, parishioners normally stop holding hands. However, we continued. Moments later, I turned to greet a woman two rows behind us with a smile and sign of peace. Her face glowed with joy and peace as she gazed at my hand clasped in Carol's! The woman and I shared a nod. How comforting that she accepted us as a loving couple. No words were ever said, but every week we sat in front of her, knowing she was nearby. That was beauty.

We experienced a gradual sense of confidence in being accepted by our local church parishioners over 30 years. Every couple of years, parishioners had their pictures taken for a directory. Initially Carol and I posed stiffly, not touching, with one of us seated and the other standing. As parishioners got to know us, we relaxed, touching and smiling joyfully as a couple in pictures.

Getting to Know Brookings-Harbor

We loved gardening and trimming our yard, and exploring the area: ancient towering redwoods, uninhabited beaches, the Harbor hills, dirt backroads, the Mount Emily bomb site from WWII by the Japanese, the aromatic Myrtlewood and colorful azaleas in groves and parks.

We wandered by car and foot up the Chetco and Wishka Rivers, down the coast to Crescent City, up the coast to Gold Beach, admiring gorgeous sunsets, brown pelicans and gray whales.

We drove through old and new neighborhoods, waving and smiling, believing everyone was our neighbor. We visited the tiny library and contributed to the fund to build a new library down the street from the only fast food restaurant, Dairy Queen. As the population boomed to 20,000, more restaurants and grocery stores opened.

We lived in a small town of 4,000 people in Curry County, where the motto was "No hurry in Curry." As tourism picked up, some people compared us to Monterey, California.

We Build More Than a Deck

Carol arranged for the handyman carpenters she met through her work to build a large deck. We designed it by walking and placing rocks as markers, laying out rope for length and width, and Carol supervised its construction.

As we cruised the neighborhood, Carol noticed a "hot tub for sale" sign.

"Let's check it out." We pulled into the driveway on Wallam Lane, rang the doorbell and became instant friends with an elderly couple. At a steal of a price, we bought it, came home and phoned the "deck work crew'" to help us move it onto the deck.

What a scene! Two trucks, cars and a trailer showed up. Using boards as ramps, with pulley and latches to tie it down, they slowly maneuvered it safely onto the trailer. The guys loved the challenge. Carol used the hose to fill our Jacuzzi. How exciting! We pinched ourselves with another dream come true. We hugged each other and the guys.

Two days later, the water was warm and bubbly, and the test strips said the water pH level was healthy and clean. We sat on the edge, slid our legs over and sank in the maroon marbled tub with underwater blue lights. Our giggles, the bubbling jets, and the creek behind us all blended into one sound, *Ahhhhh!*

"I'll turn the jets on," said Carol, playing with each setting.

"Perfect, sweetie," I said. "I like that pulse setting."

The next night, we removed the hot tub brown vinyl cover, leaned it against the deck bench and cautiously slid into the tub again. This time in our birthday suits, naked and unafraid, after ensuring that our only neighbor, Joan, could not see us.

Then it rained, drenching us and raising the water level. The rain roused fresh smells from the surrounding bushes as I tilted back to catch raindrops on my tongue.

Carol laughed. "No more of that, the raindrops are hurting my tongue."

"I think we need umbrellas. I'll be right back." I retrieved a big umbrella from the house, plopping back into the hot water. Laughing, we squeezed together under the umbrella and enjoyed a 20-minute soak in luxury love.

The next time it rained we were prepared. While shopping, we had found two rainbow-covered umbrella rain hats with an adjustable band.

"Yes, our hot tub attire!" I announced. "It will go perfectly with our outfits."

All smiles, she said, "I can hardly wait!"

We proudly wore those hot tub hats, our heads stayed dry, and we laughed hysterically with each other for years.

Our Jobs

Carol's job at the South Coast Business employment office focused on training people for new jobs and working with business owners to train people in specific markets. She met many wonderful people and they loved her joy and kindness. They treated her with admiration and respect, enhancing an atmosphere for greater listening and problem solving. She built on people's talents and improved their lives, making our community stronger and happier. She loved what she was doing and shined brightly.

I commuted 25 minutes south to Crescent City and worked for Rural Human Services as a community health educator prevention specialist: teaching classes, running community-wide programs and facilitating support groups in Del Norte County. I enjoyed working with the public and side-by-side with the public health nurses in areas of tobacco use and smoking cessation, hepatitis, nutrition, wellbeing, and HIV/AIDS. My sister Terri coined the phrase "Sister Joanie of Harbor." That was a pretty high accolade, Sis. I just tried to be the very best I could be day in and day out.

Thank you for your love, Ter!

Carol and I left our work at work, to foster and celebrate us as a couple. Still, we only shared our truth with a trustworthy few. In the 1990s, gay prejudice was real; we knew young men who had been attacked and beaten on our local downtown sidewalk. Carol and I showed zero public affection in that climate.

At work, we were honest with select people as our partnership pertained to our employment benefits. Still, we had no legal protections as a couple in case of a medical emergency, since we were not married or in a Domestic Partnership at that time. That was a scary thought! Someone other than myself would be making decisions about my lover. That tore our hearts apart!

We were listed as each other's "emergency contact" and beneficiary, and we opened bank accounts as joint owners. We were best friends in the public's eyes and forever lovers in our home.

"Gay-dar"

Our "gay-dar" enabled us to "detect" other gay and lesbian couples and singles who became "family." We had frequent delicious potluck dinners of seafood, pork tenderloin, roast, sautéed veggies, scalloped potatoes and other delights at their homes and in ours. It was so relaxing and an honor to enjoy like-minded and lifestyle company where we could truly be ourselves, and stand or sit with an arm around each other or to hold hands. Good times!

We joined the Oregon State Extension group thanks to Ginger and Marilyn, a beautiful, fun-loving lesbian couple. What a fabulous group of women with brains, leadership, energy and fun. They hosted a yearly "Christmas Bazaar" for the community and it was the largest holiday arts and crafts venue we had ever seen. It raised money for youth scholarships.

Our membership was a mix of single, married, divorced, widowed, gay and straight. Carol and I fit in as a gay couple perfectly and those friendships are strong to this day, cemented with trust and love.

Oh golly, since we did not want cable TV for 20 years, we were addicted to playing card games and other games with friends from all walks of life. It was good fun with no "shop talk" allowed. Hours of laughter, munching on snacks and meals during game intermission were a bonus.

Our house was the common meeting location; thank goodness Carol had the foresight to have Scott build us a front door ramp so Catherine and others could come inside without struggling.

Carol and I enjoyed kicking back watching borrowed library movies and we purchased several DVDs that we never grew tired of seeing. Her favorites were James Bond movies and *Sister Act*, which came out in 1992, the same year we moved to Brookings.

Carol so related to the film that she constantly laughed, sighed, moaned and cried because watching Whoopi Goldberg's performance was like watching herself.

Oh, my God! That was Carol!! Completely! Think Whoopi, think Carol! I had more fun watching Carol than the movie!

I liked watching sports, action and true story movies. Popcorn with my sweetie in our own living room was delightful. I was the one who fell asleep and Carol remembered where to resume the movie. What a sweetie pie!

Where did 30 years go? Our day to day, week to week and year to year life together in Brookings-Harbor was a dream of all dreams. Our hearts grew fonder and eternity glistened with happy, joyful memories of each other and our dear friends. Our home was bright and cheery and was our happiest place on Earth.

Home sweet home. Our Home. Thank you, God, and thank you, friends!

The Purple Couch

Carol loved the beauty and comfort of leather chairs. She dreamed of a purple leather couch. It would be the perfect eye-catching artwork to sit in, cuddle in and nap in with my head on her lap.

She talked about eating popcorn while watching adventure movies. We loved the *Indiana Jones* series, *Romancing the Stone, Jumanji, The Fifth Element* and, of course, *Sister Act*. This couch would be vibrant in color, soft and cushy, with our butts and backs melting into a restful place.

It would be long-lasting and an investment. We had socked away money and had been to every furniture store in our vicinity, but the day came to search for this gem of a sofa.

We included the Medford and outer lying areas in our search, but always began by seeing friends first. When we ended up at Joseph Winans Furniture, hope was alive that Carol could find her heart's desire: a purple leather couch. We moseyed into the elite furniture store—big as a warehouse, decorated, themed and color-coordinated.

Carol saw it immediately.

"A purple leather couch!" she exclaimed. "Joanie, look. Here it is. This is it! Can you see this in our living room? The color is perfect. It is vibrant like my dream."

I was praying that it will be as comfortable as it is gorgeous. The leather was soft, as our hands slid across the arms and back of it.

"Oh, my golly. This is really nice, Carol!"

A blond young man with a deep, happy and tender voice said, "Hi. It looks like you've found what you came in for!"

"Yes, tell me about it."

"Of course. It's Italian leather, eggplant color, steel framed."

"It's gorgeous," I said. "How much does it cost? On sale? Will you deliver it to Brookings?"

"Let me talk to my manager."

I disliked this sales strategy. *He better not be pulling our leg.*

"What's your name?" I asked politely and happily.

"Dan, Daniel."

"Hi, Dan. We are Carol and Joanie. Happy to meet you and thank you for helping us."

"So glad to meet you both. You are most welcome. It's my pleasure to assist you today. Here are the details—"

All I heard was a Charlie Brown-type mumbling. Carol heard all perfect yes answers.

"Sold!" proclaimed Carol. That was the exact amount of money and the exact sofa that she intuitively knew she would find.

She's right on again!

"Will you take a check?"

"Yes, wonderful."

I was grateful that the transaction took less than 30 minutes.

Carol asked, "Dan, would you like to join us for dinner tonight?"

"Oh, sure, that would be great. Thank you."

Wow, Carol likes this young man. Her intuition must be up to something.

At dinner, we had so much fun! First snacking on the Mexican chips and salsa before Dan exuberantly exclaimed:

"Carol, Joanie, you were my first ever sale while working at a furniture store. Today was my first day on the job."

"Really? No way!"

"Yes, really, and my manager really wanted me to have you look at the neutral beige leather sofa. I told him, absolutely not. You were there for the purple couch! I stood up for you, Carol!"

"Oh my, thank you, Dan. I don't like boring brown furniture. I can't wait 'til it comes and you'll have to come see it in our home."

"OK, great!"

Have you ever had that occasion when you knew you were meant to be friends with someone? This was one of those times! "A God thing" was what Carol and I called them. The three of us ate and shared scrumptious fajitas, beans and lots of guacamole. Zillions of questions and answers ricocheted back and forth. It was like the Australian boomerang soaring in the wind and returning with soul connections.

"Oh, I was raised Catholic, an altar boy, and I'm gay, too."

What a phenomenal day: discovering Carol's favorite color, purple, in a dream leather couch, and a new friend, Dan. Carol and I have been blessed to have Dan as our friend. We have visited and stayed in his homes in Santa Cruz, California, and Sarasota, Florida ("Once the home of the Ringling Brothers Circus," he told us), and several homes in the Medford and Rogue Valley area.

He has stayed with us in our home in Brookings-Harbor

and we have shared hundreds of moments with his family and friends, as well as ours.

Dan to us, Daniel to others, is a positive, happy, helpful person who cared deeply for humanity. Today, he's a smart, successful businessman as CEO of bookstayhop.com. His contagious joyful personality cultivates all-inclusiveness as he is nonjudgmental and open to all.

My Favorite Day of the Year is EASTER!

Ahh, I loved the magical bright, pastel and neon coloring of Easter eggs—then hiding and finding them.

My mother's family, the Morans, had a family tradition of making chocolate coconut nests with red or yellow jellybeans nestled in the delicious candy.

Easter is total JOY—the celebration that death is conquered and life is everlasting. Jesus died and went to heaven and we can all do the same.

Yes, my absolute favorite day of the year.

Carol enjoyed it as well, looking dazzling in Easter outfits that included a yellow or lavender bonnet with colorful flowered dresses, blouses and sweaters.

Bouquets of Easter lily flowers, grown commercially in our neighboring fields, adorned the church altar. Fields would sometimes blossom with the traditional white trumpet star-shape flowers, whose fragrance knocked your socks off. The center pistil was the stigma and it was sticky to touch.

After Carol's allergic reaction that caused her throat to close, we sat in the back of the church during Easter season.

"Please keep the lily blossoms outside, Joanie," said Carol every springtime.

The few times we were gifted with them in a bouquet, they were removed before entering the house. "How beautiful and thoughtful, Joanie. You know what to do."

During our first Easter in Brookings in 1992, Carol said:

"Joanie, I would love to have a big Easter egg hunt in our yard. It would be so much fun! Who could we invite? The few people we know? What do you think, love?"

"It would be fun. Yes, spectacular!"

We loved the park-like setting of our yard: level, thick green grass, lined with four, prolific fruit-producing apple and four plum trees on the east side, a humongous ten feet high blue hydrangea, and wild white and pink blossomed fuchsias. A creek flowed most of the year with water from the hills behind us. Overgrown escallonia shrubs and 40- to 60-foot-tall alder trees shaded us and were fun to watch as they swayed in the ocean breezes.

Spring and yearlong rains gently watered our park and we could literally sit and watch the grass grow. And the birds, ohhh. Quail, starlings, juncos, doves, bluebirds and scrub jays, and hummingbirds were joined by the occasional Monarch butterflies passing through on their migration travels.

Carol had great vision, artistry and design, especially with our yard and interior. She was a decorator. I was the worker bee. Fine with me. We could now put nails in a wall without a landlord issue. Way cool!

She had connections with laborers and discounted prices on wood from the local mill, so we designed a deck and she arranged to have it built, outside the kitchen window, in sun and shade about 20 feet from the soothing sounds of the creek.

After spending entire weekends taking turns pushing the lawn mower over the two-foot-high grass, she said, "C'mon, Joanie, let's go up to Sears and see about a riding lawn mower."

"Super idea, Carol. But they cost so much money."

"Well, let's go see."

Let more fun begin: after making our first credit card purchase, we owned our first riding lawn mower with an extra wide cutting blade and an automatic shut-down once the driver's butt left the seat. I liked that safety feature. We knew that we would regularly use it to cut a day's work into one hour.

"Wowie! Thank you, Carol!"

"Joanie, we can pay this off just fine and it will give us quality time for other things."

"Great idea. Your intuition was once again spot-on. Thank you, love!"

CHAPTER 14

Our salesperson at Sears, Vicki C., was super energetic, fun, efficient and knowledgeable. She was tall, thin and tan with a big smile and a friendly spirit.

"So, where do you live?" she asked.

"On the non-ocean side of the Oceanview Drive in Harbor," I said, giving her our address.

"Oh, I know exactly where that is. You have a large yard and lawn with a creek, too. I'll have it delivered and have my staff give you a lesson or two also."

"Perfecto! Thanks so much, Vicki!"

My combo extrovert/introvert sweetie said, "Vicki, we're new to the area and would you like to come for an Easter barbecue, egg hunt and potluck. Are you interested? Do you know of some other people to invite also?"

Then I added, "Our friends from Washington, Brad and Ross, will be visiting us and it would be great to know a few more local people."

"That does sound like fun," Vicki said. "I'd like to come. You two are happy, nice people. I'll invite some others and get back to you."

"Oh, Vicki," I said, "ask everyone to bring a dozen hardboiled eggs for an old-fashioned egg hunt."

Carol exclaimed, "And ask everyone to wear an Easter bonnet."

"Really? This will be fun and awesome! Thanks for asking me."

Carol beamed and I said, "You bet. Our pleasure."

One week before the Easter festivities, Vicki came by the house. We had the riding mower and used it to mow the lawn. It was a piece of cake, yahoo!

"Nice yard, you two!"

"Thanks. That rider is fantastic! Done in a little more than an hour. And our 'park' smells of fresh-mowed grass. Love it."

Vicki said, "So, I've invited people and they've invited people, probably about 30. Is that OK?"

"Wow, fantastic! Potluck, right?'

"Yes, and eggs and bonnets."

"COOL, HOW FUN!" I said.

Ecstatic, Carol said, "Joanie, we need to get to the store and buy more meat."

"Vicki, we'll barbecue pork tenderloin and ribs if everyone else can bring something to share."

"Got it! See you next Sunday afternoon."

Brad and his longtime friend, Ross, trekked their way from Olympia to Brookings and arrived the Saturday before Easter. Brad was the first to use the guest room, laying diagonal because the bed was shorter than our tall green giant, sleeping in the "dead lady's bed" from Aberdeen. Ross conked out on the living room floor in Carol's warm sleeping bag that she had used in Alaska. It was a total delight to have them here. Especially Brad!

Brad saw our happiness, our dream-come-true of living together on the southern Oregon coast. Brad put to rest his concerns for us in our new community in his mind and heart for us, Joanie and Carol, his dear, dear friends. We all knew about the imminent death that he was facing due to immune complications from AIDS. We were all joyously living and laughing together. Oh, we laughed so hard that our eyes stung from the salty tears. It was our last time with him.

So much better to focus on life, not death.

The First Ever Gay Gathering in Brookings, Oregon!

Are you ready for this? Who was hosting this first ever gay gathering? Us! The two gay former nuns!

Easter Sunday arrived. Brad, Ross, Carol and I were busy cleaning outdoor plastic and metal chairs, getting the long metal folding tables from the shed and setting up plastic utensils and colorful tulip-patterned napkins. The meats were seasoned and marinated, ready to throw on the grill.

Oh my gosh, we had about 50 people! I thought 30 would be amazing, but this was incredible.

All were gays and lesbians, except for Leonard, a gay ally, who lived next door to Tony and John.

God works in the most mysterious ways. The Holy Spirit has no limits.

CHAPTER 14

It's absolutely mind blowing.

Who could have imagined this when I said yes to joining the convent?

Who could have imagined this when Carol professed her vows?

It was the most spectacular day with a gay pride parade, too!

Guys and gals, dressed in colors of the rainbow, bright and cheery, bonnets that would look great on the San Francisco Beach Blanket Babylon stage and arms full of eggs to hide were welcomed into our yard, home and hearts.

Ross recorded the day on a camcorder: no permissions required, no fears, no bad words, nothing inappropriate, positive happy attitudes from everyone. I still have the original VHS copy on the bottom shelf of the cabinet directly behind me as I write.

Every person strutted across the emerald green, manicured lawn, proudly wearing their homemade flowered, quilted, hilarious bonnets and smiles as large as the Amazon and Nile Rivers combined.

Brad, Ross and a team of five hid dozens of hardboiled eggs while new friendships formed and new "family" ate and talked. Carol's famous question "How did you meet?" was the *Jeopardy* answer of the day.

Carol and I had decorated with spray paint—magenta, pink, yellow and neon purple—onto buckets, bags, and containers for the egg hunt. They looked darling.

It was hilarious watching grownups, with bonnets bouncing, sprint for hardboiled and plastic eggs. There were even a few tackles on the 50 yard line to get to that special plastic egg!

Carol had stashed prizes inside the plastic eggs: seashells, shiny quarters and her hand-written Chinese fortune cookie-style sayings with "I love you" and "Jesus has risen" and "You are a joy."

We shared a real communion of delicious homemade casseroles, salads, veggies, breads, chips and dips, water, soda and beer. Then we had a bonnet parade.

We were stuffed from eating and our stomachs hurt from laughing. More laughter, more love. Male couples felt free to hold hands and dance together on the deck; lesbians stood with arms engulfing their significant other and lip-kissed freely and tenderly. Together we were affectionate and intimate. At the end of the party, everyone kissed everyone goodbye. "See you later!"

Our Cup Runneth Over

This began a shared loyalty as a "family" showing generosity, respect and kindness to each other. Everybody jumped in to serve each other and to clean up. We were no longer the hosts, we were part of one big family.

Yes, Carol and I did all of the above.

Is this what heaven will be like? Or is heaven on earth?

During the BBQ, silent with arms around each other, we watched the powerful camaraderie. Faces glowed with joy; no one was alone. It warmed our hearts to see singles and widows making lifetime friends and connections, and people shedding tears and feeling supported.

Amazed and grateful, Carol and I shared hugs with everyone.

Then Vicki took the pretend microphone and said, "The prize for best dressed goes to 'The Easter Bunny'!"

The person in the Easter Bunny costume had his/her face covered, and Carol guessed their identity.

"Congratulations, Jeannette!"

The crowd went wild! More laughter emphasized all of us becoming friends for life! After the party, we patronized each other's businesses and recognized each other in town. And our celebration sparked monthly Friday evening gatherings for gays and lesbians at different homes.

Our bond endured through divorces, cancers, heartache, job transfers and deaths. Someday we will all meet again.

Never had Carol and I imagined that we could bring about such a change in our community. How fun!

Brad, your bright tablecloths and the Toucan bird artwork in the kitchen make me smile. Thank you for being a dear friend. May heaven be your happy place.

Isn't that what life's all about?

IT WAS THE BEST EASTER EVER!

CHAPTER 14

Ordinary Days

"Good morning, sweetie, Carol!"

"Joanie, good morning, love!"

Together we said, "Good morning, Jesus!"

"It's a brand-new day!" I announced.

"Never been lived before," proclaimed Carol.

For more than 40 years, Carol and I routinely blessed our day forward. Waking up together in bed, we shared tender lip kisses, soft petting strokes on each other's head, shoulders, arms or hands.

We loved our morning rhythm, waking refreshed and ready to take on the world. Carol's favorite, ancient, Mickey Mouse nightshirt was thinner than a piece of paper until it finally disintegrated in the washing machine. My favorite yellow flowered nightgown was thinning in its own old age.

Ordinary days were actually extraordinary. Being together was the love and joy of each new day.

I don't ever remember either of us waking up "on the wrong side of the bed," so to speak. Her smile was attached to her face all night long and each morning when looking out the big bedroom window as the sun came up, rising over the Harbor hills. This was true for her every day wherever she was in the world.

During our working years, rise and shine was 5:30 a.m.

In the kitchen, our *Living with Christ* book on the round table was covered with a bright pineapple fabric cloth. She read the day's scriptures and prayed. Often we read it together aloud. Other times, I'd read it first quietly while Carol performed daily skin care on her soft Egyptian face: toner, hydration and sun protection.

Prayer set the day on the right course for us. It was not just a habit or routine carried over from our morning prayers as sisters in the convent, it was us being with our best friend Jesus.

On special feast days, such as for Joan of Arc on May 30th, we had a special communion service with hosts, that we shared. Jesus filled us from the tips of our toes to the hairs on our heads as He took care of us, day in and day out.

I drove back and forth each day for work between Brookings-Harbor and Crescent City, a 25-minute drive south on Highway 101. I traveled across state lines every day, watching cautiously for broken fences, a sign of roaming Roosevelt elk.

I put in the "Alive in Christ" tape in my car stereo. Yep, in the 1990s and 2000s, my car had an old-fashioned tape player and CD combo. I also enjoyed the St. Louis Jesuits and the Damiens to pray and sing along with on my way to work and on trips, an extension of our morning glory prayers.

Carol worked in Brookings, and had a less than a 10-minute commute north over the Chetco River bridge. The view upriver to the east was packed with luscious green hills and forests of Douglas Fir trees. The view west was the river emptying into the Pacific Ocean: waters, trees and sky.

We were thankful for being employed and living together. That didn't mean everything was peachy, ultra-simplistic, and happy, happy, happy. No, there was suffering and we had our hurts, but it never dimmed our joy. Life was good!

One Bad Day

As I arrived at work one ordinary day, I walked into the back entrance of the girls' locker room at the high school where I taught PE and Health classes. High on the locker room walls were spray-painted large black letters, not just once but many times: "Lindenmeyer is f____ gay."

I was terribly shocked! I was stunned! Never before had I been so hurt at school. I immediately kept the locker room doors locked tight; I didn't want the students to see this. I didn't want to be outed, yet it seemed like I was, and I did not want their safe, private haven to be lost.

I could not let the girls lose their trust in me, as my sexual orientation had nothing to do with them, and my role as a teacher was sacred and trustworthy.

I phoned the front office, talking quickly with a wavering voice to the Athletic Director. He came to see for himself, walkie talkie in hand. He was in disbelief as well. I phoned my male Physical Education colleagues, who were in the boys' locker room next door. They listened to my upset heart and crackling voice and they felt so badly for me.

Within minutes, my colleagues who were my friends came in the back door of the girls' locker room and gave me big hugs. That was consoling, yet I teared up. *How did anyone get in and paint derogatory, ugly homophobic and demoralizing words about me on the wall?*

Photographs of the hate words, the violence, were gathered by the administration. The maintenance staff was immediately radioed and arrived—two compassionate and hard-working men carrying a can of paint. They covered it, hid it and made it go away. I was grateful for their timing, efficiency and sympathetic words.

They say, "Sticks and stones will break my bones, but words will never hurt me." So not true! I didn't cry, but I was so angry and hurt. *Who did this? Why?* Words can make or break someone.

Remind me, Jesus, to be careful in my words and actions.

Joanie, you need to be bigger than this!

With all this hurt inside me, and to combat this evil act, I dished out extra kindness and love to my fellow colleagues and students. All day, I demonstrated and taught with passion, character and resilience. I upped my game by being attentive and overzealous with my positive attitude. I turned the day into a fabulous one, not telling anyone about the incident, but instead spreading joy. I thanked my classes for their uniqueness and praised them for attending class and participating.

When I got home from work, I sobbed like a baby in Carol's arms. I told Carol the whole story, including my anger and sorrow for the person(s) who did this, the comfort from my friends, my thoughts, my gusto to continue my day and eagerness to get home so fast to be with her. Whew!

I was so glad it happened to me, not her.

She, he, or they must be really suffering to express this slander so vividly and powerfully. One bad apple out of thousands. In my heart, I forgive him, her or they. I can and did solve this with kindness! All are welcome!

Although not as personal, this hateful incident roused memories of tomatoes hitting me during my HIV/AIDS presentation for parents of high school aged students 10 years prior.

Hate happens when you least expect it. We need to always respond to hate with love. That is Jesus' way.

Fast forward to 2018 when I retired from teaching public school after giving my heart and soul to it every day for so many years. A full-page tribute was written about me and put in the yearbook, and a black-framed certificate was presented to me by my wonderful talented staff friends under the leadership of the principal, vice principal and athletic director. It hangs in my home office beside a portrait of Carol and me. It reads:

"This Certificate of Excellence is awarded to Joanie Lindenmeyer. Her dedication to the students and staff of Del Norte High School for 25 years, making these halls brighter, happier and healthier."

The standing ovation by the thousand-student body, in a surprise assembly, brought me to happy tears. They cheered louder the more my eyes streamed raindrops as I removed my glasses to wipe them away. One thousand great apples far outlive the one bad apple.

Ordinary days for Carol and me were really EXTRAORINARY!

Because it was always Jesus, Carol and Joanie at the center of it.

Jesus hold you.
God bless you.

CHAPTER 15
Health, Healing and Miracles

When we least expected it, scary challenges bombed our life. It was time to pray extra and hope for miracles upon miracles.

Carol was having problems with vaginal bleeding that started in August of 2012. I shared this in October with a friend and colleague, Irene, a nurse at DNHS where I taught.

She said, "Make an appointment with my husband." He was an OB/GYN in Crescent City, California. "Call today, Joanie."

"OK. Thanks so much."

I shared with Carol what Irene recommended, but she was waiting to have medical coverage on my policy and very reluctant to visit a doctor. In September of that year, my principal had advised me that Carol could be added to my medical insurance as a legal Domestic Partner. That was great news! Until then, Carol and I had had many conversations about getting married, but that was not yet a viable legal or sacramental Catholic Church option.

"I love you with all my heart, Joanie. You are my 'one and only' now and forever."

"Yippee! Me, too, sweetie. I love you so much!"

Now things were a little more crucial! Financially and medically. She needed to see a doctor. With our positive attitudes, we were just taking it in stride, one thing at a time. Down deep, we were both praying our hearts out and relying on faith bigger than our humanity.

"Carol, you know that I love you from the deepest part of my being. I think we need to go to Gold Beach to get our Domestic Partnership so you can be included on my medical insurance."

"Yes. we need to do that. I want to do this for us, not just insurance."

"Yeah, it's a win-win and the timing is impeccable, don't you think?"

Yep, it is.

We called our local county marriage office, and the staff person was gracious and nonjudgmental.

What a day, September 26th, 2012.

Carol dressed in her multi-colored, bright dress.

Our paperwork, with our names typed bold and proud on the counter, were like a golden tablet. That single page held a gazillion feelings and moments as large as all the sand from the world's ocean beaches.

It was where we signed our life commitment to each other in front of angels, our deceased loved ones, and our living and breathing friends and family whom we always carried in our heart. And the county court system staff.

This was a time and place that needed to happen for us and for future generations of lovers.

We had enormous smiles with Joanie's tears and Carol's giggles. We hugged and gave each other a quick lip kiss. We still felt awkward kissing in public.

"Congratulations!" and "Happy Life!" the staff said with perky, jubilant and sincere voices.

I imagined Neil Armstrong taking the first step on to the Moon in 1969. His moonwalk lasted a few hours. We believed "our moon walk" led into eternity. In fact, we needed to walk across Highway 101 to a notary to make it official.

Yes, we were now, by law, officially a couple. Yeah to the USA and Oregon!

"What a feeling! Let's dance, let's sing, let's go out to eat at the Port Hole Cafe, let's kiss, and let's watch all the sunrises and sunsets together forever."

Our good friend Maggie said, "Love is a gift and a journey of two hearts becoming one."

We were ever so grateful for the medical insurance coverage. High fives, big compliments and thanks to California lawmakers, the Del Norte School District and employees in the District office and my principal for encouraging and supporting us without discrimination.

Moving on to April of 2013, we finally went to the OB/GYN appointment. Carol held my hand during the Pap smear exam in the typical sterile, cold, peroxide-smelling exam room. Dr. John, after one try with his speculum, said, "Let's schedule a DNC [dilation and curettage]."

At last, six weeks later, that day came, and Carol and I went into the hospital—her first time since she was born. We were apprehensive, not nervous.

Dr. John visited me in the waiting room after the procedure and said, "Joanie, I couldn't continue the entire procedure. Let's have the two of you meet again when I get the results."

"OK, Dr. John. Thank you."

His eyes told me something was up; I felt nervous.

Carol had a feeling, too, that something was up.

We needed to wait for the results. The unknowns were harder than the knowns.

Carol said, "Let's just wait and see. All will be OK."

"If you say so, sweetie."

Carol and I had been together more then 20 years; believing in her intuition was imperative. And we believed this was for a greater purpose.

A few days later, Carol received the office call from Dr. John: "Carol, bring someone with you. Bring Joanie. Let's meet and go over your results."

At the meeting, Dr. John looked Carol in the eye and said, "Carol, you have stage three endometrial cancer."

My eyes welled up, but I forced the tears to stay behind the floodgates.

Calm and cool, she didn't look surprised. She asked, "Where would you send your wife to have the next thing done?"

Great question!!! I'm impressed with my sweetie.

Dr. John said, "Eugene, Oregon. Dr. Deborah Davis is the absolute best surgeon for you. She's the one I would want for my wife."

"Fine," said Carol, "Let's do that."

"Give me some time, probably a week, and I'll be in touch."

After the appointment, Carol said she knew it wasn't going to be good. While driving home, we held hands for 20 minutes and she said, "I don't want to tell anyone just yet. Let's wait until we see Dr. Davis."

"Whatever you want, sweetie, I support you."

"Joanie, it's perfect timing that I'm on your insurance."

"Yes, it is."

Yes, it's God.

Two days later, Carol got the call that we needed to be in Eugene tomorrow for an appointment with Dr. Davis and probably surgery the following morning. They said plan to stay a few days.

Carol called me right away at the high school, where it was finals week. Within minutes, Ruth Clay, the office executive assistant, secured a substitute teacher. Thank you, Ruth. I talked with Marc, my *numero uno* colleague. We always had each other's backs and did a lot of team teaching. Marc and his wife, Megan, were phenomenal teachers and dear friends.

"Joanie, go and I'll get your grades recorded," Marc said.

I was so relieved that my grades were up to date and knew Marc would get it done.

I'm so blessed. Thank you God! Did I tell you the timing was all God's time?

It was summer break–no job for two months. What a relief and what a gift. Friends went above and beyond to help. Dear friends were precious. I came home, packed and off we went, driving four hours north to a hotel in Reedsport.

It was happening at lightning speed and caught us off guard, but all was OK. Amazingly, Carol was at peace.

Trust in the Lord with all your heart. We are in this together.

CHAPTER 15

The next morning, we drove to Eugene. Waiting our turn in the doctor's office, nervous and tired of waiting, seemed like hours.

Dr. Davis thanked us for our patience and apologized for her lateness. She was kind, caring and said she had personally spoken to Dr. John, who told her about our background as former nuns and our current careers.

She put a camera inside Carol to see what was there. On the monitor screen above us, we saw the totality of cancer everywhere. Carol gripped me with "the pancake hold:" my hand was numb from being flattened like a pancake by being squeezed so tightly.

Carol said, "Joanie, move. I can't see the screen."

"Oh sorry, sweetie . . . "

"OH, that much cancer," Carol said. "It's all full."

Dr. Deb talked about tomorrow's procedure—a lengthy surgery to remove all the cancer, with a possible need for radiation and chemotherapy.

We stared long into each other's eyes. Tears welled up in mine.

Carol said, "God will take care of this! And us, Joanie!"

I nodded and hoped with all my might that she was right. With a direct line to Jesus, Carol was so strong in her faith, her intuition and oneness with the Lord 24/7. She lived and breathed right alongside Jesus, with an aura about her that no harm would ever happen. Carol trusted her Guardian Angel and spoke of her angel often.

I was emotional, but deep down felt we and she would be OK.

Adventures come in many styles. This was our biggest of all. Life threatening.

I asked for housing and the staff bent over backwards to get us a room in a Ronald McDonald-type house near the hospital.

Carol and I had a rough night. With her pre-surgery medicine, she visited the toilet every hour.

Caring, beautiful Megan, Marc's wife, called my cell to say they were praying. I was shocked but ever so grateful. How sweet of Megan! Phone calls made a huge difference when times were tough. *Thank you, Megan and Marc.*

Carol and I were ready for this day.

While I was in the waiting room in deep prayer, I looked up and was surprised to see our friend Greg, on his way home from Portland to Chico, as he entered carrying his motorcycle helmet. Ahh, so wonderful and relieved to have a friend sit with me. *Oh golly, I am still humbled by his gesture. Sharing is caring! Caring is sharing! Thank you, Greg.*

During more than five hours of surgery, I felt sick and exhausted. Now alone, tears flowed.

It's me and you, babe. Oh, God.

So I went to the cafeteria and back and forth between the chapel and the waiting room, where finally the board light flashed my number to meet the doctor in the post-surgery conference room. There I stood, hearing a skip of feet, not a walk, in the hallway. I poked my head out. Dr. Deb smiled with joy and asked:

"Where did it all go, Joanie?"

"What?"

"When I got in there," she said, "only about 25% was there. That's all the cancer: 25% cancer. Where did it go? We saw on the camera late yesterday afternoon: 100% cancer. Where did it go? I got it all, but to make sure, she'll need to have radiation treatments to make sure none of it went deeper. But where did it go?"

"Dr. Deb, you know where!" I exclaimed. "Carol has that connection to God. God took care of it! It was a miracle, Dr. Deb!" We hugged for a long time.

God took care of it!!! Carol's angels took care of it.

Dr. Deb beamed. "That Carol is real SPECIAL. I've never met anyone like her and the two of you. She is so strong. We'll have Carol do some radiation, but not chemo, to make sure the cancer didn't go deep."

I was sobbing but SO happy.

She said, "You'll see her soon. They will let you know. Just stay in the waiting room."

I cried, released, cried and thanked God.

A Miracle Was Given to Us!!

As I write this, I'm sobbing remembering the magnitude of that moment. Unbelievable . . . that's divinity.

CHAPTER 15

Dr. Deb introduced us to another doctor who would be Carol's hospital physician while she traveled to be a conference speaker. Also, Dr. Davis had arranged for Carol to start six weeks of radiation in Eugene, a five-hour drive each way from our home. We were trusting in the medical opinions and our attitude was we would figure this out—driving back and forth despite the expenses of gas and hotels.

Are you ready for another miracle?

Carol was recuperating, healing in her private room at the wonderful Sacred Heart Hospital, with one small, big problem: she was constipated and extremely uncomfortable, due to pain medications.

The nurses instructed me to walk to the farmer's market to buy fresh apricots and figs.

"Joanie," Carol said, "go now, please go get me some fresh fruit."

So I swung on my backpack and hauled buns to the market. At one stall, I recognized "Elkton" on its banner; that's a remote town of about 100 people south of Eugene. Carol and I traveled through Elkton going from the coast to Interstate 5 on Highway 38 following the Umpqua River.

"Great looking fruit," I told the high energy, talkative seller. "My friend, Carol, and I have dear friends who live in Elkton. Are you from there?"

"Oh, yes," she said. "Who are your friends?"

"Steve and Roz."

"Oh, they are my best friends."

"Really?"

"Really."

"I'm Joanie from Carol and Joanie."

"Oh, they've mentioned you . . . Brookings, right? Former nuns, right?"

"Right."

"Where's Carol?"

"She is in Sacred Heart Hospital. She just had cancer surgery and I'm on a mission to bring back fresh fruit to help her out."

"Oh golly, do Steve and Roz know this?"

"No, it has all happened really fast."

"Let me call them and tell them."

"OK, great."

Miracle again, what are the odds?

"Thanks for the apricots, figs and peaches. I may be back." I also picked up something for the nurses; Carol taught me to buy little thoughtful gifts for people.

I will carry on this tradition, sweetie!

I returned to Carol's room in the hospital and started to tell the fruit friend story to Carol and guess who walked in? Yep, Steve and Roz with a bouquet of flowers for Carol! OMG. A miracle of love!!

I was all smiles, hugs and, again, we were filled with love.

Carol was astonished.

Conversation began, rainbow colors glowing brightly, and Steve and Roz offered us their home's entire downstairs in Eugene so Carol could have her radiation treatments three times a week.

Alleluia. Another miracle!! THANK YOU GOD!

They treated us like royalty! We had our own bedroom with plush linens, a private bathroom and access to the living room, kitchen and yard—a short drive to Carol's appointments. They spoiled us with delicious, healthy veggies, salads, steak, pork, lean meats and fish, all made by Roz's home cooking and BBQ dinners.

We shared food for healing and for life, like our daily holy communion in their gorgeous, manicured backyard with decks, trees, green grass, flowers and outdoor furniture that we sank into together or separately, comforting us like a cloud on a hot day. Oh, Roz got up early and baked homemade muffins or scones and served us fresh fruit, yogurt and free-range brown chicken eggs for breakfast.

One evening, they took me to a baseball game. Steve gave me an old Padres baseball cap that I still wear with pride and love.

During week six, as Carol felt better, Steve took Carol and me on an outing of golf: sunny, blue skies, birds chirping, pine trees standing elegantly tall lining the fairway. The fragrances of trees and flowers and, of course, the fresh-mown lawn were lovely. Oh, the three of us, kidding, laughing and loving life so much.

Carol was the copilot and even drove the golf cart as Steve and I chased a little white ball around the Willamette River Valley Course. I asked Carol to putt for me. She loved it. But I loved it even more. She was ALIVE. My tears and fears had come and gone.

How many times can I praise Jesus, you ask? FOREVER!

Steve and Roz insisted they pay for everything! EVERYTHING. For the whole six weeks. Gracious, so gracious. Thank you, Steve and Roz.

For the times, Lord, when I worry about finances, or health or acceptance, I know deeply that you always take care of me and Carol.

Carol was totally cured of her cancer. Miracles just kept on coming.

Yea, God!

Jesus hold you.
God bless you.

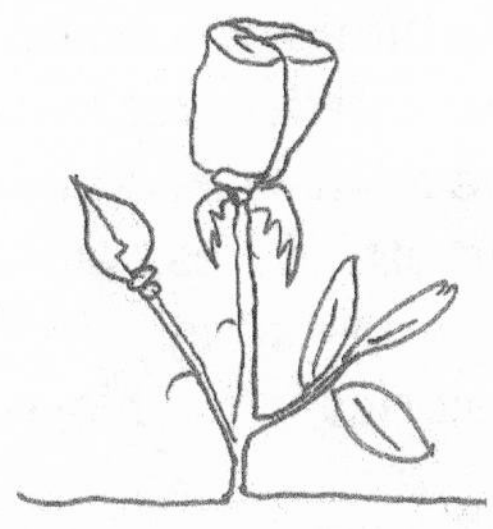

CHAPTER 16
Death Comes Calling

After Carol's dad died suddenly in his sleep from a massive heart attack, she moved into her parents' home in Paradise, California, to help with funeral and death details pertaining to the estate and to support her grief-stricken mom.

Ten months later, Carol's mom, Elsie, was standing in the kitchen holding onto the stainless-steel sink looking out the window towards the Paradise pine trees with squirrels shuffling about, when she suffered a brain aneurysm.

Carol's sister Elaine found her standing there and within seconds Mom was on the yellow patterned linoleum floor. The ambulance took her to the hospital. She fought for her life as Carol and her niece Carrie saw a shooting star outside their car window.

"Is that Grandma?" they asked, racing home with nephew William asleep in the back seat.

Situations like this shake your body with the worst emotions like an endless seizure. While gathered with her sisters, Elaine and Sara, Carol gave the final approval to take their mother off life support. This lovable mom and gracious grandmother died 10 months after her husband.

I was driving the seven-hour trip back and forth from Oregon to Paradise on weekends as often as possible to help and pour

TLC onto Carol and the family. Carol and I relished the reality of being able to gaze at each other, sleep side by side, and massage each other's skin as we fell asleep, cuddling under the sheets.

"Joanie, you're a breath of fresh air with your positivity and fun approach to work and eating," the family said. I ate like a hog, burned off the calories, and enjoyed the Tierheimer cooking. It was a win-win!

Loved Ones' Medical Emergencies

While Carol was grieving the loss of her parents, her sister Elaine, a single mother, was diagnosed with life-threatening cancer. She needed immediate surgery at the University of California Davis Hospital and would need months of radiation treatments. Another emotional blow to Carol and to the family, me included.

How do we help her and her elementary school age children? We were all in this together.

"I'll take care of everything, Elaine!" Carol confidently told Elaine on the phone. "Don't worry about anything! Joanie and I will figure things out."

Carol moved back to Paradise and became their Rock of Gibraltar. She brought hope and peace on a daily basis, being superwoman. I supported her and loved her more. Carol had always been that strong woman of her word, conviction, resilience and empowerment. I witnessed Carol's lionesque strength in mortuary settings, oncologist doctors' offices, hospital rooms and the family home, cuddling those precious kids. I heard her roars of pain and joy. We celebrated life after death, grateful for the many kind people who journeyed with us.

Hope is eternal.

Next, my family needed attention. I found tenderness and joy instead of fear, when my dad was diagnosed with cancer and my mom was diagnosed with COPD and emphysema. She died in a nursing home. I could just picture Mom's rosary under her pillow, the rosary that she had held softly in her hand countless nights, praying for her children and grandchildren.

CHAPTER 16

Being Apart

It was challenging and frustrating when we had to live apart for days, weeks and even months, but it was "our" choice to care for family and friends.

We phoned each other daily for quick updates. How delightful to hear Carol's voice! She could read my mind by the tone of my voice and it was so endearing when our hearts connected. So powerful! Zillions of times we left landline or cellphone voicemail messages, just calling to say, "I love you."

We mailed heart-decorated cards to each other. One romantic greeting card, currently in the bottom drawer of my nightstand, has cats surrounded by red and white flying hearts. Starting in 1983, we circulated this card back and forth to each other. A new date and sentimental message were added to the inside pages during an era when it was challenging to find a "woman to woman" greeting card.

We missed each other like crazy. We encouraged, cried, gave advice and supported each other: "Do what you think is best! God's got you, us!" We found joy in unexpected places and situations, and hope in the dreariest circumstances.

God bless you.
Jesus hold you.

CHAPTER 17
My Beloved Suffers a Brain Bleed

March 17, 2014 was an ordinary day that turned into a nightmare of all nightmares.

As I recall and write this, please honor me with your compassion and love. I'm flooded with tears, overwhelmed by the mental and emotional agony all over again. It was scary, heart-wrenching and I'm so glad that I had a faith to cling to. Parts of me don't want to recall this day, but I need to and you might gain wisdom from it as well.

At 7:30 pm on St. Patrick's Day, Carol and I had finished our delicious corned beef and cabbage dinner, and the house smelled great. While we relaxed in the living room with the TV on, Carol strolled into the kitchen. I heard the refrigerator door open, then it got really quiet. Then I heard the refrigerator door close.

Within seconds, she called out in a panic, "Joanie, come help me!"

I rushed to find Carol holding onto the long black refrigerator door handle for dear life.

"What's the matter?" I asked.

"I don't know." She looked weaker by the second.

"Here, sit on this chair," I said, pulling over a nearby chair. But she was wobbly and unable to move her legs, so I guided her to sit. Then I supported her while leaning for the landline phone.

"Joanie, I can't sit here. What's happening?"

I called 911 and pulled the other chair beside her. I sat on it to prop her up with my body. She leaned into me and I said, "Carol, we need to get you to the hospital. Trust me, we can do this."

"911, what is your emergency?"

"I think Carol has had a stroke." The clock said 7:35 p.m. "Get here fast!"

I turned to Carol and said, "Carol, smile for me, please. What's today? Lift up your arm sweetie."

Fear gripped our faces. Carol's cheek and lip started to droop.

I picked up my cell phone. "Aggie, it's Joanie, can you come over right now? I need you. Carol needs help."

"On my way."

Thank God for great neighbors and friends just a phone call and steps away.

When she arrived, I said, "Aggie, I'm going to move, and then you sit in this chair that I'm in. Just keep her propped up. OK?"

Aggie did, saying, "Hi, Carol. How are you doing?"

"OK," Carol said.

Then I added, "Thanks, Aggie, for coming over."

I ran to open the front screen door, turned the porch light on for the ambulance and returned to Carol and Aggie. My heart was racing as I watched the redwood clock on the wall. Scared, I remained calm and smart. I was calming myself with self-talk to keep them calm, too. My coaching-teaching-emergency part of me was strong and commanding.

Together, Carol and Aggie were leaning into each other, shoulder to shoulder. I stood in front of Carol with my strong legs leaning into hers to keep her from sliding to the linoleum floor. I was thinking about my recent high school health first aid lessons by Chuck from the American Red Cross. So fresh in my mind were the necessary care steps and how crucial the time would be in getting her treated to reverse the stroke.

"You're doing great, Carol. I'm so proud of you. Aggie and I have you. The paramedics are on their way."

CHAPTER 17

The ambulance sirens blared through the neighborhood and truck wheels crunched on our gravel driveway. It was 7:55. Our volunteer fire captain came in first.

"Hi, ladies. I'm John. We're going to help you out."

"Thanks for getting here so quickly, John. Look on the refrigerator."

John found a plastic bag with Carol's documents, including our domestic partnership copy and her medicine list.

"Please grab that for the paramedics," I said.

In walked the two paramedics with their big black box of medical supplies. One said:

"Hi, Carol."

"Hi," she answered.

"What happened?"

"I don't know," she said. "I got stuck at the door."

"OK. We can help you."

"Good."

"I'm going to check your heart and your eyes and your body. Are you in any pain?"

"No."

Aggie said, "Joanie, I can't sit here anymore; she's pushing me over."

Captain John slightly pushed Carol and took Aggie's place.

The paramedics brought in a long white gurney with black straps. It took John, me and the two paramedics to get Carol to sit, then lay on the gurney, and get strapped in. Carol's eyes were scared. I flashed my big smile, and kissed her lips. My heart was pounding; I refused to let my emotions go crazy.

"Carol, I'll follow the ambulance," I said. "We're going to Sutter Coast Hospital in Crescent City. Thanks, guys. See you down there. Thank you, John, for getting here so quickly."

Aggie said, "Joanie, I want to go with you. Let me go get my purse."

My mind and heart exploded.

Oh GOD, this is a biggie, just hold us, be with us.

Tears streamed down my face while I gathered my cell phone and charger, and my leather fanny pack. I used the restroom and pulled my hooded red sweatshirt over my head.

"I'm ready, Joanie," Aggie said.

"Coming, Ag. Thank you again. This may be a long night. Are you sure you want to come?"

"Yes, I'm coming. Carol needs both of us."

Aggie was a widow and had been our neighbor for about 12 years. She was faith-filled and prayed to Jesus wherever she went, including the casino. Many times we've shared meals, cups of sugar and game days, laughing and playing Mexican Train and Uno. She was family!

The 30-minute drive to the hospital seemed like slow motion.

I'm scared. Will she die tonight? I can't even think about living without her.

"I'm just going to go my regular 58 miles per hour," I told Aggie, driving south on Highway 101 on this rainy, dark night.

Under my breath, I asked Carol's guardian angel to give her peace and hope. *Life has changed; hope has not ended.*

"Jesus, Jesus, Jesus," Aggie prayed aloud with fear and faith sitting in the SUV.

At the hospital, the receptionist wouldn't let me into the ER.

"You don't understand!" I said. "When can I see her? I want to be with her!" I was harsh. My patience cap was not on my head. The triage nurse came out and pulled me into her cubicle.

"When did Carol have this happen?"

"7:35 tonight."

"OK. We're sending her for a brain scan, MRI."

I looked out her cubicle and saw the hospital staff wheeling Carol through the ER.

"Carol, I'm right here. See you in a little bit." I saw a very small smile on her face. And I said, "Thank you God for that small smile . . . I'll take it."

"Please wait in the lobby," the nurse said. "I'll call you when they finish."

Twenty minutes seemed like 20 years. But I was hopeful, thanks to the kind nurses and efficient, smart staff.

Let them do their job. Be kind and thankful! Yes, I can.

Having Aggie there was wonderful and comforting. So many things were going through my mind and heart. I picked up a box of Kleenex and the monsoon rains began. Just for a minute, but it was a huge emotional release. I needed to say, "I love you Carol," more often.

Not that we hadn't told each other every day, but now it was even more vivid and the only important words to say.

I was called back to her emergency room bay, where Carol was laying stiff as a board. The doctor was a visiting heart and stroke specialist from Oakland, California. She was sharp, demanding and gentle with us.

Praise Jesus, a specialist is here.

"She's had and still has a severe brain bleed," the doctor said. "We've started her on medication to stop the bleeding in her brain. We need to keep her absolutely still! We cannot move her for fear of the brain blood damaging more of the brain. We have her on an IV and will ready her for transport. I have an urgent request to fly her to Medford, Oregon, hopefully soon. You did a good job getting her in here so fast. What's your relationship?"

"Carol is my other half. We've been together over 30 years. Legally we are domestic partners."

"Great. Sit here with her. Don't let her move."

"Can Aggie, our dear friend, sit here also?"

"Yes." The nurse got another hard plastic chair.

After 30 minutes, no word yet on transportation. The area only had two life flight airplanes and both were airborne. We waited. Together. Quiet and still.

The weather wasn't cooperating, either. Minutes became hours. Oh, God. *Oh, guardian angels.*

Carol was calm, no pain, just lying there. The nurse team checked her IVs and were constantly attentive, which was very reassuring.

I was not supposed to touch her because they didn't want her to move a muscle. That in itself was so hard. I wanted to touch Carol but I did what they said, to keep her alive. Aggie and I took turns leaving Carol, going for short walks, and sending text messages and calls to family and friends asking for prayers and keeping them in the loop.

I brushed her arm accidentally, feeling her warmth. She grabbed my baby finger with her baby finger; she squeezed it tight!

Oh yes, we are connected more than ET and Elliot.

She held my baby finger tighter every now and then. It was like holding a delicate feather or a butterfly wing. I cherished the moments, hoping that they would forever be in my memory. I controlled myself to not cry, keeping it all stuffed inside, to not rattle or move or breathe heavily and upset Carol. I was pretending I was her, still and tranquil, sitting in a hard cold plastic chair.

Her body was warm; her gorgeous green eyes looked tired and exhausted.

"Lover dover, why don't you close your eyes, and just say some prayers in your heart," I said. She glanced at my eyes, then closed hers.

"Nurse, can you turn off this really bright light so she can rest?"

"Yes, for now, but once we get the OK to transport, it will go back on."

"Yes, I understand. Thank you."

At 4 a.m., great news came: a plane was flying from Bend to Crescent City to fly Carol to Medford. She was on her second dose of medication to stop the bleeding in her brain. The flight would get her to a better-equipped, stroke-focused hospital, Asante.

YES!! C'mon pilots!

Carol had a beaming weird smile with this news and tried to wink at me.

"Are you thinking of Elaine?" I asked.

Her eyes told me yes. That thrilled me to the bone that her brain was still engaged.

"No laughing aloud," I said, "but we will laugh about this later. You are doing awesome, love. You got this. Jesus has you."

A few years prior, when Carol's sister Elaine had a stroke, she described her emergency medical flight to San Francisco: "I'm strapped in with a zillion heavy metal clasps and buckles, and can't move an inch on the airplane. They announce, 'in case of an emergency, put your mask on yourself first.' You gotta be kidding: if there's an emergency, I'm going down with the plane.

I can't even move. I'm a stiff stroke body."

Elaine's laughter was contagious when she told this story. Jiminy Cricket, so funny how she exaggerated with her natural stand-up comedian flare.

I told Carol, "I've already called Elaine in Medford. She'll be at the hospital when you get there. I'll take Aggie home, pack my stuff and I'll meet you there in a few hours. I love you, sweetie. God's got us."

At 7 a.m., I called the school secretary: "Hi Ruth, Joanie here. I need to call in sick today. Carol is being airlifted to Medford with a brain bleed stroke."

"Oh, Joanie, I'm so sorry. Don't worry about anything. I'll take care of it and get you a sub."

"I have lesson plans in my binder on my desk and my roll sheets and seating charts are in the file cabinet. Thanks, Ruth!"

"Joanie, take care of Carol, please."

Back at the hospital, the flight crew asked, "Are you ready, Carol? Your plane from Bend is gassed up, checked out, weather is good, and ready to take you to Medford. I'm your nurse and we're going to make sure you're comfortable. You let us know, OK?"

Carol smiled and that meant, good to go.

Yeah, Lord.

Carol was carefully strapped into the ambulance with warm blankets tucked in on her sides and feet. The gentle but firm medical team spoke volumes to me. She was in their hands, God's hands.

I placed two gentle kisses on her forehead. "I love you so much, sweetie."

Words came out of her like a flash, slightly slurred: "I love you." I thought she'd been storing those words up for the past eight hours. They sounded fabulous.

"I love you MORE," I thought. Her eyes looked as awesome as when I first met her. We would forever be young lovers, even though our gray hairs and wrinkling skin were growing old with wisdom and grace.

Aggie kissed Carol's forehead, too.

Carol had cancer, was cured, had heart afib, had a pacemaker—and every one of those medical challenges turned into miracles.

OK God, will you do another miracle for us? Please?

Through the years, Carol and I had received fantastic medical care—nonjudgmental and nondiscriminatory along with bedside manners and attitudes full of love, compassion and equality of service without gay discrimination. *We've been blessed.*

Sadly, our gay friends had told ugly stories about poor treatment in hospitals, care facilities and doctors' offices. I prayed that Carol's treatment would be fair and excellent.

The Brain Bleed Continues in the Medford, Oregon ICU

Running on adrenaline and gratitude, I drove 25 minutes to return Aggie to her house in Harbor. I thanked her immensely for being with us.

I packed a suitcase of clothes, mine and hers, grabbed our black "to go bag": medicine, extra cash and some food. During the three-hour drive to Medford, I was in task mode—proud of myself for always keeping the car gas tank full in case of an emergency.

After a blur of a drive, 30 minutes faster than usual, I pulled into Rogue Asanti Hospital, where the desk attendant directed me to the ICU. Elaine was in the waiting room. We hugged and her eyes were big as saucers. Trembling, she looked scared to death.

"They won't let me see her." Her voice was wobbly.

I pushed the intercom button and talked with a nurse: "I'm Carol's domestic partner and I really need to see her."

The nurse said they had started her on a stronger medicine, hoping to stop the brain bleed.

"Carol has been asking for you," she said. "You can go to her room for 10 minutes only."

That gave me AMAZING hope. The nurse activated the big metal door to open and I dashed in.

Carol was hooked up to IVs, tubes and machines amidst a

menagerie of beeps, lights and flashes. In the cold and sterile room, she looked very calm and peaceful. She either heard or sensed me entering, and glanced at me with foggy eyes.

"Hi, sweetie love," I said. "I'm here with you, love."

Her eyes closed and she wiggled her right hand. I kissed her hand in a long, loud smooch. She wiggled her fingers. "Elaine is in the waiting room. We are all with you! And Jesus, too!"

The nurse explained that Carol could not respond, but she could hear me. She encouraged me to talk more with her. So I did. I held my composure, using my strong, confident voice, hoping she would feel confident, too. No tears would be shed. It was all about Carol, not my emotions.

While Carol was taken for a CT scan, I talked with the doctor and the nurse at the counter.

"She's had a massive brain bleed and we can only give her up to three rounds of this medicine," the doctor said. "We've given her one and let's see how she does."

"Will she make it?"

"She might," the doctor said. "Hope so."

"She has a real strong will," I told them.

"We see that. Go rest and we'll call you if anything changes."

"Can her sister Elaine sit with her?"

"Yes, but not now," the doctor said. "Did you give permission for Elaine?"

"No, how do I do that?"

"Nurse, will you take care of that for Joanie?"

"Thanks, doc."

As I left the nurses' desk across from Carol's room, someone called, "Ms. Lindenmeyer." It was one of my former high school students, who was now 20-something.

"What are you doing here, Ms. L?"

"My other half, Carol, is here with a brain bleed."

"Oh, I'm so sorry."

I lost it! Tears flooded out. The nurse handed me a Kleenex box and asked, "How do you know this young man?"

"He was a student of mine at Del Norte High School in Crescent City."

"He's a wonderful worker and will become a nurse someday," the nurse said. "That's great."

Then my former student added: "Ms. L, I'll keep an eye on Carol for you! I'm in charge of all the supplies in the ICU. I'll come by and watch her for you!"

How sweet. "Thank you so much!"

Thank you God, that's how 99% of our life is: connections just happen. You got us, God.

While Elaine stayed in the hospital waiting room, I went to the chapel, put Carol's name in the book at the altar and sat and prayed to our God of life and miracles.

Your will, oh God. Let me accept it all.

Then I drove to Elaine's apartment to sleep. Since Elaine was on dialysis, Carol and I had frequently visited her on weekends and stayed in her second bedroom. Now Elaine and I communicated by cell phone, taking turns waiting with Carol or in the ICU waiting room.

I called local friends Joyce and Scott E, Kelly and Steve, and priest friend Father Jim C. who was the chaplain at nearby Providence Hospital. Joyce and Jim started prayer chains.

After 24 hours, her brain was still bleeding. I hardly left Carol's side. March 18th came and went.

Carol was in a comatose state. I sat with her or in the ICU hallway or waiting room as minute by minute and hour by hour ticked by. Time warped with increments of despair and rays of hope in my positive outlook glass. I prayed and looked at her, prayed and looked at the machines, and her body was not moving. Over and over my eyes wandered, hoping for a sign of life. I talked to her aloud, reading from the *Living With Christ* scripture book, knowing in my heart she could hear me. I believed it!

I said silly things like, "The weather report for the day is . . . in the sporting news today . . . the cafeteria tapioca was good, but the chocolate pudding better. The chapel is filled with sunlight and bright lights with gorgeous stained-glass windows; the colors are bright reds, yellows and blues. I keep adding your name to the altar book every time I go in and tell Jesus 'Hi' from us. We are making a book."

I told her about the people praying for her: CSJ sisters, Terri and Billy, Elaine and Sara, Dan and Andrew, Tim, Gail, Doris, Aggie and everyone who loved her so much.

Elaine visited with Carol when I took a break. I called our good friend Father Jim on his cell phone to ask, "Can you come and please give Carol the anointing of the sick sacrament?"

"Yes, of course. I will be there soon." Jim was an Augustinian. He had taught at Saint Augustine High School in San Diego and had been the parish pastor in Central Point, Oregon. He was an excellent friend of our longtime friends, Joyce and Scott. Every year we cheered for Villanova in March Madness basketball games and Jim, Carol and I texted back and forth during games.

I went to the hospital cafeteria for nourishment and casually talked with a man whose wife was not doing well. It was the first normal thing I had done in two days. I realized that other people were also going through difficult times. We held each other in our hearts.

Good thing God's clock is endless and forever.

I returned to Carol's ICU room. Her sister Sara had arrived, and with Elaine and Father Jim, they had all been present to administer the sacramental blessing. I thought that this was great, fantastic: it was meant to be that her two sisters and Father Jim were together for the sacramental blessing.

March 19th: St. Joseph's Day

March 19th was the wonderful, happy anniversary of the day Carol had professed her life to be a nun. This was also my anniversary of when I surrendered and accepted the temporary vows. The day! It was also the most important feast day of the year for the congregation of the sisters of St. Joseph of Carondelet. It was bigger than our birthdays.

It had been 48 hours, with periodic CAT scans. Carol had received her third and last medicine dose to stop the brain bleeding without causing loss of brain activity. This was serious!

The medical team had done everything possible.

Alone with Carol in her ICU room, I sat in dim light, the machines beeping and bleeping. Breathing on her own, she was lifeless and motionless.

I'm exhausted. I have no more tears. I am numb.

With my low voice, I said, "Carol, I give you over to God! It's St. Joseph's Day!" I knew she heard me and I know God and St. Joseph heard me, too. I just knew.

I stared at the ceiling. Suddenly all the lights in the room flickered. The ceiling looked brighter—completely lit up, whiter than white.

The nurse came in and asked, "What happened?"

"I don't know. I just told Carol I gave her over to God. It's St. Joseph's Day!"

"Did you turn the lights on?"

"No, I haven't touched anything."

Then, Carol opened her eyes! A squint that told my heart *I'm home! I'm back! Here I am!* It was Carol's version of life.

I looked at the nurse, who had leaned over to look at Carol. Then Carol, with her eyes open, looked at me.

I was speechless!

Wowowowowowowowowowow!!!!!

"It's Saint Joseph's Day, Carol!" I said. "I gave you over to God and I guess He didn't want you yet."

She cracked a crooked smile.

The best smile I've ever seen!

I smiled and kissed her hand with big, long smooches.

The doctor and more nurses entered. Everyone was smiling!

"Thank you, thank you, thank you!" I yelled. "Everyone was praying!" Yes, it was a miracle. Yes, Carol was a miracle!

The lights were on!

Venturing onto New Roads

Carol embarked on a courageous journey, inspiring me and hundreds of people over the next eight years.

Accepting the new Carol was extremely difficult for herself, for me, and all her family and friends. We discovered who the winners and whiners were.

First, she was elevated to an upper floor in the hospital.

She was paralyzed on her left side, unable to lift or move her left arm, fingers, leg or toes. She was unable to eat, swallow or talk. She had a catheter and IVs.

The good news was that she thought clearly, remembered the past, understood today and hoped for the future.

I was at her side and together we would make this work. We learned to appreciate and celebrate the things most people take for granted.

Her Hearing Returns

Oh, another miracle: her hearing returned and she no longer needed hearing aids. A miracle within miracles! Yippee!

Physically, we were exhausted. She was sleeping, napping and looking better: her skin color was getting rosier and her green eyes sparkled more. A 20 minute power nap did me a world of good.

Emotionally, Carol was fired up! She was willing and open to any and all help. Speech therapy, physical therapy, occupational therapy—she wanted it all. After a week of being on the hospital's third floor, she re-learned how to talk, eat, swallow, sit in a wheelchair and live with only half of a working body. I was so proud of her! I went to speech therapy with her and the drills that Carol said were funny and childlike. But they worked and invigorated her laughter.

"Can we do a do-over?" I asked. "Is that an English or French word?" We cracked up.

Carol loved having me there and I wouldn't have wanted to miss a second of it. What an opportunity!

She was making tiny, incremental progress with the body parts that were damaged and had lost strength, flexibility and coordination. She was performing her "slight edge" technique of counting her reps while adding one more. She inspired her trainers and others. She trained harder than Olympians and professional athletes.

I learned and earned the right to steer her wheelchair down the hallway and to the recreation room's window to watch the trees and sky. She told me where to go, when to turn, to slow down and to speed up.

I slept for several nights on the windowsill bed in her room. We said good night and good morning, face-to-face with soft kisses on lips and cheeks. The staff ordered me meals with hers; we spilled and made a mess, but so what.

They saw our love and commitment were strong and true. We were a witness of God, gay life and profound love. We continued to believe in the unbelievableness of life.

We cried together a little; the loss was major! But we were excited to have days and nights to still hold hands, kiss and dream. I encouraged her and myself because we needed to know the things that would help her when she came home.

I asked many questions: Does she get to go to the acute rehab floor? So what's next? Is she going to go to a care facility?

I love what happened next. I was sitting in the large recliner in her room, and a therapist came in and said, "Carol, try this." Nothing happened. And the therapist was ready to end the session.

"Wait!" Carol yelled. "I want to do it by myself. Let me do it! I can do it!"

We didn't know it, but outside her door was the doctor who was NOT going to accept her on the upper floor of acute rehab. With Carol's vim and vigor attitude, he changed his mind.

He walked in to meet her and me. "Welcome to the specialized rehab floor, Carol," he said. "You'll move up there and start today."

"YES!" we answered and smiled, crook and all.

What a miracle! Thank you, God.

Oh boy, mixed deep emotions and feelings about all of this. Worse than a PMS or hormonal imbalance. Sadness, frustration, depression, fears and fragile emotions raged inside both of us. It was evident in our harsh voices and hard stares. Expressions of these wild feelings pounded us like crashing winter ocean waves.

She slept more and cried in her sleep—murmuring, yelling and begging God for help, "Lord, help me, Lord Jesus. I need you. I can't do this. This is so HARD!"

I cried and sighed, turned my car stereo up louder and saved my patience for when I was with Carol. But with some other people, I was abrupt and intolerant.

After two nights, I had to return to work: a perfect solution for us. She was grieving and figuring out how to do life. Her sister Elaine would visit her every day. I would return Friday by 6:30 p.m. and stay till Sunday about 5 p.m.

Care Facility Bad News

After two weeks, Carol "graduated" and was shipped out to a care facility in Medford because no bed was available at Curry Good Samaritan Care Facility in Brookings. I was so bummed. I wanted her nearby with her Brookings friends who wanted to visit her. I knew she would feel better back on our home turf. The staff and therapist were top notch. How could I make this happen?

The Medford care facility was Bad News! A nurse called me at 4:30 a.m. Carol had been thrown out of her bed! I talked to our attorney Peter Spratt on my cellphone as I carefully drove in the dark through the narrow, winding Smith River Canyon to Medford.

I arrived at 7:30 a.m. Carol had a lemon-sized welt on her forehead. Her right, non-paralyzed leg was in excruciating pain, and her lip was swollen with brown crusty blood. Her bed had no safety bars, and was surrounded a quarter-inch thick, two-by-five-foot black pad on the linoleum floor. Carol had a wrong-size inflatable mattress that had malfunctioned and pushed her out of bed, and her forehead had hit the baseboard heater. So BAD and so WRONG. I was furious! I was sick to my stomach!

The nurse apologized.

I was a fierce tiger. Fangs and saliva spitting out of my mouth. My eyes shot sharp daggers. "Did you call the ambulance?"

"No."

"She needs to go to the ER!" I exclaimed. "She had a brain bleed two weeks ago and this is a head injury. Don't you get it?"

"The doctor won't be in until 9 a.m."

"I don't care. I'm calling 911 right now. Carol needs to be evaluated."

I couldn't believe it. My first experience of a faulty system, underpaid staff and no accountability.

I followed the ambulance to Asante Hospital. In the ER, the nurses couldn't believe the story I told them. Immediately the VP of the hospital was at my service.

Carol had a CAT scan. Results: a mild concussion, no bleeding in the brain and a hairline hip bone fracture. No available beds in the hospital. Back to the care facility, darn it. No, damn it!

Dr. Jekyll and Mr. Hyde, good cop/bad cop came out of me. I saved my pleasant loveliness and demeanor for Carol! I was going to keep her on the loving, positive healing groove.

When I went to take care of business with the administration and the nurses, I let them have it. This was unacceptable. I would not tolerate it. My attorney had been notified.

I saw certain staff that treated her with respect and kindness. I complimented them in front of Carol as much as possible. It brought out even better results when I played songs on my phone for Carol when she was in the therapy room. The next day, the therapist had her phone with Carol's favorite singer: Neil Diamond.

For those who were rude, unprofessional and demeaning towards Carol, I spoke with them privately and informed the CEO. It was here that I first heard nasty, derogatory name-calling towards other patients. They did not have a family member or advocate. I found myself being one for so many.

Words do make a difference. Carol was called stroke victim, disabled, handicapped and needy. How about calling her by her name? Carol, joyful lady, big smile lady, colorful dress you are wearing, beautiful, courageous, faith-filled, lovely, friend and sweetie.

It's choices; it's free will.

I filed a written report and conducted an oral interview claim with the State of Oregon about her fall incident. The care facility was put on a six-month probation. I was pleased because many patients did not have an advocate, a family or friend to stand up for them.

CHAPTER 17

Protecting Carol from Further Harm

I would not let Carol see me arguing, fighting and making things right with the care facility CEO or doctor. I told her, "I'll be right back, sweetie. I need to go take care of something."

"OK, love, if you say so," was her new pat answer. So cute.

A week of ugliness continued at the Medford care facility. I was there for long weekends, taking a Friday or Monday off from work. I observed her alone at mealtime in the cafeteria, unable to open her packet of butter, unable to take the paper off her straw, and unable to cut her chicken. And no help was provided. They plopped her tray in front of her and let her eat it like a dog. It was disgusting. I raised hell for that, too. They said I couldn't sit with her because that would distract her. I was furious to see her helpless with no one willing to help her.

"Hi, sweetie, am I in time to share a meal with you?" I asked.

Oh, her smile radiated and tears welled in her eyes. This was big. Carol was not the teary-eyed type.

"Hi, Joanie. I'm so glad you're here. I want to go home! They stole my dress."

"What?"

"They stole my favorite colorful dress!" She started to really cry.

"OK, let me see if they took it to the laundry. Yes, I'm working on it to get you home. Actually to Brookings at Curry Good Sam. Once you get stronger, you'll be home with me. How does that sound?"

"Good, the sooner the better!"

"Have I told you how much I love you, Carol? And how good you look today? You are AMAZING!" I leaned over and kissed her on her lips.

She kissed me back, then flashed a big smile.

"Let's share a little of this fruit and juice, OK?"

"OK, I'm so glad you are here!"

"Me, too, sweetie. I'm here all day with you."

"You got the day off?"

"Yep. Oh, can I go with you to therapy, Carol?"

"Of course, Joanie."

Joe's Sour Cream Breakfast Cake

At therapy in a nice big room, there were orange bands for Carol's leg lifts, a large blue ball to kick, and a big red balloon to play volleyball. My cell phone played loud tunes as Carol, the Filipino PT lady and I grooved to the music.

"Do you make lumpia?" I asked. This triggered Carol to talk about her favorite foods too, including her dad's sour cream breakfast cake. Carol was engaged and initiated conversation. She was alive and kicking.

By the way, readers, the recipe is at the end of the book. Enjoy, compliments of Carol.

Thank God for Elaine, Joyce and Kelly who visited Carol every day at the care facility. They brought her better food, made her lap blankets, clothed her, hugged her, smiled with her and believed in her. Thank you, dear angels. You made a huge difference.

Carol hung in there for three more days until the arrangements were finalized for her to come home to Brookings.

I Forgave the Person Who Stole My Dress

I often wondered what I would say to the person if I ever saw someone wearing Carol's stolen dress? Oh, before Carol died, she said she forgave the person who took it.

Thanks to numerous phone calls to Curry Good Samaritan Village Care in Brookings and visits to the center by dear friends Aggie and Doris, Carol was approved for admittance. She was transported by ambulance, paid for by Curry Good Sam donations. I followed behind in my SUV loaded with her new supplies: her walker, manual wheelchair with footrests, armrest for her chair, and hospital pads.

I asked Doris and Aggie to greet Carol with balloons, hugs and kisses, a real welcome home surprise by the staff and her new home for several months. She was delighted and showed her thankfulness with lots of wows and, "You did this for me? Thank you, Aggie, thank you Doris." Carol had a private room and the staff was fabulous, attentive and caring.

CHAPTER 17

Guardian Angel LIGHT

After work every day, I drove directly to "Good Sam" in the middle of Brookings, excited to see my sweetie.

One day around 3:30 p.m. on a partially sunny, high cloud day as I drove through Smith River and was about a football field length from the Oregon-California state line near the agriculture bug inspection station, I saw something, and I felt something.

It was the brightest light in the sky, but not the sun. It had a glow and a sparkle, not a flicker. I said, "OH, are you Carol's Guardian Angel saying hi to me?"

It got bigger, wider, brighter and sparkled more. I was talking out loud to a real person, a spirit and an angel. "You are reading my mind, Guardian Angel. You know my deepest thoughts. I feel you here!"

I had been agonizing, with a heavy heart as I drove, about how life had changed. I was really nervous about it that day. Would Carol ever be able to come home? Would I need to bathe her, roll her multiple times at night, move her in and out of bed, take care of her bathroom needs, and do all the cooking? Did I have what was necessary to DO it all? 24/7? Work, finances, upkeep of our home, her care and my stamina and sanity? *How is this possible? Am I strong enough?* I surely knew I loved her enough!

The light was still in the sky. I gazed at the ocean on my left, then through the front windshield. In my rear view mirror, no cars were behind me. I slowed to 30 miles per hour in the 55 mph zone.

The light became brighter, like the miraculous day in the ICU hospital room. It was so big! Bigger than the moon, smaller than the sun, and brighter than an LED light. I felt light and relieved—no worries, only peace and joy. The light, strong and bold, hung in my front window view for a mile. Definitely a strange phenomenon. It was a miracle. The light was Carol's special Guardian Angel.

"OK, I get it angel/God! It's not all me. We will be fine because YOU are our light! There is no need for me to worry. YOU will give Carol and me what we need when we need it. Thank you! Bye."

And she, the Guardian Angel light, disappeared like the snap of a finger!

I pranced in to tell Carol, "I met your Guardian Angel on my way home."

"I know you did."

We looked into each other's eyes, missing the sights of gray hairs on our heads and eyebrows, wrinkles more than dimples and our lower vocal singing chords. Shivers went up my arms; no other words were needed between us. Carol knew her Guardian Angel had visited me on her behalf.

Carol's gifts of seeing before it happened, her intuition and her true faith were alive and well. The brain bleed never blocked her direct line to God. Our loving smiles reaching our ears were still the ageless facial expressions we had shared 35 years ago. We knew each other inside and out. She was a holy woman—yesterday, today and tomorrow.

Good Sam is Great

Carol had a single room with a large window overlooking colorful rhododendron bushes and a bubbling fountain in a courtyard. She operated her bed with a remote control, and I enjoyed sitting in a power recliner or a metal chair kept in the closet. Outside her door sat a manual wheelchair with a left arm support piece, as well as a Hoyer lift. With this luxury and service, she was in good spirits, waiting for me to walk in.

I leaned over her, we kissed; I hugged her and rubbed her back. She encircled me with her big hand and arm around my shoulder from her propped position in bed.

"Tell me about your day," Carol said.

Exuding gratitude, I perched on a metal chair beside her and we chatted up a storm.

This was our routine for the next three months of afternoon visits during these Monday through Friday work weeks when she had twice-daily, intense workouts of physical and occupational therapy. How cool to see Carol regain strength and confidence, and her acceptance of her God-given abilities. She was an inspiration day after day, said the nurses' aides, therapists and residents.

She had a new family who loved her for who she was. Activities were fun as she painted rocks, did crafts and watched movies on the big screen in the Activity Room, her favorite place to hang out. The kitchen staff helped cut her meat, aides removed the paper off the straws and she could eat with whomever and wherever she wanted.

Help was around the corner. Rose, Mary or Letty helped her dress in her chosen daily outfit. I picked up her laundry weekly and nothing was stolen. Father Bernie and wife Paige loved Carol's theology, spirituality and prayerfulness when they visited her several times a week.

What a joy to be a cheerleader with her at therapy, to see her sit on the edge of her bed by herself, stand with a walker, take one step with her walker, take two steps, three, four and more. Eventually she was able to walk the length of the Good Sam hallway, followed by me pushing her empty wheelchair.

Oh God, how incredible that you gave our bodies and minds the skills and will to put one foot in front of the next. We praise you, Lord. We give you thanks! Amen.

Fast forward a few weeks to our afternoon chat, when she shared, "Well, today I was asked 'How'd this happen? Why are you in a wheelchair?' I told him, 'I used to be a boxer!'" Carol beamed!

I burst into laughter. "Ha, ha, ha! Good one, Carol. What a hoot! You will always be the surprise of the day!"

Carol said often as she was struggling, "It takes courage to get older."

"You bet," I chimed in.

Life had changed, not ended.

Jesus hold you.
God bless you.

CHAPTER 18
Gay Marriage and the Catholic Church

Love Is Meant to be Shared!

Carol and I prayed individually and aloud together in the prayer corner of our Brookings home that the Catholic Church would open her heart and policy in accepting gay marriage as a sacrament, which is a religious ritual that imparts divine grace, such as being baptized and receiving communion.

That was our main reason to get married: to be a sacrament!

We waited and waited for the Catholic Church to progress, to move forward and to update her teachings. We had prayed fervently together since 1983 for a wider spread of our Lord's love within the Catholic Church.

So, here we are in February of 2023 and Pope Francis has told the world that "being homosexual is not a crime." As he said this, 67 countries and jurisdictions worldwide criminalize consensual same-sex sexual activity. That's "unjust," he said.

Meanwhile, the Catholic Church stance on gayness and gay marriage seems contradictory. It's OK to be gay and celibate or chaste, yet it's not OK to be gay and share intimate love or to be married.

Prayer leads to action, thus let us pray fervently with open minds and hearts, recognize, move forward and celebrate LGTBQ committed relationships in the ACT of Marriage.

May Jesus be the light of truth in our lives.

Psalm 62 was marked in Carol's Bible with a laminated bookmark I made from a dried flower that I had picked in the Navajo Nation as a novice. "Truly my soul finds rest in God; my salvation comes from Him. Truly He is my rock and my salvation; He is my fortress, I will never be shaken."

While the world celebrated the legalization of gay marriage in the United States in 2015, it was not sanctioned by the Catholic Church. Carol and I did not want a civil marriage. We wanted a sacramental marriage, which means blessed by God within a church. The deeper meaning to us was that the Church would recognize we were living out God's love; our marriage was not just a governmental legal entity.

If it is meant to be, it will be. Somehow God will provide.

The 1980s were a time rich with a new world awareness, changes in the Catholic Church, and new social issues. Yes, opposition to how things had been was alive in protests, civil rights court battles and people asking questions of their governments, their churches, and themselves. Gay marriage was one of those questions.

The Catholic Church was still incorporating and growing with Pope John Paul II's 1962 Vatican II progressive modernization through folk Masses and the adoption of Rite of Christian Initiation of Adults (RCIA), a process through which non-baptized men and women can enter the Catholic Church through religious education, that had begun in 1974. Pope Paul VI reinstated Latin Masses, tridentine, on special occasions set by the bishop of each diocese. Leadership by regions was extremely varied and hard to understand as universally Catholic. Things take time to implement.

Though it was a tumultuous time, our motto was: "Expect great things to happen." Carol had plenty of smiley face stickers and a rainbow sticker with her name on it. She loved the colors and knew it was biblical for God's promises.

All the while, it took time and patience for our internal self-discoveries, requiring deep down self-trust to understand and accept who we each were. One helpful tool was journaling. Carol journaled in small, lined notebooks, covered in cutesie flowers, rainbows, sunshine stars and smiley faces. She wrote poems, sketched pictures and had fun with it. My journal books were lengthy written sentences to Jesus and letters to myself, including big bold words on a single page, such as:

"HELP ME, JESUS. I WANT TO DO YOUR WILL! I AM WONDERFULLY MADE. LIFE IS THE BEST. BE THE BEST ME. THANK YOU GOD FOR MY LIFE WITH CAROL."

We also strummed on the folk guitar with church songbooks, chords written in large black letters. Music enabled us to know each other better.

Pope John Paul II was inclusive and had begun dialogue to modernize the Church and welcome new members. Pope Benedict came next and he agreed that bishops of local dioceses should make the local parish decisions. He promoted the traditional male leadership. We could not see that anybody was petitioning the Vatican to make changes for becoming more inclusive. This was a frustrating time for Carol and me.

Our House of Prayer

We had designated prayer tables and areas of our house that were our mini sanctuaries of God's goodness. Sitting on our shelf or wooden table was our Bible or scripture reading booklet, symbolic river stones, flowers from the yard, pictures of those we lifted up to God, and a ceramic nativity scene. The aqua-colored glass beads that form the shape of angels helped us live in prayer. Taking the time and energy to be with Jesus was and is peaceful. We showed up with questions, doubts, fears and thanksgivings. Jesus listened.

We prayed for Catholic-sanctioned gay marriages, more laity involvement and more women positions in the church. We prayed for leadership at local parishes to ignite the love of the Lord, know their congregations, stand with them in a personal way, visit and listen to them without their pre-agenda, and truly get to know them without being superior or hierarchical.

We prayed for open mindedness to have honest discussions and dialogues about real life issues, whatever the topic! Do you think that Jesus had LGTBQ disciples and friends? If so, I wondered what things they discussed. We read, sang, reviewed and prayed the eight Beatitudes, Latin for abundant happiness, starting with, "Blessed are the poor in spirit . . ."

Since 1968, and in 2009, 2012 and 2015, other denominational churches have discussed gay marriage for more than 39 years. Hmmm. That was our number of years as a couple. What a coincidence!

So, we waited longer . . . still hoping for change within Catholic teachings.

Some of our local parishes were filled with "Kindergarten Catholics": those who knew their church and faith by memorizing prayers and answers either from their childhood or from a book of do's and don'ts. A few parishioners said they had a personal relationship or friendship with Jesus.

Many others, like Carol and I, saw "Catholic" everywhere, anytime and anyplace, universally. It was way more than a building or memorized repetitive responses. It was in walking, talking and seeing Jesus in ALL people. We were personally involved in others' lives by delivering fresh-baked goodies, calling people to chat and surprising them with flowers as we visited their homes. In Carol's words, "Be the best you can be and bring out the best in others."

Carol and I were ecstatic and hope-filled with Pope Francis: a Jesuit Priest, a common people's servant who became Pope in 2013. Change took time because hearts had to change first. I, with Carol's input, personally wrote him a letter introducing ourselves and thanking him for being our servant leader. Prayers to you, Pope Francis.

Our gay friends wanted support from the Catholic Church. They wanted to remain Catholic, but were struggling to fit in. We believed that a person could be both gay and Catholic. Some people and authors speak, theologize, and write about the

Catholic Church and gay life and marriage. We lived it!

But our questions remained: can an LGTBQ person or married couple be in "good standing" with the church? Receive communion? Have a sacramental marriage? Other people showed numerous examples of a smorgasbord approach to being Catholic: individuals could pick and choose which teachings or laws to follow, such as a straight married couple choosing to use birth control. However, LGBTQ couples, such as us, were excluded from inclusion based on not conforming to the Church's strict rule to remain celibate, as we could not be married in the Church. Jesus answered these questions in Carol's and my hearts and Jesus can do the same for you! Be quiet and still; peace will come.

We were involved in the Catholic Church for years as leaders and members of sponsored guilds and councils. We shared meals, listened and executed ideas for fun parish retreats, prayer services, crab feeds, bake sales and picnics. We fed people's stomachs and hearts with joy, love, kindness and peace.

We received Eucharist or Holy Communion every weekend or at daily Mass. Only one time in 50 years were we refused to have a host placed in our pyx, (a container that holds the host—the wafer which represents Jesus) while visiting a neighboring church. A priest would know by my having a pyx that I was a practicing Catholic, and I was at a loss to understand why I was refused. I got it, the priest didn't know us. But our thinking was, if someone wants Jesus, give them Jesus.

We were a huge part of Catholic faith communities, and of course contributed financially. Some knew we were gay; some did not. It didn't matter to us. We have no idea what was said about us and we didn't care. We were never asked and we never flaunted it. We were simply Carol and Joanie, friendly and kind to all.

One disappointing sermon that hit both of our hearts hard was when a Catholic pastor said from the pulpit that he was asked by a parishioner, "Is it OK to attend a friend of a family's gay wedding?" The pastor explained that marriage is between a man and a woman and the bottom line was, "No, you should not attend the wedding." The pastor looked directly at Carol and me.

Sitting in the pew beside Carol, I gently touched her hand and she squeezed it. I whispered, "It's up to us and Jesus." She squeezed my hand again. At the next week's Saturday night Mass, the usher invited us to carry up the offertory gifts of the bread and wine while joining the choir with "One Bread, One Body."

Gay Church Leaders

LGBTQ persons could have an important role in any local church if the leadership of that church, organization, institution or diocese were willing to open their arms and hearts. We had seen some churches that allowed LGBTQ individuals and couples, either "out" or "not out," to become ordained ministers, Catholic school teachers, RCIA Catholic leaders, youth leaders, hospital or prison chaplains, and hold administrative and liturgical positions.

Our dear friend John was in the seminary and after he left it, he met his male lifelong partner, married and lived happily ever after as a monogamous, loving couple. John was absolutely one of the best singers for our parish liturgies. He sang his gay heart out in both English and Latin. His prayer melodies filled the entire church with joy and praise. John died in 2006; his memorial Catholic Mass was standing room only. We, the parish, tried to sing loud and happily, but we just didn't sound the same. In 2022, I bumped into his sister during a vacation in Newport, Oregon. We reminisced about the funeral Mass, the overflowing reception, the graveyard service and John's love of the Lord.

Carol and I had a wonderful friend, Joyce. She was a little older than me, a beautiful woman, who was the kindest, most compassionate and smartest RCIA leader, besides Carol, that I've ever known. She had, for more than 30 years, walked the spiritual path with so many people who wanted to be baptized and confirmed Catholic. She and her husband, Scott, have two sons, one of whom is a happily married gay man with hopes of having children. At his wedding, Joyce and her husband gave him away to his loving and handsome husband. Their other son was a proud, loving brother on that special wedding day and every day.

A calm, meek man, another John, comes to my mind as a single gay individual who taught his entire career in a Catholic elementary school. He was well educated, credentialed, peaceful, articulate, fun, creative and a phenomenal religion and academic teacher, whom everyone loved. I never knew if he chose to be "out" at the school or not, and if his school either never knew or didn't raise a red flag. He was a good and Godly man.

We saw some churches lose LGBTQ members because they did not feel accepted: people glared at then in disgusting ways, avoided them at church events and did not support them to grow spiritually.

A Beautiful & Joyous Gay Wedding

Carol and I were thrilled and honored when our dear friend Dan asked us to give him away at his marriage to Andrew at Hyatt Lake, Oregon.

Their joyful celebration included a meaningful ceremony, family participation, close friends and scrumptious catered food and drinks; no one got wasted or out of control. We loved how they both planted a living tree, using scoops of soil to unite and extend their "roots" for the rest of their lives.

That cold April wedding day was picturesque with patches of snow and huge, fragrant pine trees surrounding the outdoor deck decorated with white calla lilies and strings of white lights.

Dan and I walked down the aisle arm in arm; I gave him a cheek kiss and then stood next to Carol. Carol, sitting in the front row, held his held his personally written marriage vow script in her hands like an angel holding her cherubim. She nodded and gently handed him the vows when the time came for him to give his all to Andrew. And Andrew to Dan.

Carol and Dan exchanged super eye contact, a holy blessing of approval as Andrew and I watched them. The look of these two beautiful men, holding hands and gazing deeply at each other, spoke of eternal love. It was a very moving ceremony.

Carol and I sat holding hands, fingers entwined, realizing that we were witnessing our best friends united with Jesus, the all-wonderful, loving God and the Holy Spirit of grace. Carol's huge smile and my teardrops were heartfelt in the families' and friends' faces as well.

With total acceptance of gayhood and family love, we all agreed to support them forever. We were asked to be lifetime witnesses and to be involved in their lives. The "I do" was all-encompassing and beautiful; it reminded me and Carol of when we had made our sacramental vows to each other.

Dan and Andrew arranged for us to stay overnight in our own cabin nearby. They had a designated crew that moved the rented portable ramps needed for Carol's powered wheelchair, so she was included in all the festivities. Dan and Andrew were truly selfless and pre-thought what would be best for our comfort.

We were loved by his family and friends and vice versa, and it was a beautiful gay wedding day for Andrew and Dan.

What is the Will of God?

In the context of gay marriage and everything in our lives, Carol and I often asked, "What would Jesus do?"

Henri Nouwen, Thomas Merton, Thomas Aquinas, Pope John Paul, St. Ignatius, St. Augustine, Saint Joan of Arc: what would they say about the Catholic Church of our century? Was the church currently doing God's will? Were we doing the will of God? Was I doing the will of God today? A song goes, "Abba, you are the potter, we are the clay." Theologians, saints and Popes since the time of Christ have had one common theme, **to do the will of God!**

So when I said the will of God, it meant listening to your heart, your intuition, your gut, your higher power, and when you truly listened, you would receive pure answers. That was the will of God. For us, the will of God was that Carol and I were meant to be together to share a life of love and joy with each other and every person we met.

FREE WILL: What is it?

Free will was Carol's hot topic and the center of her soul. She wove it in naturally during counseling sessions, in friendships and throughout her life.

CHAPTER 18

"What is free will, Joanie?" Carol asked one day.

"Huh . . . let me think. I think free will is God giving us choice: giving me and you and us the absolute free will to make our own decisions and choices, unconditional trust and love from God. It's all based on a friendship I have with Jesus."

I asked the same question of Carol as we were courting. Carol described free will as saying, "YES to the Lord. It is prayer . . . purpose of prayer to surrender your life to God. Which begins with wonder, not trying to get an answer, just the truth. It all ends with surrender. Pray about the things in your life: calm and peacefully turning to scripture. Prayer is the ERUPTION of God within you, focusing your mind on a point. Prayer is for the whole person, body and spirit. The body is alert, put in a position of reverence: sit up straight, take a few deep breaths, relax the body, arms hang, and close your eyes. God gives you the free will to choose."

Carol and I chose to believe that someday, we would marry with the blessing of the Catholic Church.

Jesus hold you.
God bless you.

CHAPTER 19
Patience, Prayer & Travels Lead to Marriage

While Carol and I waited for change, the Catholic Church had zero dialogue about gay marriage. That was frustrating. We knew in our hearts we were called together, but no system was in place to make that happen.

Our Freedom Trip

In September of 2018, Carol and I took a 30-day, awesome road trip to celebrate my teaching career retirement as OUR FREEDOM. We were as excited as two glimmering hummingbirds. We had planned our trip a year earlier, coordinating with friends and family, and allowed for "Flex Mode" if we wanted to make changes.

We hit the road in our double 007 James Bond cranberry colored mobility Buick Terraza. We had loaded our most important items: our suitcases and her medical supplies, and our "game bag" with games and ping pong paddles. I felt my mother's presence and love every time I carried, zipped or unzipped it.

Carol was a master at driving up the ramp to get in our van. It was equipped with a retractable side wheelchair ramp, and safety hooks and cables to fasten Carol's wheelchair to the floorboard. Once in the dance floor, as we called it, provided tight but ample room for Carol to turn and drive forward into the front seat position. It was a close fit with only inches to spare on each side. My eyes were glued to her as she made this maneuver that put her at risk of crunching her toes and sandals. We took our sweet time—15 minutes—to do this right. Once buckled in, we gave each other a high five and I put her leak-proof water drinking cup with a neon green straw into the cup holder.

"Carol, do you want your sunglasses?"

"Yes! I like wearing my Oregon Ducks sunglasses."

Carol would belt out our road tune: "Hit the road, Jack, and don't you come back no more, no more, no more," and often it became "Hit the road, Joanie..." Our trips always started giddy laughter that expressed our excitement at being free and footloose. Yippee!

She never failed to say at least once, "Thank you, Joanie!" as I patiently cared for her every need.

"You bet, sweetie! Thank you, too!"

I loved that Carol was the designated navigator, co-pilot and map reader. Often she would say, "Slow down, watch that truck, did you see that blue heron? Look, there are the elk."

Part of the fun was her fantastic memory of the highway directions, back roads and locations of wheel-chair accessible rest stops or restaurants. We kept track of our stops in a spiral notebook with Tinkerbell on the cover, stored in our glove compartment: was the floor level? Any bumps or ridges she would have to drive over? Was there room for Carol to maneuver her wheelchair inside? Is the bathroom stall large enough and with a grab bar on the right hand side? At each stop, Carol waited patiently in the van while I scoped this all out. A few times, we had to move on and try again.

One bathroom stuck in our minds forever: at the North Rim of the Grand Canyon was a 150-square-foot National Park bathroom. It was one room, no door inside, with just a raised commode and a sink. It was perfect!

"This is the best bathroom ever!" Carol shouted. It was a five-star bathroom!

Unpredictable situations could pile up fast. Once when I was gassing up the van, a man approached Carol's open window and startled her.

"Joanie!" she called with a frightened tone.

I skedaddled around the car, where a transient was standing at her window. "Hey, sir, what's up?"

He left. After that, we only opened her window a fourth of the way when we stopped. A safety habit, not a nun habit. That was a joke.

Our Freedom Trip started by trekking to Southern California, where our experiences in Oceanside nudged us closer to seeking a sacramental marriage.

We spent seven glorious, warm nights in Oceanside, California, with the sounds of the surf, the smells of salt water, the sights of the waving palm tree branches, and the warm sun gently kissing our faces, making my freckles say, "Hi, World."

On the agenda was a huge family reunion with all of our family, hers and mine, combined for the first time. Yippee! So awesome was the anticipation. My sisters, Terri and Gail, had sent emails and texts announcing, "Carol and Joanie are coming to town. Let's celebrate!" This was the family bugle call.

When we arrived, our relatives sounded like the TV commercial, announcing, "Aunts Joanie and Carol are here!!" Haha.

That September day we had sunshine, blue skies, toasty warm temps and a little breeze. Ages ranged from two years young Lyndi up to Carol at 76. It was truly the first time both sides of our families got to know each other, a "one big family" event! Nephew Dusty and grandnephew Byron flew in from New York. Niece Carrie flew in from California's Bay Area and stayed with her brother Will with us in our three bedroom condo overlooking the pools, tennis courts, kids toys and the distant Pacific Ocean.

Chef Carrie spoiled us for days with her home cooking and masterfully created lasagna Bolognese that we froze for our continued trip to Arizona.

We celebrated more by sharing a huge sheet cake decorated with "Congratulations Family," flags and people's names for that year's celebration events: birthdays, milestones and achievements. It was ingenious how Gail honored so many people on one cake. Thank you, Sis! We played ping pong, pickleball and basketball, and swam in the kiddy pool and jumped in the five-foot-deep big pool. We talked endlessly, enjoying quality time together.

"I really do belong to a family," declared one niece.

I think many, including myself, were thinking how great it was to belong to such a fun loving group of old farts.

Heads nodded, smiles flashed on cell phone snapshots and we thoroughly enjoyed getting to know one another. It had been several years since our families had been able to be together. Our families were growing. When Carol and Joanie came to town, all clans united in harmony.

Carol wore her multi-colored dress and it matched her lime green powered chair. I wore my mint-colored shorts with my deep purple top. We felt like matriarchs of a dynasty. For the family photos, everyone had an arm or hand on someone's shoulder or leg. Cool! How fun! Love is the best; it's never hateful.

One teenage family member said to me, "Where's the flag for your and Carol's wedding? Aren't we celebrating that?"

"Ohhh, thanks, sweetie," I replied, "but we're not officially married. We have a domestic partnership."

"Oh, I thought you were married!" she exclaimed with a big smile.

"Someday," I responded. "We keep holding out for a Catholic Church marriage."

The Freedom Trip Continues

We never knew what we would run into on our road trips. Oh boy, the sunny day when the huge Roosevelt elk herd was eating the grass at the Highway 101 off ramp near the Prairie Creek State Park.

As we pulled off, lo and behold the big daddy elk, about 800 pounds with six-foot wide antlers with sharp points began approaching our van. As he walked closer to Carol's window, she talked gently to him—until he was too close. My eyes were getting ready to pop out of my face as I imagined those antlers breaking her window and denting our van.

"Joanie, drive away," Carol said with a higher pitch. "He's taller than our van. So beautiful and so BIG."

"I think we disturbed him." I hastily drove away. More laughs and more memories.

The Joy of Clothes

One of Carol's greatest joys was sliding open her glass closet doors, smiling and selecting her outfit from her marvelous fashion choices—sometimes changing three times each day.

Her stroke changed that; now I helped her dress in the morning, as she could not pull anything over her head or put on her socks or shoes. Her outfit had to last for the whole day, especially when we traveled. Hats were special because she could select one and put it on herself.

"Looking good, sweetie. You look so darn cute in a hat!"

Thinking of each other's needs first enhanced our excursions. It was really special that we expressed this in our own ways. "Selfless" was best described as when I held a door open for her, did her laundry and home care. While traveling, Carol often ordered me a drink and an appetizer while I went to the restaurant's restroom, then we raised our drinks to toast.

"To you, oh special one." That was my secret code name from Carol.

Solvang, California

Our next overnight, in a special needs room, was in Solvang, California. A policeman in his SUV saw us that evening in the street, not on the sidewalk, because it was too dark for Carol to see.

"Are you two up to something tonight?" he asked.

"YES, we are," Carol said. "It's too dark on the sidewalk so we are cruising Solvang streets tonight."

"I'd love to do the honor of lighting your way, Miss." This gentleman officer, using his high-beam lights, escorted us four blocks back to our condo. How fun was that! Our special needs room was spacious and delightful with a roll-in shower. We called it Spa Night. Romance in Solvang!

Yuma, One Stop Before Tucson!

With a sandy desert, warm winds and desolation, Yuma reminded me of the old cowboy movies, where people and snakes moved slowly.

A simple hotel, clean and thanks be to God, had a restaurant directly across the parking lot. That meant Carol did not have to maneuver into and out of the van in her powered chair, which we called "her other legs."

We entered the restaurant through two big doors that the staff opened for us. We thought we were stepping into Mexico itself. The tantalizing food smells, lively music and vibrant colors spoke to us of adventure! Yahoo! We were graciously welcomed and seated.

Sitting across from us were two young men and an older man who lit up our "gay-dar"—the intuitive spark that recognized other gay people's spirits. Carol and I flashed big smiles and said hi. We had fun watching and somewhat listening to the couple with the older man. Of course, they were eyeing us, too. Isn't that the LGBTQ way? Always looking out for one another, in curiosity, safety and delight.

We felt them watching us, noticing Carol's protective cloth on her chest to catch food (we never called it a bib) held in place with a clip and covering her dress. We thanked God that her dominant hand was still fully functional. Her gusto for life, going on this trip and today out to eat was a treat! We didn't take anything for granted after her stroke.

Thank you, God!

We didn't care what others thought about us, but we recognized that we stood out. We wanted to be noticed for our beauty and joy, not because of a disability or being gay. We flashed smiles and had naturally energized voices, which projected our happiness. We loved chatting with people: "How are you doing?" or "How's your day going?" or "Where did you two meet?" These questions with our positive attitude helped servers, hostesses and new acquaintances relax and enjoy the moment.

Our stomachs were growling! We split a fabulous, platter-sized chili relleno dripping with cheese and sauce. Sizzling fajitas arrived with marinated meats, carne asada, shrimp and veggies on a 16-inch dish. The homemade taco shell was crisp.

We shared a margarita with crushed ice, salted rim and two lime green straws. Carol had to bend over to drink, and she always came up smiling. We freely dove into each other's plates with our forks, and we were in food heaven, topping off our meal with flan, a Mexican dessert.

We asked for a to-go menu as a souvenir and for Carol to enjoy looking at later. Our glove compartment was loaded with to-go menus, which we placed in a our brightly decorated container in the living room. We'd circle what we ate and mark if we would return there. Looking at them, we remembered the good times and salivated in dream land. How fun!

Then we began our nightly routine. Everything took longer helping Carol, a differently-abled, mobility-impaired person. Carol wore Depends (not diapers), which I helped her change. The good thing was she still enjoyed doing her skin care, brushing her teeth and brushing her soft, shiny hair by herself.

"Tuk-son" Javelina

We arrived on the luscious desert grounds of Worldmark Wyndham Tucson Rancho Vistoso, and I skipped to the front desk to check in. The kind resort team agreed to help us unload the van. Yippee.

We drove to our building, gawking at flowering cactus, shrubs, saguaros, sand and blue sky. Carol announced that it was time for her to use the restroom, so I quickly scouted the three-bedroom condo to determine that the best bathroom for her would be the one next to our master bedroom.

Together we entered and she transferred to the commode. I stood at the sink, unwrapped the soap for washing our hands and got the towel ready.

"Watch out for that CAT!" Carol exclaimed.

I looked down. It was about six inches from me. But it wasn't a cat!

I screamed and chased this huge thing into the living room.

Five more of these animals were there!

Shocked, I tried to identify this creature: 80 to 100 pounds, with coarse dark hair and white tusks. I chased them from one bedroom to the next, trying to make them leave through the sliding glass door. They had entered through three outside doors left open by the condo helpers.

"Get out of here!" I commanded in my PE teacher coaching voice, stomping and waving my arms. "Get out of here! Get out of here!"

"Joanie, take a picture! Call the office!"

"Not yet," I yelled.

Two of these short-legged, weird-nozzled animals were smashing their faces into the glass sliding door. Snot and slobber dripped down the glass. I thought these creatures were deaf and blind because it seemed they could not hear me or see the glass.

Finally, I got within a foot of them to guide them out the door.

OHH OHH, relief! After 10 minutes of crazy mayhem, they were all outside. Carol was waiting patiently on the potty. Haha.

I found my phone, snapped a picture as the animals walked by the pool fence and I called the office. In a hyper tone, I told them what happened.

"Did they attack you?" they asked.

"What? No! I think they were afraid of me! I sure was afraid of them."

Someone knocked on the door, but I checked on Carol first. I was laughing hysterically while calm and patient Carol sat like a queen on a throne, wondering what was happening.

The four maintenance staff used their pass key to hurry in and check on us.

Standing in the bathroom doorway, I said, "What were those things?"

"Wild javelinas," they said. "Wild boar pigs."

"Oh, they were really scary looking!"

"You're lucky they didn't attack you," the staff said.

"That was quite the Tucson welcome party," Carol said.

I told them I had to go help Carol. As I entered the bathroom, she said, "I've never heard you yell that loud before, Joanie. Are you OK?"

"I think so, my heart is still pounding." We laughed. What a hoot. Or what a snort! Wowie!!

Thanks be to God for keeping us safe, entertained and blessed with all good things. Years later, Carol and I still laughed and retold this startling story.

Our Trip Inspires the Urgent Need to Wed

On that long and beautiful road trip, Carol and I had a few short and sweet conversations about getting married. We both felt that we were married. We had always gone by our own first, middle and last names and would keep it that way when we married. We, as a couple, had been so loved by our family and friends for decades. They already looked and treated us as a married couple. There was just one missing component: the Catholic Church's sanctification. We decided that when we got home from our 3,500 mile road trip, we'd make some calls to our Catholic Church friends and priests.

Something just clicked that we needed to officially marry! We needed it to be OUR sacrament, for the three of us—Jesus, Carol and Joanie—JCJ. Carol and I were delighted to move forward in this quest and we had two holy men, our friends, whom we wanted to do the honors of marrying us. We had both their cell phone numbers.

Will You Marry Us?

We made a late-morning call to an ordained person in our Catholic circle whom we'd known for a very long time. "We've decided to get married and we were hoping you would do us the honor?"

He sounded positive, yet apprehensive. "Umm, let me get back to you after checking with my superiors."

"OK, sounds good."

We waited two months. No return call. No return communication. Very strange.

"Carol, why hasn't there been communication with __________?"

"I don't know, Joanie."

So, we called him again. "Hi, Carol and Joanie here. We have you on speaker phone."

He said, "I apologize. Oh, I guess I forgot to get back to you?"

Forgot to get back to us?

"It is very important to us to get married. What did you find out?"

"No," he said, "I can't marry you because it is against Catholic teaching. I would lose my ordination over it."

"Oh, that's a bummer! OK. Carol and I disagree with this, but we understand what you're saying. Bye."

"Bye."

"Joanie, call________ [another ordained person]."

"OK, great idea. He'd be so fantastic!"

"Hi ________. Joanie and Carol here. How are you?"

"Hi. Good to hear your voices."

"The reason we're calling is that we want to get married in the Catholic Church. Would you marry us?"

"Oh, Joanie and Carol, I'd love to! But I cannot with the way things are. I would lose my faculties. Oh, I am so sorry. I wish things were different. I would really be honored to marry you two, but I can't."

"Ah, you are so sweet. Thank you and that meant the world to us to hear what you just said. We don't want you to lose the great work that you currently do."

Carol's voice cracked with disappointment as she said: "I guess in time, just not ours, Thanks. Bye ________."

"Stay in touch, OK?"

"We will."

"Love you."

"Love you two, too."

We Believe

We were both so down from these two phone calls. We knew the rejection wasn't personal, but it felt personal. It was bigger than personal. In our minds and hearts, it was systemic institutional wrongdoing. Together, Carol and I had served the Catholic Church and its people with our heart and soul for more than 100 years combined. We loved God and each other with our whole being.

Forgiveness is an amazing act. In fact, Carol always said, "Reconciliation was the most important sacrament."

"Carol, you know what sweetie? I forgive the Catholic leadership for being so unloving. I feel for these two great men. They know you and me, yet their hands are tied. That's a shame. I truly forgive the church."

Carol peacefully said, "You've heard me say it before that it is 'from within that demise happens.'"

"Yes, I get it."

Carol and I quickly determined that neither these two people nor the church were going to destroy us and our path of love. *Love conquers all. God is love. God's timing will come.*

Next Option

"Carol," I said. "How about Father Bernie from St. Timothy's Episcopal Church? He's been a dear, Good Samaritan Care Center minister with you and me. He's been a prayer friend for eight years or more."

"YES! Go for it, Joanie. Call him!" She was all smiles and my heart was beating with high hopes.

"Hi Bernie, Joanie and Carol here. How are you doing today?"

"Hi, Carol and Joanie, doing great. Working on my homily for the week. What's up? Everything OK with Carol?"

"I'm great!" said Carol.

"Good to hear, Carol. What can I do for you two lovely ladies?"

"Bernie, would you marry Carol and me?" I asked enthusiastically.

"Absolutely. Yes! I'd love to. How about Wednesday? This coming Wednesday?"

"Perfect, you are the best, Bernie!" Carol said. "Thank you, thank you, thank you! It's a sacramental marriage, correct?"

"Yes, of course! You, God and all of us!"

"Will 2 p.m. be good? Paige, my wife, will come with me."

"Fantastic. Yes, at our house."

"Do you have rings?"

"Yes, we are wearing them."

He said, "You've just increased my odds for lasting marriages, making it three out of four for gay marriages that I've celebrated! Thank you for asking me, Carol and Joanie."

"We are so happy you said yes!" I exclaimed.

"Thanks Bernie," proclaimed Carol. "Oh, we have a song, Bernie. 'I Feel You Everywhere.' Do you know it?"

"No, I don't know that one. I'm sure it will be wonderful!"

"OK. Bye, thanks again!"

"Bye, you two. See you Wednesday for your big day!"

Carol burst into song and I added more; we danced, hugged, and kissed, and I cried. Carol was one big smile, looking radiantly happy. Excitement popped inside me like a bag of popcorn in the microwave. *ALLELUIA, ALLELUIA. I've got that JOY, JOY, JOY down in my heart!*

"Our marriage will be a sacrament, Joanie! I love you so much. God did this!"

"Yes! For sure! I love you more, Carol, sweetie!"

Our 39-year wait was over and the blessing of God's love through the Episcopal Church was His way. Who could have imagined that?

Nun Better than the Holy Spirit!

Marriage License

Carol and I booked an afternoon appointment at the Gold Beach courthouse to get the marriage license paperwork. We smiled as I parked curbside.

"Back in a bit, sweetie," I said, plopping my N95 mask on my face to protect us from COVID. I skipped into the old building, noticing an outdoor handicap accessible elevator sign.

Oh golly, that handicap entrance looked really small.

I dashed up 10 steps. With delight in my heart, I entered the room, where several worker bees were behind a long counter.

I announced, "Good day everyone. I'm Joanie and we spoke with Renee this morning about getting our marriage license. Carol is outside in the van in her powered chair. What do we need to do?"

Renee popped out of a nearby office. I shared about this momentous occasion, that Father Bernie would be officiating our marriage, and that it would be a sacrament and legally official. After 39 years, it was time.

The kind, efficient man got the necessary paperwork and a friendly lady was politely asking questions regarding Carol's mobility. I paid a $50 fee with my tie-dye debit card. Renee approved the lady to walk outside with me with a brown clipboard, pen and license document for Carol to sign. In the sunshine at the curb, the van passenger door opened and the lady greeted Carol with a big smile. Papers were signed and she said, "Congratulations! Have fun on your wedding day."

We thanked her for going out of her way to make this happen.

She said, "This is our first time doing it this way. It's my pleasure!" I followed her inside and gave me the signed marriage license and explained where Father Bernie and our two witnesses would sign. "Return it by mail or bring it in person after the wedding."

"Okey dokey!"

We were ecstatic! I showed Carol our signatures on the document and she said, "Joanie, let's go to the Port Hole Cafe for fish-n-chips and celebrate!"

"Great idea, Carol. Let's get you buckled in."

During the five-minute drive, I touched her arm and we held hands at a red light. We were happy! We sat by a sunny window in the Gold Beach restaurant, watching boats, seagulls and pelicans. Seated nearby was a widowed friend with her new husband; they congratulated us and asked to share the great news with their son, Michael.

Wow! Finally, our love will be official for the world to know and see. I guess we are your messengers and witnesses. How good you are, God.

We enjoyed our food, giggling like teenagers because everything seemed silly and wonderful. We devoured the fresh fish and onion rings while smiling at each other. Our eyes were on fire; our hearts burning with passion and I started to cry.

"Oh, Joanie!"

"Yep, sweetie."

"Your food is going to get soggy." We laughed.

That's everlasting love.

Hopefully, the next gay Catholic couple won't have to wait 39 years. Driving home along the Oregon coast, we started planning the details of our wedding day: August 5, 2020.

"That's your favorite number, Joanie, the number 5!"

"Oh yeah, it is!" I said. "Cool! It is Jesus, Carol, and Joanie Day! The best! Carol, where would you like to go eat and celebrate after our marriage ceremony?"

With COVID, it was safer to be outside, so we called Zola's On The Water, which was happy to serve us on their patio overlooking the fishing dock and harbor. We pre-ordered food from the dinner menu for our party of seven. Our dear friend Marilynn, the best pie maker ever, agreed to bake us two pies. Yippee! Doris was super excited for us and thrilled to pick up balloons and decorate the tables while we were at the ceremony.

Because of COVID, we kept our celebration small and intimate in our home. Sara and Tim were honored to be our witnesses. We texted and called family and friends to announce the wedding, ask for their prayers and thank them for being in our lives.

We insisted: "No gifts please; your love is the best gift of all. Please spread the word: it's a big, big thing that we are finally getting married, a sacrament by the Episcopal Church."

Our Wedding Day: August 5th, 2020

Carol and I were awake, lying in bed, my arms engulfing her body. She grabbed my hand and held it gently but with extra gusto this day as she lay on her right side. I kissed her shoulder a bunch of times. She squirmed with delight.

"Good morning, Joanie."

"Good morning, my lover dover. How'd you sleep?"

"Like a rock," she giggled, our pat answer from a song.

I asked, "Are you good?" (Meaning does she have urgent needs or not.)

"I'm good. You go first."

"Back in a bit."

I turned the blinds to see daylight. *Oh boy, it's a foggy day.* I used the restroom, smiled at myself in the mirror, brushed my blonde-silver hair, and put on soothing skin care. I entered the second bedroom where my clothes are and slid into a pair of shorts, polo shirt and my blue and white Air Monarch leather tennis shoes.

Then I went to greet my Carol, carrying her walker. She was patiently waiting for me, playing Neil Diamond on Alexa. I so admired Carol, her spunk and tenacity.

"You have to be courageous to get older," she said.

I gleamed with smiles. "Are you ready to get up?" Opening her mirrored closet door, I removed her bright yellow, orange, pink, purple, teal and green flowered dress with her teal jacket. "Still thinking this is your wedding outfit, love?"

"Yes, it is."

"OK, what color bra, yellow or white?" I asked.

"Yellow."

"Got it." I hung them on her armoire and closed the mirrored doors. What color socks? Bright pink? Yes, bright pink. Sandals? Multicolored? Yes, plaid sandals. And so it went.

Our Morning Routine

First in our routine was to loosen the sides of her Depends. Then socks and sandals went on her feet while she grabbed the bed rail. I slid the blue hospital pad and together we pulled her to a sitting position on the side of the bed where the walker was stationed. In methodical, slow moves, she used her strong right side and I assisted with the left side so she was standing and balanced holding the walker with both hands. I removed her soiled Depends, and she was ready to step and pivot to the commode.

"Perfect, sweetie, well done!"

She/we resumed dressing while she balanced on the commode, helping as much as she could. We took our time, about 20 minutes.

"Fabulous outfit that makes your eyes pop!" I said. She stood with the walker, looking sharp today. I moved the commode out of the way, quickly and efficiently. I put the black manual wheelchair behind her while she reached for the purple washcloths that covered the arm rests. She squatted, then sat up tall and proud! All done quickly and safely.

"Are your feet up?" I asked.

"Yes."

I steered Carol in her chair, backing through the tight hallway corner and into the bright orange kitchen with the pinkish red tablecloth on the round table. Carol glanced out the kitchen window, noticing the fog circling around the yard of wildflowers.

"It's a brand new day," I began.

"Never been lived before," she continued our morning mantra of happiness.

When Carol was perfectly positioned at the table, we shared a quick kiss, and I placed a red cloth over her chest. Thanks to her physical therapy and vast improvements with her left hand, she groomed her face in a high-powered mirror and wiped her soft Egyptian skin with a warm washcloth that I provided. Her once totally paralyzed left side arm, hand and fingers now enabled her to apply facial skin products. Her left fingers were floppy and bent as if lacking ligaments or tendons. I loved to touch and sooth her soft hands and she enjoyed that, too.

"Looking good," I said.

She smiled and said, "So do you." I laughed and said thanks.

Then I entered chore mode: making the king bed with the purple bamboo sheets and her hospital blue pad, tidying the room and laying the patchwork quilt from the Idaho nuns on top. I emptied and cleaned the commode and moved her walker into the living room near the next commode, a larger seated white one from Lincare that she used after breakfast.

I then threw her nightgown and bed pad into the washing machine. Almost every day I ran the washing machine to keep the house from smelling like a care facility and to see Carol's face light up with the use of soft, clean towels, bibs, wash cloths, etc. It reminded me of my siblings as they raised their young children.

The scripture booklet was on the table. "How about I read it out loud," Carol proudly announced.

"Great." I sat and listened to her proclaim the first reading and psalm. "Wonderful, sweetie. Thanks for reading today. It's a holy day, huh?"

"Yes," she replied, "Our day." She puckered her lips in an air kiss, making a loud smack. I jumped to catch the kiss and received it with my puckered up lips. We smiled and she laughed at me, with me.

"I want to read the gospel to myself," she said.

"OK, I'll do that too, after you. Yogurt or smoothie today, Carol?"

"Yogurt, please."

"Blueberry or peach?" I asked.

"Peach."

"I'll have the berry. Here's your water for your pills and vitamins."

This was our morning routine, give or take, for the past six years since her brain bleed stroke. Each day was a great day!

Wedding Day Surprises

The doorbell rang.

"Who's there?" she yelled excitedly.

I dashed through the kitchen and green-carpeted living room, where I'd already opened the curtains to see the morning fog. I opened the front door festooned with a Flora Pacifica dried cranberry wreath.

A large box sat inside our screened porch.

"Look, Carol, from our sister and her family." I carried it into the kitchen.

"Chocolate covered strawberries!" she exclaimed. "Wow! Wowie! So nice!"

How exciting and it's not even 9:30 in the morning. Oh golly, we are so loved.

The fog rolled in thicker and it was really chilly outside, even though the hydrangeas and gladiolas were showing off their purples, yellows and blues. The small birds, juncos and sparrows, were swooshing up the feeder and circling the house in rhythmic form. It was amazing—a complete fast-circle race around the house and back to a feeder. First come, first served: bird etiquette.

Carol ate her yogurt while gazing at the box of chocolate-covered treats. Yes, we each indulged in one delicious chocolate-covered strawberry after reading that the strawberries spelled out CONGRATULATIONS. So cute! Yummy, yummy, as the fresh ripe berry juice dribbled onto our hands and we licked the chocolate from our fingertips.

"Very berry delicious," Carol said with a smile. "Thanks, Gail and family."

Using her colorful, child-sized toothbrush with a large grip for better control, she brushed her teeth at the kitchen table and spat into the container that I placed in front of her, along with her small Coca-Cola water glass with a neon green flex straw. She took her time to not spill a drop on her pretty dress. Yahoo! "See, look ma, no cavities," she said, shining her pearly whites.

"How fun you are, Carol! I love you!"

The doorbell rang again. Carol was flabbergasted! This time the local florist shop delivered a gorgeous bouquet of colorful daisies, carnations and other fresh flowers. This thoughtful gift was from Terri and her family.

"Look at all of the colors, Joanie!"

From the book, *The Five Love Languages*, Gail and Terri knew that "gifts" were Carol's primary love language. Carol loved every minute of it, from the doorbell ring to the opening of the cardboard boxes, to adding the flower powder to the vase. Suspense and delight were prisms in our house today and every day.

Carol's CSJ sister in Tucson called. They chatted with laughter and excited voices. Meanwhile, I cleaned up the bathroom and kitchen for our guests who would arrive in a few hours. More phone calls and text beeps brought more joyful wishes for a beautiful day. The Disneyland Main Street electrical parade song played in my mind and Carol enjoyed Alexa favorites, including Susan Boyle's dream song going nonstop. Carol absolutely loved watching *America's Got Talent* performances.

Friends, Sisters of St. Joseph, and blood family were telling us:

"It's about time."

"So happy for both of you."

"I thought you were already married."

"This makes me happy."

"Glad you are celebrating in the middle of COVID."

"Your marriage is such a blessing."

"You're the first family member to not get pregnant before you marry."

I really belted out a laugh with that one!

Carol used her commode and transferred to her powered chair. She had freedom to drive in the living room and kitchen; she sometimes aimed for the windows to watch the birds, trees and flowers. She then settled in her designated corner spot with a view of everything: nautical artwork, Alaskan work by artist Barbara Lavalle, the original sculptured wooden salmon and orca, family mementos of painted rocks, an abalone shell the size of a dinner plate, and the take-out menus holder shaped like beach flip flops and hamburgers in bright yellow, orange, green and pink that belonged to her sister Elaine. She could see the TV, the table, the front door and the kitchen entrance.

"Would you like a warm blanket on you?" I asked.

"Yes, please, and help me wrap my shawl around me, too."

"OK. How's that?"

"Wonderful!"

I dressed in my wedding attire of Capri pants with bright, large flowers of reds, pinks, greens, blues and yellows and my soft pink short-sleeve sweater. I had on gray flat leather sandals showing off my magenta toe nail polish. I proudly wore my pearl necklace from Carol's sister Elaine, rest in peace. I felt GREAT. I looked good, too!

On my left ring finger was our wedding ring from years ago; it was my mother's gold wedding ring with a few small diamonds on the side, centered by the emerald stone that Carol bought for me. Carol wore her sterling silver necklace with the sun and moon ball that I bought at the San Diego Pride Parade festival 39 years ago. On her right hand, due to the stroke, she proudly wore her gorgeous gold custom-made amethyst ring I had purchased for her.

She was decked out with two fun and snazzy bracelets on the same wrist: one was blingy, shiny black and gold and the other one was silver with dangling beach charms. She looked AWESOME and exuded SUPER HAPPINESS.

Tim arrived first, in the foggy wet drizzle. He was as happy as a wild trout! Tim is our outdoor river fishing fanatic. "Hi Carol. It's your day today!" he said as he approached her with a smile and kissed on her forehead.

"It sure is, Tim," Carol said. He wore a long-sleeve shirt, cuffed three quarters length, and a bold colorful tie. He looked spiffy and great with his short darkish curly hair and goatee.

"I think we'll have the ceremony in our living room," I said.

"Good thinking, Joanie."

Sara, Carol's sister, wore a nice, tight-fitting black and white dress with high heels. She was dressed to the hilt for this big occasion. She was all in! How fun! She looked stunning.

Father Bernie wore his light blue shirt and priestly white collar and his wife, Paige, sported a colorful skirt and jacket. They entered our home carrying a Bible, a folder and a gift bag. Both greeted us with smiles and loving eyes with masks on . . . No hugs because of COVID carefulness.

Let the Ceremony Begin

The ceremony began. Carol sat in her powered chair while I was in a chair to her right. The three-foot-tall angel metal sculpture created by Hobart Brown was behind us. We were in the middle of the living room where there was sunshine from people, not the skies. Keeping our social distance due to COVID, Paige sat at the dining room table, near the buffet table that came from Carol's parents' house. Tim sat four feet from us in the plaid chair with large wooden armrests. Sara and Father Bernie sat at opposite ends of the long leather couch.

Father Bernie began with, "Blessed be God, Father, Son and Holy Spirit. Blessed be God, now and forever. Amen."

Then he said, "Dearly beloved, in the name of God and the Church, we have come together today with Joanie and Carol to witness the sacred vows they make this day as they are married and reaffirm their commitment to one another. Forsaking all others, they will renew their covenant of mutual fidelity and steadfast love, remaining true to one another in heart, body, mind as long as they both shall live.

"Let us pray that God will give them the strength and for the wisdom to see God at work in their life together."

For the entire ceremony, about 30 minutes, Carol and I held hands, basked in a spirit of living in wonder, thankfulness bursting with fire from our twinkling eyes, expanding our gargantuan smiles, pure and divine.

The Scripture readings were about God's faithfulness in Ruth and Paul to the Corinthians . . . how faith hope and love abide . . . and his everlasting covenant and Jesus' humanity and divinity as taught to his disciples. Father Bernie read The Beatitudes from the Gospel of Matthew.

Then Father Bernie asked, "Carol, do you freely and unreservedly offer yourself to Joanie?"

"I DO!" Carol responded.

Then he turned to me and asked, "Joanie, do you freely and unreservedly offer yourself to Carol?"

And I answered, "I DO!"

Then Father Bernie said, "I invite you now, illumined by the word of God and strengthened by the prayer of this community, to make your covenant before God and the church."

Father Bernie recited each of the following lines, and Carol repeated them to me while looking in my eyes: "In the name of God, I, Carol, give myself to you, Joanie. I will support and care for you by the grace of God—in times of sickness, in times of health. I will hold and cherish you in the love of Christ—in times of plenty, in times of want. I will honor and love you with the Spirit's help—in times of anguish, in times of joy, forsaking all others as long as we both shall live. This is my solemn vow."

Then Father Bernie recited each of the following lines, and I repeated them to me while looking in Carol's eyes:

"I, Joanie, give myself to you Carol. I will support and care for you by the grace of God—in times of sickness, in times of health. I will hold and cherish you in the love of Christ—in times of plenty, in times of want. I will honor and love you with the Spirit's help—in times of anguish, in times of joy, forsaking all others as long as we both shall live. This is my solemn vow."

Bernie blessed our wedding rings, but first we needed to remove them from our fingers and then put them on each other in a symbolic, never-ending circle of love. From our first "commitment love rings" purchased at JC Penny's jewelry store and now in our living room, our circle of love had expanded beyond our wildest dreams. Our rings, emerald and amethyst, were blessed! We giggled and told Bernie about our first rings in 1987.

He read a blessing prayer and asked Tim and Sara, as witnesses, to commit to protecting us, sanctifying our love, honoring and being accountable to both of us. They said, "I do." This was very moving. We both loved this involvement and commitment on their part. Sara and Tim took beautiful pictures throughout the ceremony.

Father Bernie concluded the wedding by saying, "Now that Carol and Joanie have exchanged vows of love and fidelity in the presence of God and the Church, I pronounce that they are married and bound to one another as long as they both shall live. Amen."

We were overjoyed.

"Please greet the happy couple," Father Bernie said.

We were so peaceful! The sacramental marriage vows of our everlasting love had been sanctified. We committed with our entire heart and souls our unity and oneness that we had lived for in the past 39 years. I felt like I was speaking in front of thousands of people proclaiming the greatness of God and the acceptance of Carol as His precious gift, loaned only to me. This was my solemn vow. Our living room was holding the world of true lovers and loves. With her calm, holy, peaceful demeanor, Carol's green eyes looked into my watery, exuberant, tear-filled eyes as she gave herself to me in promise, word and prayer. This was her solemn vow.

Till death do us part.

We are a sacrament!

Next, I jumped up and entered the kitchen. We had pre-set the compact disc on our 30-year-old BiMart stereo and I pushed the play button for our wedding song. Turning the volume up, the music and lyrics of *I Feel You Everywhere* blasted into the universe as Carol and I joyfully sang every word. The four of them sat in amazement, staring at us as if we were on stage in the Hollywood Bowl. We shared with Pastor Bernie that this song was about God singing to each of us, us singing to Him and us singing to each other.

Pastor Bernie said: "I now pronounce you married! This is the time to kiss each other."

YIPPEE!!! ALLELUIA!

We already had our lips puckered, locked lips gently and profoundly, in front of what seemed to be the whole world.

Carol took my hand to her face, kissed my hand with many smooches.

I stood up, squatted in front of her seated in her powered chair and tightly wrapped my two arms around her shoulders and chest, engulfing our bodies and our faces, cheek to cheek.

Carol and I shared another long, gentle lip kiss as a married couple. How wonderful. How profound! Absolutely Holy and blessed. We hugged tightly again and smiled to the moon and beyond. We were immediately swarmed with affection and hugged by Tim, Sara, Bernie and Paige.

Laughter, joy, peace—the years of waiting were over.

The Episcopal Church and The God of Love prevailed.

Tim and Sara glided to the dining room table to sign, as witnesses, the official marriage license document.

What an AMAZING love story! Carol and I, quiet and still, watched them add their approval to our story. We tenderly held hands, fingers interlocked, her in her powered chair and I by her side. This was a blessed moment filled with internal and eternal happiness!

Bernie presented us with the sacrament of marriage document. "YES!" we said chorally in unison. Giggles erupted from all of them. What an incredible ceremony.

God's plan all along. Thank you, Jesus. One Spirit, many churches.

I didn't realize until days later when they brought us the photo prints that I was tearfully happy as we pledged our everlasting love. An emotional joyous long-awaited celebration.

Our marriage celebration continued with fabulous fun, food, and delightful companionship at Zola's Restaurant. Doris had three connected tables decorated with white linen cloths borrowed from St. Tim's Church, fun kazoos and colorful confetti. It was a combination of a kid's birthday party and a royal wedding. She outdid herself!

We pigged out on three kinds of shrimp, fresh Greek salads, pizza, meatball sandwiches, decadent chocolate desserts and Marilynn's fresh-baked apple pie.

We took turns making a toast, raising a glass of soda, water, coffee or cocktail with words of fun and wisdom. We laughed, told stories, and enjoyed a wedding fest with everyone sitting at the head table—the only table. It was a communion of saints.

Jesus hold you.
God bless you.

CHAPTER 20
"In Sickness and in Health"

One morning during our regular routine on June 28, 2021, Carol lost her balance while attempting to pivot to the bedside commode with help from me and a walker.

Wearing a black and red nightgown, she collapsed, falling fast. All her body weight struck the medical equipment. Her walker smashed into the porta-potty and her body was mangled between the bed, the walker and the commode.

She screamed.

I was beside her, but could not stop this ugly accident.

I grabbed the walker to prevent it from crashing into her head. I eased her butt to the floor and leaned her against the bed frame. She was shocked. We were stunned by how fast this happened.

I quickly moved the commode to the other bedroom so her legs would not be twisted, and took the walker to the kitchen, snatching my cell phone from the table.

She was amazingly calm and said, "I'm so sorry, Joanie."

"It's OK, sweetie. You'll be fine. Let me call. We need the paramedics now. Are you hurting anywhere?"

"No."

"OK. That's good. Let me see."

While pushing 911 on speaker phone, I saw a puddle of blood on the carpet. Blood gushed like a faucet from an eight-inch gouge with gaping skin and muscles beside her shin bone. Her leg must have hit the bolt on the bottom wheel of the walker.

"Carol, you split your leg open. I need to get clean towels from the hallway closet to put pressure on it. I'll be right back."

"911, what is your emergency?"

"My spouse, Carol, just fell and split her leg open. We need to get her to the ER."

"What is her name, your name, your address?" The operator asked. "The paramedics are on their way."

I laid her more flat onto the floor, with a pillow under her head and a red plaid comforter over her.

"Are you more comfortable, Carol?"

"Yes, I'm fine!" Frustration tinged her voice.

No blood was coming through the towel, thank God. "You are doing perfect, sweetie. Help is on the way."

I told the 911 operator, "Thank you, the porch light will be on."

We had made several calls to 911 in the past years, so we were actually pretty calm.

"One thing at a time, right?" I asked Carol.

"Right," she answered with a ton of more frustration in her voice.

"It will be OK. Breathe in, breathe out, together, let's breathe in and out. Good, believe. Say Jesus' name as you breathe, sweetie."

I sat with her on the floor and giggled.

"What?"

"You always do things in a big way!" I said.

Giggles . . . "YES, I DO!"

The local staff knew of us and arrived within 10 minutes with their "bag of goodies" as Carol and I called it.

"Good morning, Carol," a paramedic said. "What did you do? Are you in pain?" And the 20 questions began, "What day is it?"

"I don't know," she smiled and looked at me and said, "It's a brand new day."

I responded with, "Never been lived before."

Her wit surprised the paramedics and me.

They smiled. "Where are you?"

"I'm home. In Brookings."

"What year is this?"

"What do you think?! It's 2021."

She is sharp and her feisty self. Thank God!

Long story short, they gave her the entire full-body, head-to-toe look-over, checked her vitals and bandaged her leg. She was following their directions and I watched, wondering, "How bad is this?"

Then the tricky part: getting Carol up into the manual wheelchair, rolling it into the kitchen and getting her onto the gurney. It took three of us to lift her with a sheet and get her into the manual chair. The bedroom/hallway corner was a very tight maneuver to back her out into the spacious kitchen, and then on to the gurney. It was about 8 a.m.

All done. Carol had a free ride thanks to CAL-ORE membership and medical insurance. The ambulance lights flashed with no siren.

"I love you," I said with a lip kiss. "See you up at the Brookings ER on 5th Street. I'll follow you with our van."

I figured I'd better load a few things and her powered chair for her return home.

Carol was in the ER and the nurse gave her a shot. The doctor was sitting on his round chair with wheels to scoot around when another nurse led me in the room to be with Carol.

"Hi, sweetie!"

"Hi, Joanie. They gave me a shot."

"Oh, for what?"

The nurse spoke up, "Two shots: an antibiotic and a shot to numb the leg."

"Sounds good. We don't want you to get an infection," I said. "Thank you for helping Carol. Hi, I'm Joanie, Carol's spouse of 40 years." Carol and I smiled at each other. We had found that things go more smoothly "to say it like it is" when we dealt with medical people.

"Carol, how are you doing?" the doctor asked.

"It doesn't hurt anymore."

The doctor was about halfway done as I calmly watched him, the nurse, and Carol. I held her hand and looked in her eyes with love and confidence.

"You are a super dooper, sweetie. Do you want to close your eyes from the bright lights?"

She did not like bright lights in her face. Never had and never would.

"OK, if you say so."

"Maybe when the doc has finished, we'll turn the light down."

"OK, if you say so."

The leg oozed blood as the doctor used a heavy duty stapler. The nurse was right there mopping up the blood that leaked out from every staple that connected the skin and muscle. Yikes, it looked terrible.

Wow, this is a big injury, and on her good leg. Help us, Lord! How is she going to stand and go to the bathroom?

"All done," said the doc. "You've been very quiet and still, Carol. You're a model patient."

She and I both smiled.

"How many staples did Carol get, doc?"

"Twenty-two staples?" he asked. "Nurse?"

"Twenty-seven!" she said.

"It was deep and you'll need to keep it elevated."

I asked, "Can you make a referral to home health for us?"

"No, you'll have to see your primary doctor."

I told Carol to stay here, I was going to see if Dr. Manuele would do this for us since we were there.

It took about 15 minutes, but I fought through the channels or systems to get the referral. I delivered the ER paperwork to them to expedite the referral to home health.

Today was the beginning chapter of more complex mobility issues and struggles for Carol and me. Her brain bleed stroke in 2014 resulted in her left side paralysis and now her good side, her strong right leg, was wounded.

I prayed triple prayers. Relying on God one more time, surrendering to His ways.

I was so proud of myself that I had brought to the ER a clean Depends (sanitary brief), a clean nightgown and her shoes, along with her power wheelchair.

I asked the nurse if she would help change Carol's Depends. She called for another nurse and with the numb leg, plus all of our help and a walker, we changed her soiled Depends and bloody nightgown.

Thank you, God, for the help. This will give us a few hours before we will deal with the bathroom issue at home.

She stood and pivoted strong and powerful, to sit in her powered chair.

"Yes, I did it!" she exclaimed.

"Yes, you are doing this!"

I am relieved.

She drove up the van ramp, I got her buckled in as co-pilot, and we drove home. She drove her power wheelchair down the ramp, onto her black asphalt pad, and up the wooden ramp to our front door. I latched the screen door open and she went into our home. She headed to the kitchen and positioned herself at the table. "Let's eat something, Joanie."

"OK, great idea. First let's—"

"Oh, yea, let me do my face. Can I have a warm washcloth, please?"

"You bet."

She used the large mirror for her face toner, moisturizer and protection cream. Carol used her left hand and chest to hold the containers and her right hand to twist them open. She was a pro at making things happen. All through her life!

I admired her in so many ways and that was why we both smiled so much! Little things were actually big things. We didn't take anything for granted.

I was glad my blood type is "B+": must be why my attitude is always "Be Positive!"

Life Changes Keep Us Going Strong

Fast forward—Carol slept with pillows under her legs, under her arms and behind her head in her powered chair in the living room every night. No bed. Yucko. But that was what we needed to do for now.

Every morning between 7:30 and 8 a.m., for four years, our angel neighbor Carolyn was a burst of sunshine in helping meet Carol's needs. She had been there at a moment's notice and walked the 30 steps from her yard to ours, entering through the back door, any time I phoned or yelled for her.

"Good morning, Carol. How are you today?"

"Hi, Carolyn."

"How'd you sleep?"

"Like a rock!" Carol said with her singing voice.

"What colorful clothes are you going to wear today?"

"I don't know. Let's see."

The routine was sweet, tender, all good and not rushed. It was all part of the constant care that we shared.

"I'm on my way" were the sweetest words Carolyn spoke on the phone to me for eight solid years. She loved Carol, and me, and vice versa. How blessed we were for each other.

We devised a way to get Carol to the porta-potty and back to her chair, safely and confidently, along with easy ways to dress Carol for the day.

Coastal Home Health was a life-saver by sending an RN, Christie, two or three times a week to check on her leg. Professional and caring, they brought all the required medical supplies.

Carol's physical therapy resumed July 14th, thanks to Mike and DeeDee.

Hygiene care, personal care, and mini "spa days" for bed baths with Kathy Dovey were the best! Kathy was a welcomed soft hug with shoulders I could cry on. She and Carol had private time to talk, too. The Home Health team was our team and had been on and off since 2014. Thank you, God.

We were family. They knew our life, adventures and stories as ex-nuns, gay and in love! They supported us physically, mentally and emotionally!

Love was round like a circle, not a one-sided, dead-end road. It was exhilarating to be loved unconditionally, especially after all the decades that Carol and I poured out love. Now we were the recipients. A huge difference. And much needed.

Carol and I were very humbled with this new way of living. Things were not the same as yesteryears. Carol spoke and showed her terrible, agonized feelings with her loss of independence. She hated it.

"I can't do anything by myself! This stinks! I wish I could die!"

I hated it, too. Carol would never be the same! I released my anger and frustrations by going into the yard to pull weeds and whack at the wild growth.

Carol had to figure out other ways to release her frustrations. Sometimes it came out directed at me, other times in her tears from a book or TV show.

I hated accepting it. Thank goodness pity parties were few and far between. We would say, "Good thing we are not 'down' on the same days."

Yep, we kept each other going!

But it was better than this.

"Joanie, I don't want to be a burden for you!"

"Sweetie, you are never a burden for me. We're in this together, every day and every night. You'd do the same for me, sweetie."

"Yes, I would!"

Carol's mind was better and sharper than mine. Her memory, short and long term, were fantastic. I was on the verge of jealousy, *just kidding.*

She was devouring Sue Grafton, Stewart Woods and other authors' books, sometimes two books a day. She loved phone calls with her cousin Marylou, her nun friends Celia and another sister, Frances and Suzanne, her friends in Idaho, Arizona, Southern California, her family, Will and Carrie and Harley.

I don't know how I did it. I had given her 24/7 care since I retired in July of 2018.

Actually that's not true; I know how I did it. I didn't think about it as work, do this, get this done, etc.

I did it because of LOVE!

Live each day to the max! I love Carol so much and she loves me so much. That's all that matters! The other stuff is just stuff.

We stopped going for rides in the van and going out into the yard. Instead, we told each other "I love you" a gazillion times a day!

We showed our love with touches, hugs, kisses, blow kisses and big smiles. I wore bright clothes and saw miracles in the smallest events. Everything felt new!

We prayed together with The God Minute every morning like clockwork on Alexa or on our cell phone app. We played rummy tiles and Quiddler every day for hours by ourselves. Sometimes Doris, our other happy loving neighbor friend, would join us and bring her homemade cookies.

Honoring Family Members in Heaven

A family gathering to sprinkle cremated ashes in the ocean in Brookings was scheduled for July 3rd. Carol's deceased sisters Elaine and Sara and brother-in-law Bill, who died of COVID, would be remembered with stories and lunch at Zola's restaurant.

Family from Arkansas, Will and Carrie, and from Colorado, Harley, Nicole and Kai, and friends from Oregon and California were here. After tears, laughter and faces white with nausea due to seasickness for a few on the boat, we all left with a touching memory in our hearts.

At home, things were getting rougher, harder; Carol was still sleeping in her chair, not the bed.

Between August 28th and 31st, we had four consecutive days where Carol, Carolyn and I called paramedics for "lift and assist." She lacked the strength to transfer from her powerchair to her porta-potty, so we would ease her to the floor, call 911, and wait for help.

It was heart-wrenching. We all cried. A lot! Me the most: when the flood gates open, I let it flow!

She so wanted and willed to be better and healthier. But no go. God had other plans.

We could not get assistance with a hospital bed at home and we were on a waiting list to get Carol into Curry Good Samaritan Care facility. It was like the world was falling apart every day.

All I could do was pray and make more phone calls.

God, I know you are giving us time to prepare for her last days of life on earth. Hold us closely. I, we trust in your ways but, wow, is this hard. A little letting go each day. OK.

Carol finally was able to be admitted to Curry Good Sam on Sept 9th, nine weeks after the fall that split open her leg. She was trying her hardest with therapy, the flavorless foods, missing me and me missing her. My daily visits just didn't do it. We craved each other immensely.

We tried to keep a stiff upper lip, making her new place a happy place, but deep down, it was lonely for both of us.

COVID restrictions were lessened as we had been vaccinated and boosted. I had to become a volunteer in order for me to go to the dining room to eat with Carol. Every day I brought flavorful, home-cooked food for us to share. It was like an indoor picnic.

I was extremely sad when Carol lost physical strength and was "stuck" in her bed. Her left hand and arm were too weak to hold or balance a book.

I had fought for and monitored her meds, care and treatment. She had lost more than 50 pounds and was sleeping more and more.

Eventually, therapy wasn't working at all; her internal organs were wearing out due to complications from her stroke and loss of mobility. She was unhappy, cried, and, according to the nurses, wailed at night. It was so terrible to see the person I loved the most deteriorating in body and in spirit.

The skin on her hands was beginning to be paper thin, and if I gripped too tightly, she would bruise. Her eyes were lost at times, looking through me and not at me. Her voice was mellow, not feisty or happy. She lay in bed, immobile, not feeling alive. She would tell me, "I don't want to be a burden to you."

"You are never a burden to me. You are the joy of my life." I would hold my tears back until I was in my car alone. These conversations and observations with my love prompted me to find something to give Carol choices, independence and self-empowerment.

I realized that an Alexa Dot could do some physical tasks for her. It was all about giving Carol some dignity and control over her world. She could tell Alexa, "Call Joanie's cell" or "Alexa, play the God Minute." Alexa was waiting for her voice commands to play her favorite Celine Dion and Neil Diamond songs at her selected volume whenever she wanted. Without her bodily controls, balance or strength to hold her Bible, "Living with Christ" readings on The God Minute on Alexa were the best!

Her life was changing and so was mine. Two months had passed and it was now November. We needed hope!

I am Preparing You a Room

"Carol, I want to hire someone to remodel our bedroom so you can come home. How does that sound?"

"Yes! I want to come home. Now?!"

"Not quite now, but it will happen. You are coming home."

I am preparing a room, a mansion for you, says our God; I believe God is telling us this is what I need to do: bring Carol home.

This gave us the spunk to live and was evident in our smiles, giggles and increased appetites. She had a reason to be alive.

She told everyone, "I am going home! Joanie is making my room new and I am going home!"

Our joys and deep kisses sprouted like wildflowers. My eyes turned from dull to sparkling and so did hers.

I made sure her care facility door, room 202, was closed as we tenderly touched each other's faces and French kissed until we couldn't breathe. It was fun! She couldn't take her eyes off me.

Oh boy!

"I love you so much!"

"I love you more!"

There was hope! Big time!

It took three weeks. But worth it all! The remodel included a wall opening that was cut to make a wide door to get her Hoyer lift and powerchair through, new electrical wiring with grounded outlets for medical equipment, and new non-skid carpet for her roll-in apparatus. And I painted the walls and ceiling. Curry Good Sam gifted us a hospital bed with a vertical lift. They were in the process of replacing patient beds and, wow, did we luck out!

Was that a God thing or what! What perfect timing!

Yes, there were tangible gifts and physical accommodations

and all the while our emotional and spiritual gifts were growing in strength and surrendering.

I took pictures that I showed her daily. I brought in paint chips so Carol could select the colors. She chose off-white walls, a purple accent wall behind her head and a purple door, multi-colored carpet and her favorite pictures of family and artwork. Making these decisions and designing her own room gave her gusto for life. It was extra work for me to collect all the samples for her to touch and see, but it was worth it.

Tim, one of our best friends, and I built and dug into the ground two bird feeder stations next to the bedroom window. Fred and Tim installed more safety bars and a smart TV with a wall bracket for her James Bond movies.

We had to make this the best homecoming for Carol, knowing that we needed to confirm everything for her death and resurrection. Carol and I both knew she was coming home to die. Everything fell into place.

We were eager to have alone time and be "us." We were tired of the institution where she had been. They provided her care, but it was not the same as being cared for by a loving spouse. She wanted me with her 24/7 and I wanted the same.

Jesus hold you.
God bless you.

CHAPTER 21
Voices from Angels

Carol's Passing

Oh boy, here goes. Oh, Lord, and oh, Carol, please type the words today. My memories are still fresh, alive, tearing and joyful as I recall Carol's last weeks, days, hours, minutes and breaths.

The stroke created internal and external medical problems that, after eight years, ultimately took her life.

During this time, my heartbreak and heart ecstasy were summarized in the artwork on the cover of my prayer journal. It had two sailboats showing off their tall masts, quietly sitting and rocking in the glistening waters, and shadows encroaching on the blue waters. The blurry structures behind kept the sailboats as the central focus until your eyes glanced at a person with a white-brimmed hat, dark face and white bulging eyes. He wore a long-sleeve beige shirt. He was steering his smaller white boat and concentrating on the main two still-sail boats. The boats were really not alone and it was a brand new day, of sorts.

I opened my journal very slowly to read, remember, and re-live an amazing, miraculous set of events.

December 7th, 2021: Finally, Carol is Home!!

My journal entry for this day had a huge smiley face drawn on the page.

After a $5,000 remodel of "our"—now "her"—bedroom, it had a new door, new blue-green carpet selected by Carol, freshly painted walls by yours truly, a gifted remote-controlled hospital bed, and a used but recently purchased remote-controlled medical Hoyer lift. This medical equipment has a sort of sling attached to a machine with a hydraulic lift that transfers the person from a bed to a chair or vice versa.

Carol's spirit was improving tremendously because she was leaving a care facility and would be in our home with our non-stop loves and joys. She was coming home to DIE, but we would be together!!

All had been arranged with hospice and homecare aide Kathy, the most positive and out-of-this-world caregiver who became our friend. Kathy had been an integral and very personal at-home shower-bather for Carol off-and-on for the past eight years. She was 5'9" with long, light brown hair. Strong, funny, joyful, real and common-sense smart, she could turn any sourpuss person's day into beams of sunshine.

Our hospice nurse, Shirley, was our knight in shining armor. We nicknamed her "fabulous Shirley." She was Brookings' Mother Teresa, short in stature, maybe five foot, but her heart was larger than a blue whale's 400-pound heart. YEA!!

Carol didn't have the strength to sit up, so she was in bed 99% of the time. Only four times she was willing and able to use the Hoyer lift to transfer into her new powered chair. Twice it was for only a few minutes; she couldn't get comfortable sitting. After that, she, Carolyn and I accepted Carol's 100% bedridden life.

After just three days of being home, Carol was absolutely tired of fighting, struggling so darn hard to live normally. She relinquished her abilities. I didn't blame her one bit. I loved Carol so much that I totally supported her choice to enjoy life from the comfort of her hospital bed. We make life meaningful by being human beings, not by our human doings.

Looking out the big bedroom window, Carol watched the black, gray, yellow and blue birds, sometimes 50 at once, scratch around on the 12-inch square bird feeder on a pole, which Carol called "the birds' dinner table." They flew in and ate the seed on the wooden platforms held up by tall poles.

Tim and I positioned the feeders exactly where Carol could see it all happen right outside the bedroom window: a bird's eye view! Carol and I loved to watch the sky colors change from bright sunshine to streaks of clouds and light, ever changing. Carol and her voice-activated Alexa were two musical friends and Carol giggled when Alexa said her name.

Neighbor Carolyn was a BIG, BIG help caring for Carol, only a phone call away as she would stomp across the lawn and greet Carol every morning, "How are you today, Carol?" We kept Carol cleaned and turned. Lots of smiles. Every day was precious.

Journal Entry for December 10th

Nephew Will visited for one full week! Awesome! He came to give Aunt Carol a hug! He spoiled us, helped us and had QUALITY time with Aunt Carol and with me. We all knew it's God's timing. PEACE was everywhere!!! God was all around.

Will paid for a lot of things: an electric blanket and two chairs with wheels so people who visited could scoot around in her room and be with her. He also assembled the chairs in front of Carol. He brought treats of groceries and left us with restaurant certificates. He took me to the jeweler to get my wedding ring repaired and he paid for that, too. I wore it every day and Carol liked to touch my finger with it on it.

Carol's was eating very little. She had Roku on TV and she loved the movies she had heard and seen a thousand times. We shared and gave lots of kisses, words and "love you"s. She gave her all and I gave my all, spiritually and in other ways.

For the last six months together, we talked, shared and wrote both of our obituaries, hopes, and dreams, as well as what to do when she died. What should I do? "Live each day to the max," I promised. She said, "You'd better!"

So grateful for Hospice, Kathy, for calls from so many: Dan and Andrew, Tim and Fred. Doris came over and we watched the Rose Bowl Parade on January 1st. I made the famous Carol "egg impossible" with fresh duck eggs from Peter and Taylor's sausage topped with avocado. Carol loved the flavors and the softness of that dish that she could swallow it without chewing. She ate a bite or two of the tasty, hot casserole brunch, served on her small multi-colored plate with her choice of a fork or a small spoon. She asked me to help feed her one bite.

Giving Away Brings Joy

Giving things away meant a lot to Carol. I brought in boxes of lifelong pictures from the shed and the office that I spread out on the living room table. While she watched movies, I sorted them into categories with people's names on yellow stickies.

As she sat up in bed, I presented about 10 at a time and asked, "Who would you like to send these to?"

She would hold the pictures, as her brain, eyes and smiles reconnected the love moments of her life. We sent text pictures and we slow-mailed envelopes of pictures to her friends and CSJs. All the while, we were remembering stories, laughing, crying just a few tears and releasing. What a wonderful life.

God was so pleased with Carol . . . she was SO CALM. She was accepting! Both of us were letting go after 40 years of sharing profound love. Humbly accepting the calls, cards and texts from the sisters of St. Joseph, especially.

January 5th: She Stopped Eating!

Poor Carol, she had thrush in her mouth, tongue and throat. Never complained!! We focused on playing music, reading and saying prayers. Our morning routine continued with me having my coffee and biscotti while we listened to the God Minute app, placing my cell phone on her red and green plaid comforter on her chest. She listened and talked with friends throughout the day and evening. Her thinking was slowing down, but her eye contact with people was profound. It was like she was pouring out love, peace and hope with intense kindness from her eyeballs.

Really, it was the face of God. She was changing right in front of me. So hard to describe and put into words, but there was a calmness and serenity going on. Such grand support from local and far-away friends and family for me and with Carol. We were feeling blessed and highly favored.

Her voice and mind were sharp. I thought if it were me, I would be a basket case, a grouch, in pain without food, but she was alert and joyful. Amazing! I loved being with her. Hospice came regularly and people came for 20-minute visits. She was loved: people were bringing cute cards, bright flowers, baby roses and azalea plants. We set up two coffee tables in the bedroom for her gifts.

Literally and aloud with Carol, I had said, "Goodbye Sweetie Carol. I'll see you in heaven when it's my turn. Go be with God, family and friends." At this point, Carol was unable to talk but I had a feeling as I lovingly gazed into her green fuzzy, non-clear eyes that she had one foot in heaven and one foot on earth.

On Carol's last couple of days before she passed, Sister Ruthie, age 95, her first communion teacher and a dear, dear friend, called and told me, "Joanie, you need to tell Carol that she needs to let go of you."

"Really?"

"Yes, she's holding onto you even though you have told her good bye. She is still holding on."

"OK, I'll do that. Thank you."

"Sweetie, Ruthie just called. You know how wise she is, right? Well she told me to tell you that you need to let go of me. You know I'm going to be fine. We've had an AMAZING life together. We know how much we love each other. And we know we'll be together again in heaven someday."

In my strong determined voice I said, "Carol, repeat after me: 'Goodbye Joanie, Goodbye Will, Goodbye Carrie.'" In her silence, non-voice, I sensed Carol let go of me, our love and our life. She let go of me and her family.

Where did I get this strength I thought? Silly me, this was all about God. Anything was possible when you believe. Sister Ruthie knew the truth about her friend Carol ever since she was in her first communion class at St. Bernadette's. Thank you, Ruthie, for your wisdom and being the messenger we needed.

I promised Carol and God that I would live each day to the max and Carol told me, "You'd better."

God is everywhere and everything. Lead me on, Lord, I pray.

I remember Kathy from Hospice telling me that when the time of eternal life comes, it would be up to me when I called Hospice, when they would arrive and when it would be time to remove her body from our house. That wisdom gave me immense peace; I could be with the love of my life for a little longer yet I knew it was only a body. Her soul was the most important part and that was without question a heavenly solace.

Carol's smile was contagious and tender in her shrinking face. Her cheek color was less pink and more beige. I carried on to keep myself healthy and alert, too. She encouraged me to eat and I ate some of my meals with her in her bedroom with the colorful coyote artwork staring at me. Other times I ate my meal at the living room table by myself. It was strange to do that but I did it. I cherished those times of eating in her presence because I knew the day would come when we wouldn't be together for meals and conversations. That was ok, but I was not ready yet.

Joanie, don't be selfish, put yourself in Carol's shoes.

God kept helping me to let go of Carol. *She was more ready than I will ever be.* I thought I had let go and then it sprang up from my deep crevices.

The Hoyer lift was now in the living room and all medical necessity supplies were in dresser drawers or in the kitchen, so Carol only got to look at life, not medical stuff. We were in comfort mode. God was with us. We were together.

It would be 25 days of no food and seven days of no drink before her new life awakened.

Holy Moly, a few days before Carol died, I woke from a sound sleep and thought someone was standing in my bedroom. I heard, **"I bring glad tidings of JOY!"**

I got out of bed to see who was there. A clear distinct voice! I walked; no one was in the kitchen. *Who's there?*

Again, I heard, **"I bring glad tidings of JOY!"**

I walked into the living room, again loud and distinct: **"I bring glad tidings of JOY!"**

I walked into Carol's room; she was wide awake and full of spunk.

"Did you hear—"

Carol interrupted me, "Yes, I heard. Who was it?"

"I'm not sure," I said, "but maybe your Guardian Angel?"

"Oh yeah, that's who it was. Go back to bed."

Was that really her Guardian Angel? I think so!

I returned to bed feeling fine and safe. Carol's snoring soothed me to sleep.

I remembered the years of she and I sleeping together and she would say, "Put your back into me and let's go to sleep."

I have surrendered Carol completely to God in the last 12 hours. She was ready and had screamed many times before, "Oh Lord, take me. I don't want to live here anymore."

She had many episodes when I walked into her bedroom, and she spurted out loudly, "HI!"

Is she talking to me?

I said, "Hi!"

There was complete silence. She did not look at me or acknowledge my presence.

Then it hit me, Carol was not saying Hi to me! She was communicating and being greeted from heaven by her family and friends. They were excited to see her. And she was super excited to be with them again.

Journal Entry: January 28th and 29th

Two days before Carol died, at 2:30 a.m., I sat next to her in a black office chair with wheels on it. I wore my lavender hooded sweatshirt over my nightgown with an extra blanket on my lap. I had been praying so hard from my gut, my real deep gut, asking Jesus to bring her home now.

"Please, Jesus?! She has suffered enough."

Her breathing had changed and her gasping echoed off the walls. Emotionally, I was drained. She was lying more comatose and lifeless. The pitch dark room matched the dark night outside.

All of a sudden I saw flashes of lights, like vibrant blinking stars, like an eye examination at the optometrist office. For about 20 minutes, all over her bedroom were these lights that had stopped blinking and were now stationary beams of bright white, high-beam lights. I counted them: one, two, three, 10, 15, 20—so many I couldn't count. *This was a miracle!*

"Hi, Angels and Saints!" I said aloud. "Hi Joe, Hi Elsie, Hi Mom, Dad, Elaine, Sara, Marilyn, all of you, saints and angels, we are so glad you are here!" This was truly a miracle from heaven!

Carol was not moving a muscle, flat as a board as she lay warm and cozy on her bamboo fabric purple sheets with the green electric blanket and the red comforter on top. I was wrapped with the maroon blanket over my nightgown, my Ugg slippers keeping my feet warm, gawking at the angels' and saints' lights that remained starkly bright all around on the walls and ceiling.

I was, and we were, in the company of holy people and holy spirits. I sat quietly mesmerized. I reached under Carol's blanket to feel her arm. She was WARM! She was resting; we were resting in the divine world.

Carol's gurgling and rattling was awful sounding. She was now on morphine, from the comfort care pack of medicines that had been in storage in the refrigerator for a week. The Hospice nurses had taught me how to fill and use the baby syringe. I squeezed the morphine into Carol's back cheek as needed. Nurse Shirley had advised me to use it every four hours beginning January 29th at noon.

A big tear flowed from Carol's right eye. I wiped her eye tenderly with my finger, knowing that this was rare and beautiful. I had only seen Carol cry about a dozen times in our 40 years together. I prayed she was not in any pain. I phoned the nurse on call, Joyce, and she said that she had never known anyone to cry at the end of life being on morphine. The morphine should eliminate any pain. Maybe that tear was Carol not in physical pain, but an expression of her love for me.

I feel you, sweetie.

I was crying more and more that God would take her! I played lots of Catholic songs on my cell phone, or had the bedroom Alexa play Neil Diamond and John Denver, too. Her favorites.

She was looking more ashen, her eyes were gone, unresponsive and drugged out.

Oh . . . social worker Jordan came over at 6 p.m. and we counted how long before her next big gulp of air: one minuteand 40 seconds. She told me three minutes means no brain function without oxygen. I thanked Jordan for coming by, but I wanted this special time alone with Carol.

Journal Entry: January 30th

At 2 a.m., I got up to check on Carol; it was past her four-hour morphine regime because I overslept. She was breathing more quietly, less gasping. She was slightly cold when I touched her face, forehead and arm. But so peaceful!

I said, "Hi sweetie. Should I give you another .5 morphine or not? It's been about five hours." She looked so calm, so beautiful. Then I told her, "NO more meds! Let's let God do this!"

I kissed her forehead long, with a loud smack!

"Love, I don't need to be here when God takes you; that's between you and God. I'm ready when you and God are. I love you dearly, sweetie, and I know you love me dearly, too. It's time."

I walked to my bedroom and went back to bed, totally exhausted from the past three days and three nights of being at her side; tonight it was just the two of us. It seemed like our Lent journey, since December, our Holy Thursday, last suppers, our version of the cross on Good Friday, would soon be finished. Good thing we knew the end of the story. Yes, Easter would be here soon!

Journal Entry: January 30th, 3 a.m.

It had only been one hour, but I woke up with my ears and mind hearing stereo-sound blaring and lots of voices singing, "All are welcome in this place." These were not sounds from Alexa or our stereo in the kitchen.

I laid in bed five to 10 minutes listening to the repeat of this choral song: "All are welcome . . . " Then the song ended.

My body felt light as a feather and the house was extremely QUIET! SO QUIET!

No noise from Carol. It had been longer than three minutes.

I awaited her breath gasp.

Nothing.

I turned on the hall light and entered her bedroom. It was quiet, so quiet. I stared directly at Carol—her mouth and eyes were open; her face was yellow-whitish. I touched her arm under the purple sheet and her body was COLD! I moved her head—dead weight. I leaned over her to feel her breath. No breath. I checked for a pulse. No pulse. I tried to close her eyelids, but they were fixed open; I tried to close her mouth, but it was stiff. She was so cold and stiff.

She had died peacefully in her sleep.

I yelled, "I'M SO HAPPY!" My heart was unbelievably so JOY-filled! More than I had ever experienced before.

THANK YOU GOD!!!!!! [LARGE SMILEY FACES IN MY JOURNAL] YEA GOD!! REJOICE IN THE LORD ALWAYS! [DRAWING OF HEARTS] I SING, I DANCE, I CRY, I SING AND YELL ALLELUIA, HER SOUL IS IN HEAVEN!! I'VE GOT THAT JOY, JOY DOWN IN MY HEART. WHERE? DOWN IN MY HEART . . .

She was cold except for her warm knees. I rubbed her feet like I'd done a thousand times. She loved foot rubs and if I had the chance over, I would have delighted her more by giving her longer and more often those tender, loving foot rubs. I didn't feel alone. I felt wobbly, I felt strong, I felt a mix of joy and sadness. It came in waves of tears, smiles, heartaches and amazing joys.

Her right fingers were not clinging to the bed side safety bar. SHE HAD LET GO!!! SHE HAD SURRENDERED TO GOD AND GOD WANTED HER WITH HIM. THAT IS THE VICTORY OF ALL VICTORIES. YIPPEE!!! AMAZING!

I called my sister Terri, no answer. I called Tim, no answer. I called our friend Fred, who would be the Redwood Mortuary person to pick Carol up, no answer. I texted nephew Will, niece Carrie, Ter and Tim. No response. I was OK with that. They said to call them right away. Oh well, no biggie, I said to myself.

I was talking out loud to Carol, "No one is awake, sweetie. It's you and me, babe." She was wearing her black nightgown with red trim and I kept the sheet and red comforter on top of her. I told her, "I'll be right back; I'm going to grab a biscotti and heat up a cup of coffee."

Looking at Carol, 40 years of memories flashed at super speed and I visualized as if I were there again, our first kiss in Lewiston, Idaho, me as a novice and her a professed sister of St. Joseph. The most amazing kiss in the world.

I felt hope. I got dressed, out of my nightgown and into my jeans, a bright purple polo shirt, and white and red tennis shoes with pink laces. I told Alexa to play Neil Diamond and her favorite song came on; play John Denver, "Sunshine on My Shoulders," Marty Haugen, "All are Welcome."

We sat with music and coffee, and suddenly I saw her lips twinge and really move. OMG, I was startled. Maybe I was wrong.

"Are you alive, Carol? Or are you dead?"

Immediately, with both of my hands I placed them on her cheeks lightly shaking her. Zero response.

Oh, relief! Carol was dead.

I was not losing my marbles. I must have been in some sort of shock, relief and joy all at once.

I sat back in the black rolling chair nearest the window, opened the blinds and sighed. The sunrise was spectacular over the Harbor hills. I snapped a cell phone picture and said, "Carol, your first brand new day in heaven. Way to go!"

I started to bawl!! A flood of emotion, realizing she really was no longer with me.

I stared out the window, looked back at her, stared at the sunrise sky, the oranges and streaks of pinks and then at her ashen face.

All beautiful, I thought as my emotions created a flow of tears. Kleenex tissues, one at a time, forget that, make it a blob of tissues to catch my snot and salty tears that I tasted by the liter. I held her hand, kissing it gently, its soft skin warped by her cold stiff fingers.

Joanie, let go of Carol. Look outside: she is FREE. She is racing to her parents. She's not stuck in a bed; she's not stuck in her chair; she is leaping the mountains. She is being swarmed with more love in heaven than can ever be on earth! She is an angel singing and laughing with all the angels and saints that were just in this room a night ago.

THANK YOU JESUS. I will take the u out of mourning and make it morning. It is a brand new day, never been lived before!

Journal Entry: January 30th, 5 a.m.

Calmly, feeling it was time, I used my cell phone to call Hospice, using the already recently programmed number that I had called frequently over the last three days. I spoke to a nice young male voice and told him, "My spouse, Carol, has just died." He said he was having his first night on the job, handling the switchboard.

"Oh, what do I do?" he asked.

"It's OK," I said. "We're not in a hurry. We are not going anywhere. Please call the nurse, Joyce, who is working on call this weekend." He called her and somehow the three of us were on a conference call.

"Hi Joyce, Joanie here. Carol has died."

"Oh, Joanie. I'll be right there."

"Joyce, please don't hurry. It's dark out and cold, maybe icy. We are fine."

"OK, I'll see you soon."

"Alright, the porch light will be on."

"OK."

"Can I hang up now?" asked this gentle, kind, teary-sounding voice.

"Yes, thank you so much."

Joyce arrived and gave me a huge hug at the door and then entered the bedroom. "She looks so peaceful, Joanie."

"Thanks, Joyce. Yes, she was and is."

"Let's make the official time of death 5:55 a.m., Joanie."

"Perfect, that's my favorite number, five. This has to be an angel Carol thing."

Joyce did her RN duties and checked Carol's body from head to toe. She was gentle, soft, and slow. Very respectful and solemn. She asked, "Joanie, would you like Carol to remain in these clothes for cremation?"

I told her no, as Carol picked her sister Elaine's animal printed nightgown to wear. Fun and special.

"Can we change her together?" I requested.

"Yes, of course."

Turning Carol's body was strange. Just a body; her soul was what was alive. We undressed her, leaving her protective panties on her in case she defecated, Joyce said.

"Let's put on her pink and black fuzzy socks that always make her smile," I said.

"Yes," said Joyce.

Carol looked cute and ready for the next adventure.

Joyce started to call the mortuary, but Jake from the mortuary was calling me. I told Joyce. She hung up and I put him on speaker, "Hi Jake. Joanie and Joyce from hospice here, on speaker."

"I'm so sorry, Joanie."

"Thanks, Jake."

"Joyce, the guys will be there in about 45 minutes."

"OK, thanks."

"Jake, you'll be in touch with me later, right?" I asked.

"Yes. Joanie. I or Mary will call you in a few days."

"Is Fred the one coming?"

"Yes."

"Perfect, that's who Carol wanted. Thank you!"

Joyce and I sat in the kitchen and Joyce dissolved all of Carol's medicine that had been on the kitchen counter or in the kitchen cupboard into a baggie with water. *I'm grateful for her thoroughness.*

I had never done any of this before. I was rolling with every step, being kind and feeling happy and relieved at the same time. I was impressed with professionalism, but more than that, I was so thankful that Carol and I had lived in this small community and developed really good friendships for the past 30 years. Ever since hospice, we had been on the receiving end of love and compassion. There was a season for everything.

At 6:45 a.m., Fred and Leo from the mortuary arrived. Fred gave me a big, long hug and then Leo did the same. Very consoling. I appreciated that a lot, Fred!

Fred said, "I brought a colored sheet just for Carol because she loves bright flowers."

"Yes. Thank you, Fred."

"We'll be right back, Joanie." They went to the van, and returned with a gurney with a black bag and straps like the ambulance uses.

All four of us entered the bedroom. Fred went over to Carol's face and just stared at her. He had tears in his eyes. How touching to see this. I thought of the Bible story when Jesus cries when his friend dies. Fred and Carol were good friends and Fred loved to kid with her and she dished it right back to him, too.

Fred and Leo put on their blue gloves and showed me the yellow flowered sheet. I smiled big.

"Joanie, would you like to help us?" Fred asked.

"Yes, of course. Thanks." Together we wrapped and tucked Carol's stiff cold body warmed by her sister's hand-me-down animal print nightgown and her bright pink and black fuzzy favorite socks. She looked so darn cute dressed with her feet warm and toasty into the daisy sheet. Her body was lifeless, her head and face were now covered in a tight sheet.

I will no longer see her! That was difficult! *She will only be visible in my mind, in my heart, in pictures and in memories.* It was very emotional, yet I was at peace. I was not even shedding a tear. I knew she is in the happiest place ever, heaven.

Am I still in shock? My tears have disappeared. Is Carol giving me this internal spirit of peace and tranquility? Or am I so exhausted from years of wondering when this glorified day would happen? I bet the angels and Jesus are holding me, surrounding me and Carol is making sure that I'm feeling what she is feeling. Total love!

I got a flash memory picture of Carol in our living room seated in her new powered chair with colorful wheel rims of neon sky blue and plum purple. She was sitting tall, poised, and peacefully at our big prayer window facing the 30-foot-tall green trees, the mowed park-like grass, and gray feathered doves with white rings around their necks, prancing around on the grass and flitting from the wire above. I was sitting, also peacefully, in a chair next to her, when she said, "Joanie, do you know that heaven is on earth? Jesus is here on earth as much as in heaven."

"Yep, that's cool! Thanks, Carol, for telling me that!"

It was a miracle statement as powerful as all the miraculous angelic voices and songs along with the blessed holy apparitions that have occurred in our last three days. Unbelievable, unless you're a believer. *God is with us all the time. Don't ever doubt it.*

Fred said, "On one, two, three." We all lifted Carol, completely covered in the sheet, onto and into the black bag on the gurney. Her body was heavy, but we were strong. My emotions were numb. It was quiet except for the directions that Fred was telling Leo. Their voices were low.

Carol was now in the long black heavy vinyl bag and Fred said, "Joanie, would you like to do the honors of zipping up the bag?"

"Yes, Fred, I would!" It felt like such a quick response out of my mouth that I surprised myself. Was that the Holy Spirit speaking for me?

I took my right hand to reach for the zipper at the bottom of the bag where Carol's toes were. I matter-of-factly zipped it up. Strange, emotional yet not emotional. I felt her body under the sheet as I zipped, being careful to not catch the zipper in the sheet. I just knew I needed to take this opportunity, this blessing, this final act of servant love, our married love, to the everlasting domain of us as lovers: friends and gifts from God.

Fred and Leo strapped her in.

That would be crazy bad if she slid off the gurney.

For my final words with Carol, as they cautiously guided her out the front door, I said loudly and proudly, "Carol, it's your last ride! I'll see you in heaven!"

Standing alone outside this cold morning, the sky lit up the day and I watched the van exit the driveway onto Oceanview Drive. No longer in my sight. She was gone physically.

"Joanie, do you want me to stay with you?" Joyce asked.

"No thanks, Joyce, you've been great. I need to make calls and get something to eat. Thanks for everything!"

"You call us if you need anything or just to talk, OK?"

"OK. Will you call nurse Shirley for me?"

"Yes, of course."

"OK, bye."

Right away I called Ter. She cried with me and said, "Can I come?"

"Yes, come!"

She called me back in five minutes or less. "I'll be in Crescent City tonight at 6 p.m. Can you come get me?"

"Yes. Thanks, Ter!"

Last Entry: 7:25 a.m., January 30th

Carol died January 30th at 3 a.m.

I LOVE YOU CAROL! AND YOU TOLD ME, "I LOVE YOU, JOANIE."

Ter is coming for nine days. I'm so grateful. I need her!!!! Ter will bring joy, noise, tender love and spoil me!!!

I am a widow with an angel in heaven.

Grief is a super incredible, individual journey and eventually "our" will become "mine.'" I'm still not completely there yet. Or who knows if I will ever be there. Megan Devine's book *It's OK to Not Be OK* is superb for grieving people and for people wanting to know how to help one in grief. So many benefits from the hospice grief support group.

Thanks to my new friend Jenny, whose husband died five days after Carol: we are kindred souls and have been able to journey this harsh grief path together.

"The deeper you love, the deeper you grieve," said dear friend Sister Suzanne.

Jesus held me and will hold you.
God blesses all of us.
Miracles happen.

CHAPTER 22
Creating the Rose Garden

Through the years, we wrote responses to questions in our blue, hardcover book. The title was *My Favorite Things* and on its cover was a white heart that held pictures of cars, flowers, a camera, a phone, a basketball, fork and knife, dolphins and palm trees.

"Carol, sweetie, if time and money weren't the issue, where would you go, what would you do?"

"Oh, I'd travel anywhere and everywhere or nowhere as long as we're together," Carol quickly responded with a big, romantic smile.

"You are so sweet, Carol. Thank you and I agree. With you is always the best."

These words, written in Carol's handwriting, were in our little blue book of favorites. They spoke of volumes of fun, adventures and love: "bags of M and M's, boxes of See's Candy, travel to fun places, looking at the night stars, going out to lunch at odd places, listening to people sing, wearing hats that were odd, holding hands with each other, lodging in large gorgeous rooms, going on a cruise vacation and creating our own time schedule."

Another page asked, "Which favorite people have guided you?"

Carol listed: "Joanie, Dr. Gerald Hershey, a freshman in college, you changed my life, Bishop Treinen."

I added: "Sister Mary Ellen, Tim, and you, Carol." We had fun telling stories and learned a lot about each other's past, present and future with our little blue book.

It was inspiring and touching for us. Carol was always thinking outside of a box. Actually, in her world there were NO BOXES and no labels. We chose quality time versus watching hours of TV in the evenings. Did you know that for 20 years, we did not have cable TV? Didn't miss it a bit. We chose to watch an hour of a DVD movie, play games, play guitar, read or write cards to people. Or just plain talk, sit and be.

Our living room was a haven created by both of our families' furnishings and mementos. It was our space of rest and joys.

I reread the hundreds of sympathy cards, celebration cards and faith-filled cards, and centered myself with a note from Suzanne: "The deeper you love, the deeper you grieve, Joanie. You and Carol were one."

The Healing Serenity of Our Rose Garden

In the summer of 2021, Carol and I had calming, heartfelt conversations about the end of life.

"How should we live after one of us is gone?" we asked each other. We didn't know details, but believed that God would take care of each of us, our friends, our families and everything.

"Carol, do you want donations for a scholarship, or whatever? Friends will want to do something to remember you when you die."

"Joanie, I want something where people can see lots of color and they can visit you."

"OK, how about a flower garden?"

"Yes! That would be AMAZING. Have Dan and Tim help you do it."

"A rose garden?" I asked.

"Yes, beautiful!"

"OK, sweetie, done!"

And so as I grieved with tears streaming down my face, I mowed the lawn, missing Carol, our fun life and our relationship.

Then I donned my old Nike tennis shoes, walked into the shed, found the old can of white paint, popped off the lid, stirred the thick gunk and grabbed an old paint brush and the tape measure.

Walking down the ramp, another memory of Carol driving up and down it in her powered chair, I was all smiles. I faced the house, the sun at my back, the birds chirping and began sketching, painting a line to mark the future garden's boundary.

"OK, sweetie, how big do we want this garden?" I asked aloud. "Alrighty, 20- by 40 feet. That will be just perfect."

I dug up 30 or so gladiola bulbs and replanted them in front of the kitchen window. *Here we go, Carol, it's one step at a time! I know you're watching me. I feel you. I love you!*

Then I said, "Just in case, I have a feeling that more roses will be coming, so let's do another plot by the light pole. How about 15 by 20?" I painted the lines.

I asked my neighbor, a business guru who had heavy equipment, "Do you have time tomorrow to come over and scrape out the grass for the two areas I've marked? Also, remove and replant two big shrubs?"

"Of course, Joanie. I'll get Richard to help."

"Thanks so much, Joe!"

"You bet, how are you doing?"

"OK."

The garden designers, Dan and Tim, set forth, with brains, dreams and muscles.

Dates and times were easily put together because I told them that Carol's celebration would be March 31st and people would be bringing roses to plant them. As I invited people to her celebration, I said Carol had requested "no rosary and no Mass." She wanted an "all are welcome" lunch at the local Wild River Pizza restaurant and for guests to bring a big smile and wear bright colors. Then I added, "A rose memorial garden is being built if you'd like to contribute."

Yep, that was Carol's desire!

My heart leapt every time I invited people. And I invited everyone!

Oh golly, the first rose arrived on the front porch from Patty and Tom Finn-Fitzmaurice from Southern California, and then from Aunt Fran in Oklahoma, and cousin Vicki and Paul from

Temecula, California.

I coordinated with Dan and Tim about the construction details. Tim event suggested a "rock creek" from the gutter spout. We went to Home Depot to buy 30 bricks for the border.

Joe drove loud, heavy equipment, and I gave instructions how where and what to do. My grief thinking skills were on the slow side but I was so happy that Dan and Tim were my guardian angels of my heart. They loved Carol so much and I often forgot that they were grieving, too. Sorry about that, guys.

Tim, Carolyn and I found some river rock and slate for the "creek" and stepping stones in the garden.

Dan and Tim used shovels and wheelbarrows to move the dark rich soil dirt onto the scraped areas. Good old hard labor! Tough and strong, with big mushy hearts. It was fun to watch them talk, pace themselves and sweat a little. I heard them laugh and then it got quiet.

Time for cheerleader Joanie to go compliment and encourage them. "Hi guys, looking great!! Wow, you moved all that dirt. I'm impressed. How about a water break?"

Then I was back in the house prepping the lunch food: making a green salad loaded with bell peppers, carrots, radishes, tomatoes, olives and onions. I turned the marinating chicken, made burger patties and a few extra hot dogs ready for the BBQ.

Dan had informed me that he had four staff workers coming to help, too. "Let's throw a few yams in the oven. More beer and water in the fridge to get them cold."

"How fun," I said. Carol would be loving this day!!! I was doing her job in the food department, pinching myself as I welled up with both grief tears and joyful tears. The waves of grief were surprises that sprang up when least expected.

They rolled out the white weed cover cloth, cut it to fit the length and width of the garden dimensions, and each with a hammer, nailed in the pegs to hold it in place. They kneeled to do this and I swiftly grabbed the old chair cushions from the shed to soften it for their kneecaps.

Tim had started placing the river rock in the "creek." Dan and I unloaded the rocks from his truck. Tim had walked thousands of miles in creeks and rivers as an amazing fisherman, and he was definitely the pro about this.

The other crew arrived! That gave Dan and Tim relief; their faces glowed with dirt and sweat. Perfect timing.

Someone burst into song, "Hi Ho, Hi Ho, it's off to work we go!" Laughter and whistling chased through the marine air.

The new younger crew, dog included, wheelbarrowed and shoveled the dirt in the second garden plot. Though they had started with clean blue jeans, now everyone looked like Linus in *Charlie Brown* with flying dust and dirt making halos above their heads.

Ten roses were planted in the main garden!

"YIPPEE!" I yelled, with my vocal chords cracking with grief and joy. "So awesome, everyone! I now see the vision that my Carol had. A big thanks to Dan and Tim."

Visionaries are leaders!

God, thank you for their gift of believing before seeing!

Me, the playful grasshopper, I learned to cut the cloth, peel it back, dig the hole, put in the fertilizer, plant the rose, cover it with dirt, water it and say, "Carol, it's up to you. Grow with delight in the Lord's name."

Oh, so cool!!!

They were only green canes, stocks, brown sticks; some had a few leaves but were so barren. Their roots were long and thin, configured like an umbrella or an octopus with many arms reaching for hands to hold. I wondered, "God how do these grow into such fragrant and unique blooms?"

Is this like death and resurrection?

Is this like how you formed me, God?

Is this similar to me discovering who I really am?

Yes, be patient, sit with me, and believe.

They looked tiny in the massive garden spaced about a foot or more from each other. My mentors taught me to give them room to grow.

Hope was a good thing! My heart was so happy.

This was an eight-hour day easily. The team was tired and hungry.

"Let's eat in about 15 or 20 minutes," I announced.

"Yeah," the workers said. "Food, glorious food!"

Dan cheered, "Fantastic work today everyone. Well done! We couldn't have done it without each of you. Thank you!"

"I second that, Dan. Yes, thank you to all of you."

In the kitchen, before we loaded our plates, we said a quick prayer of blessing the food and giving thanks, always a tradition in our house.

"Grab a plate, silverware and help yourselves."

Some ate inside, gathered around the table in the living room, laughing, talking, eating, relaxing and enjoying each other. It felt so good to have a house full of people, the first time since Carol had died. Carol and I had had hundreds of occasions sharing meals with friends in our house. We loved doing it. It was fun!

"Compliments to the cook," they said.

"Raise your hand," I said, "if you've ever been to our house for a meal or gathering."

All their hands went up.

"We were the hostess with the mostest."

Some crew wanted to eat outside with beers or water to toast and salute Carol. *May the roses grow and brighten our world.*

How cute and personal! That meant a lot!

The Garden Looks FABULOUS

Dan and Tim, fearless leaders who took charge, Richard, Joe, Jerry, Fred and Dan's friends, Carolyn and I turned the front yard grass and shrubs into a landscaped garden party—simply paradise. It had a rock creek, red bark, a curving border of stone-colored bricks, a black metal bench near the roses, and a blue heron sculpture as the guardian spirit.

It took sweat, dirt, weed cloth, rocks, blisters, a few Band-Aids, jugs of water, food for the crews, laughter, tears of healing and grieving, all to prepare for the growth of new life. It was fun and it kept me busy and active. I needed that.

Word spread! Rose plants arrived on the porch daily by mail or FedEx or in person.

Monetary gifts flowed like honey to buy trellises, rose food, bird feeders, gloves, clippers and even dirt. It was hilarious when I heard on the car radio a country-western song about how you can't purchase happiness, but you're able to buy dirt, on the day I ordered the dirt.

Every day for a month, I was stunned as plants kept arriving. I and others dug holes, placed them in the ground after soaking the roots in water for a day, then said, "OK, God, OK, Carol, help them grow. It's all up to you."

It was healing, and I never held back my emotions. I felt my smiles getting bigger and happier.

The roses came from her family and friends, young and old, poor, middle class and wealthy. From straight, gay, religious to atheist. From brown eyes, black-skinned, red-freckle-faced, Alaskan, white, and Egyptian and German ancestry. It was all inclusive, nonjudgmental lifelong and recent dear people. It was a world of colored roses; it was an expression of love.

My heart was so happy and full.

With so many roses, we prepared a second garden. John from Numotion planted the first one, followed by neighbor Maggie, who was also grieving the loss of her husband, Mike.

Are you ready?

50 rose bushes total! 5-0. Fifty!

Jesus hold you.

God bless you.

CHAPTER 23
Smile Big, Wear Bright Colors

Carol's 80th birthday was February 1, two days after she had died. Of course, we celebrated fun-loving Carol at Cazadores Mexican Restaurant in Brookings-Harbor.

Our best friends, Carolyn, Charlene, Tim, my sister Terri and Doris, carried Carol in our hearts, as we skipped inside. We toasted her almost-80th birthday, raising our cervezas, margaritas, sodas and water. We shared words of praise with salty tears in our eyes, Carol's new life as an angel living in her heavenly world. We laughed, told stories of her great love of going out to eat and how she loved her favorites of succulent shrimp, chili-flavored carnitas, and perfectly grilled carne asada.

Being together with funny, loving friends put smiles on our faces. We joyfully sang, "Happy Birthday, Carol." We missed her dearly, but we all knew she left her joy inside each of us. We were arm-in-arm, hanging tightly together to comfort and support each other, physically and emotionally. Tears streamed down my face despite my joy that she was no longer suffering and was where she needed to be. I was still living the Carol and Joanie way: food, friends, love and bright-colored clothes.

My New Ways

My sister Terri flew from San Diego to comfort me after Carol's death. Her love, fun and kindness were exactly who and what I needed.

Together we enjoyed morning prayers with The God Minute podcast. Father Ron Hoye and team streamed from the Alexa Echo Dot sitting on top of the antique dark wooden china cabinet, the family heirloom from our Grandma Ruby. In the prayer corner of the living room, we displayed colorful angels and the "soccer picture" of Christ. There was a ceramic statue of Sister Giggles in her black and white habit with arms raised to the sky in jubilation with an energetic smile. She reminded me of us and our joyous life.

This peaceful, quiet sanctuary was a place for listening to Jesus.

Every morning prayer with Carol was a joyful blessing as we surrounded ourselves with love hugs from God. Oh, I missed her so much as I sat in the prayer corner as a grieving widow, with waves of sorrowful pain. Half of me had died, but here I felt whole, unafraid, unstressed, alive, comforted, protected and peaceful.

I asked the Lord to heal me and just be with me through this struggling, yet special time. I would regain complete joy of life in His time. My mind and body told me to be patient and kind with myself, take naps as needed, stare at nothingness whenever and sob and smile at the same time.

House Projects

Best of all, Terri and I started "Carol-related" morning routines beginning with converting "our" house to "my" house. For the past eight years, our house was door-less to accommodate Carol's wheelchairs. So we retrieved the glass shower doors and the bedroom door from the shed, then cleaned, painted and re-installed them. We also rearranged furniture.

Though I was relieved and excited to create my new home, grief hit me like a cracked baseball bat on a fast pitch.

Lastly, Terri and I set up my folk guitar with its stand in a music area in the living room filled with natural light. How sweet to have it out of its case, a chair beside it, making it comfortable and easy to pick up the guitar and strum, "How Good You Are, God."

This morning routine of prayer, breakfast and house projects established a pace to get things done and allowed my emotions to ride a roller coaster with my eyes closed, with internal and external screams.

By 1 p.m., we went for hikes!

Life is everywhere! The trees, the ferns, His excited voice, my deep breaths. *Life has changed, not ended.*

At times Ter let me cry, sob or be in my grief fog whenever the wave of pain and loss hit like a crashing wave that knocked me to the sand. But she also brought out my smile joy and love of life. This was all a transition.

How do I go on without Carol? I am not a couple. I am a widow. Lord help me with my heart full of memories. Lord lead me on to create new memories.

My words were often stifled. I couldn't make complete sentences, so she did most of the talking the first few days.

Ter retold Carol stories and kept her in conversations: "Carol loved the color purple! I remember when Carol, you and I picked those delicious fresh-picked blackberries from your yard, and made light and melt-in-your-mouth crepes from her dad's famous recipe."

Get To's

My eating and sleeping patterns were bizarre for a while and Ter was phenomenally patient, sensitive and compassionate. If you've lost someone recently, I can tell you it does get better. I hope you have a gentle, loving soul to walk on this journey with you as my sister did for me. There was no timeline for peace; I learned to crave it, live with it and let it be. No have-to's, only get-to's. Some days or hours were better than others, life in flex mode. Life does go on in strange ways.

Only God planned for me to have such a beautiful sister.

During the first weeks, I was so honored and humbled to receive dozens of sympathy cards, notes, emails, texts, flowers and even surprise visits from friends at the front door. To read and reread the kind words, the consoling messages, their grief heartaches as well, was profound. Carol was loved so deeply by so many. This outpouring blew me away! I thanked God multiple times every day for our 40 years together, and I thanked Him more for the sincerity and love from others after her death.

Now she was with God, the angels and saints. I needed to remind myself that I was also with God.

My friend Maggie said, "Now it's time to take care of you as well as you took care of Carol." Such wisdom and heartfelt advice. But my heart was broken, really broken! I hoped and prayed for my own healing. I knew that others held me in their thoughts and prayers and wow, was that comforting.

Yet friends were a blessing and a curse. Sometimes I just had to say, "I'm not able to talk right now. I'm really not able to listen to you, and let's continue this another day." Most friends were understanding, but a few kept on talking. "I gotta go, bye."

Celebration of Life, Colors and Smiles on March 31, 2022

As I contemplated how to move forward, I reflected on conversations with Carol before her death, specifically her celebration of life as COVID remained a threat.

"I want people to wear bright colors and have big smiles," she said. "I don't want a rosary and I don't want a Mass. I want all kinds of our friends to come. I'd like it to be at the Wild River Pizza Restaurant." That was it. Simple and clear, like the song, "All are Welcome."

I selected March 31st for Carol's celebration of life, the day COVID face masks were not required but recommended, and public gatherings were allowed in the State of Oregon.

Months before Carol died, we had written our obituaries in ink on lined white paper, smiling and crying all the while. It was so intriguing to hear how important Carol thought of her upbringing, family times, her Catholic elementary and senior high school friends, nun experiences and our AMAZING adventures. We laughed, trying to synthesize our lives into a few paragraphs. Family, friends, God and joy summed it all up!

Carol's life celebration, her memorial rose garden and her

obituary card all intertwined for a phenomenal end-of-life tribute. About 75 friends from all walks of life attended: church, school, business, out-of-town friends, in-town friends and neighbors, retired, employed, gay, single, married and non-married couples, elderly and young friends. We socialized, ate plenty of cheesy, mouthwatering pizza, munched on green salad and demolished tasty fried chicken and thick, fried potato wedges. Water, soda, beer and wine topped off with the deserts of homemade scrumptious cookies baked by our Christmas Bazaar ladies group.

I gave her eulogy and told hilarious and tender stories about her by using the six pictures on the obituary program as my outline. People laughed as I described her 79 years of living a joyful life with the first picture showing Carol as a young child, fishing rod in hand at Virginia Lakes, California, then her post-Vatican II 1960s portrait in her partial nun habit as an elementary teacher, the 1980s newspaper article photograph of Sister Carol winning a recipe and cooking award, and her 2005 pose at the Philadelphia Phillies baseball game where she flexed her bicep muscles and appeared on a national television commercial. The picture on the back cover illustrated Carol's huge smile about life and "dessert first" philosophy as she prepared to dive into a chocolate cake.

On the large wall-mounted monitor screen, I showed a video of Carol's vibrant and joyful life. *This was your life, sweetie!*

People shared, "How did you meet and know Carol?" They spoke 15 minutes and could have continued for days, but I graciously interrupted them to move the event along.

I shared how she and I met as nuns 40 years ago: "It all began with a phone call and a kiss—"

Then the spirit surprised and moved me to ask, "Would you like to hear about Carol's last month and days of her life?"

"Yes!"

So I shared my heart, crying and stuttering, exclaiming and telling of miracles, God's presence and her peace. People wiped tears with napkins. They laughed, gasped, said amen. It was a Jesus moment as their gazes fixed on me. I wondered if his disciples shared this experience they gathered after Jesus died.

Dan shared how Carol's life modeled love. He heartfully explained how he learned to connect his gay life with the Catholic Church, without guilt, from his upbringing of being an altar boy to an adult reconciling the harder stuff. He complimented Carol for always being kind and direct. He softly choked up, gazed into the crowd, and said, "Her hands and words were always gentle and firm . . . and that is what made her a beautiful person."

Tim described his bond of everlasting friendship with Carol. A bond that will live on in his big heart, filled with precious memories and gifts from her: trust, honesty, strength, hope and happiness. Tim then shared the story of Carol giving him her father's prized bamboo fly fishing rod with the oil from his hands saturated into the rod. I'm sure that for years to come Tim and Angel Carol will fish the rivers and lakes, catching and releasing wild rainbow trout. Fishers of people.

People hung around longer, with contagious tears, giggles, and laughs. It was a holy, happy event! Many people said this was the best memorial celebration they had ever attended.

As a Carol-thing, there was ample left-over food for people to take home in to-go boxes or wrapped in foil. Carol knew the human and divine power of the loaves and the fishes. Even dead, Carol was making smiles bigger.

This event revitalized my laughter and happiness, as Carol lived on in spirit and memories.

Oh, that was the last day I wore my wedding ring, sweetie.

Grief Group Relieve and Release

"On the Road Again" by Willie Nelson and "Grieve Not" by Lori True were heartfelt and faith-packed lyrics that kept me going. Music pushed forward along with the hospice grief group that I attended twice a month.

The only reason I attended the grief groups was to make a new friend. I was surprised that seven of us had recently lost our spouses, including Jenny, whose husband had died five days after Carol. We were experiencing the same stuff simultaneously. Both young and vivacious, we would look into each other's eyes and say, "We can do this!" Our friendship led to weekly hikes together, phone calls, texts, movies together and sharing books and resources.

We lived alone in a quiet, dreary, empty house, but we were not alone.

Taking Carol with Me on the Road

I took my first solo trip on April 11, 2022. It was a biggie for me. My desire was to keep putting one foot in front of the other, so I felt gutsy and exhilarated to embark on a 35-day road trek!

I planned to spend two nights in hotels by myself, to eat in restaurants by myself (not fast food), and to share quality time with family and friends by myself. Yes, without my lover and love of my life, Carol. "I can do this! I want to do this!"

And I did it! Along with many fun adventures and with more to come, this was the beginning of my new life—age 64, healthy, widowed and single.

I was on a mission to show and tell them how much Carol loved each of them. We had sorted and labeled her belongings and she determined which friends and family in Southern California and Arizona would receive: 75-year-old photographs; numerous newspaper clippings highlighting Carol's achievements as a nun and not as a nun; unique artwork; her professional attire—blazers, dresses and skirts, casual, fun and colorful sweaters and psychedelic socks and shoes; musical instruments she played at churches, at retreats and for pleasure, including her harp-sounding omnichord; her favorite books, jewelry, and lovely self-made stained glass hearts and hummingbirds; and knick-knacks from her world travels to Hong Kong and beyond.

Tim guided me as we carefully and methodically stacked, balanced and arranged the cardboard boxes, suitcases, manilla envelopes, See's Candies bags and plastic bins in my SUV cargo areas. Thank goodness for Tim's detailed personality to make sure things would be unloaded in the correct order by the arranged itinerary, dates, times and places. Each container had a handwritten label with the name and destination, secured with packing tape. I planned for the least amount of work for when I arrived at their homes.

As she wished, I transported Carol's collections, honored and peaceful as I transported this loving cargo to the homes of friends and family.

Watch out, FedEx and UPS, Joanie's delivery service is taking over.

Fun and Celebrations

During this healing trek, I celebrated Holy Week and Easter Sunday with Terri at her parish, Saint Martin of Tours Catholic Church in La Mesa, California. There I rested my head and heart, allowing my grief and joy to explode as I sang with their excellent music liturgical director, Frances, a friend from way back in elementary school at St. John the Evangelist.

The first celebration of Carol's resurrection and Easter happened at Terri's and Billy's house, and included coloring, hiding, and finding duck eggs and making our traditional chocolate coconut nests with a colored jellybean on top. My high school friend Ruthie helped Terri make the Easter treats.

With hugs and laughter, we bonded. My new Easter outfit included an orange shirt with two geese that said, "goose bumps" as the birds fist-bump each other with their wings. Perfecto! So much fun! Add the hacky-sack play time, and the gorgeous, warm San Diego weather, and it was an *eggcellent* Easter day.

We all missed Carol, but she lived in our exuberance.

That night in my bedroom, I cried with joy and sorrow. But much, much more JOY! This reminded me of the Native American proverb: Don't let yesterday use up too much of today.

In the morning, sitting alone on my balcony with a mourning cup of coffee, watching the palm trees sway, I sobbed. "This too will pass," I heard my sister Gail's voice in my head, after her dear husband, Jim, died a few years ago.

I celebrated Carol's passion for sporting events by pre-purchasing tickets for San Diego Padres baseball game for Mag, Gail and me.

Gail asked, "Do you know that that game is Out at the Park?"

"No, what does that mean?"

"Oh, Joanie, it means it's gay night."

"Oh, how fun! Are you good with that?"

"Yes, of course! I get to be with you!"

I wished Carol had been there so we could hold hands at a ballpark and not stick out like a sore thumb. That was a dream of dreams. All in God's timing.

I was coming back to life while splurging and eating at many outdoor and indoor California restaurants with Terri, Maggie, Gail, Sister Ruthie, Loni, Melissa, Dan, Armando, Chris, Jamie and even alone.

Next, I drove to Indio to meet with Carol's oldest cherished childhood friends, Suz and another CSJ sister, who delighted me with Carol stories, while I surprised them with Carol's gifts.

Maggie, aka Mag, who had flown from her home in Tucson to San Diego, drove with me 1,000 miles north to Oregon, listening to my expressions of grief. I felt so comfortable talking with Mag, trusting her explicitly!

This trip was a journey of the past, a healing present, and hope for the future—humbly, graciously and spiritually with never-ending love.

Cremation & Freedom

I was excited when I picked up Carol's cremated ashes at the mortuary office. With her ashes squashed into a black box, I felt that we needed to go for a drive to the ocean for fresh air. Just the two of us!

We sat and watched the breaking waves crash, roll and foam onto the shore. Seagulls danced with the wind from the sandy beach to the rocky jetty, chased by a free spirit. Salty tears welled in my eyes, yet smiles and giggles from my soul bounced around in the closed up car. I put Carol—"the box"—on the front dash so we could feel the sunlight. As 20 minutes passed, it felt like 20 years.

"Carol, you are as free as a bird!" I exclaimed. "No worries, no needs, no nonsense. Thank you for our love and life!"

At home, Carol's box sat on the dining room table for one day. We were waiting for the windy weather to change, so I could take her out to sea, hoping to set her free. The winds were not cooperating. Carol's wish of being "dumped into the ocean" from a boat was a lost cause. It was definitely not a Carol thing to be "boxed in."

I called Tim and said, "We need to let Carol out of her cremation box. She needs to be free and travel around the world by sea to spread her joy."

"Joanie, I'll be there. Yes. I'm on my way."

Silly me, that was also my way of saying I needed to move on because she had moved on.

On February 9th, God blessed us with a superb, sweltering-hot day on the coast. I dressed in true Joanie style: black O'Neill shorts, waterproof heavy-duty, duck-rubber boots cuffed at the top, a long-sleeved pink sports blouse and my purple OR (Outdoor Recreation) hat with a black toggle chin strap. Tim wore his long-sleeved mint-green fly-fishing shirt, jeans and tennis shoes. He was emotionally strong and compassionately spirited as he drove five minutes to Crissy Field Beach near the California border.

I removed the plastic bag holding Carol's ashes from the black box and carried her like a golden purse. I was ready in mind, heart and soul— excited to free her from the box and send her on.

As the wind whipped the plastic bag, I held it tight and Tim read a really sweet poem. With my arm around his waist, we stood on the dark-colored, hard beach sand as waves crashed towards us.

He held both of our cell phones with cameras ready, and I bolted to the ocean, splashing into the two-inch-high surf.

I was excited to set her free. To set me free.

Grabbing a handful of Carol's ashes, way more than a smudge on any Ash Wednesday, I threw her into the waves!

"Go, sweetie, go!" I yelled. "I love you and now you are free."

I took another huge handful of her old bones and skin, throwing her further out into the wild Pacific Ocean. "You lived an incredible life, Love, and I thank you."

Then a surprise wave drenched me from my thighs down. As

water gushed into my knee-high boots, I laughed my heart out. Then I quickly dumped more handfuls of her remains.

"Circle the globe and spread your joy!" I yelled into the wind and the sea. For the last little bit, a nun thing to never waste anything, I waved the bag, emptying her final tiny pieces of ash into the now calmer breeze and watched the specs circle onto the clear ocean water near my feet.

Carol, you always made me laugh, and now I can barely walk out of the ocean with my water-filled boots sinking me deeper into the sand. Joy is everywhere, sweetie.

Her ashes had vanished. Laughing, I high-stepped out of quicksand and onto dry land. It was AMAZING. She was now on a world cruise with a new mission to spread joy in a brand new way.

I could visualize people in far-off places, walking beaches and feeling peace and joy. They would speak different languages and wear bright clothes. They would know in their hearts that today was a special day, lovely in the Lord.

I felt so happy, so very happy. Freedom for her and freedom for me. Freedom for all!

My Prayer Journal Entry: May 28th, 2022

Good evening, Jesus. Hi, sweetie pie, Carol. Here comes the tears with loving thoughts of You. Oh, the two of you.

I was so wonderfully surprised last night at 2 a.m. Carol, you called my name: "JOANIE." I heard your voice, it was your voice, and you said, "Come, check this out!"

It was lovely to hear your voice, Carol! So distinctive.

What did you mean, come check this out? Yes, I heard you, love. I feel you. I don't consciously think of you anymore but deep down I know you are always with me. BOTH of you!

I've been teary-eyed the last two days. It's a gift from Jesus that I truly feel other people's PAINS!

What a realization.

It's like I see right into another person's heart and feel their pains. So those people, hurting people, wherever they are, I give them to you, Jesus.

Tonight Lord, I have prayers for the dying, those in pain and I give thanks for LIFE. Thank you, Carol and Jesus, for calling my name.

My Prayer Journal Entry: June 25th, 2022

Thank you, Jesus!

I heard and felt you last night, Carol, as I calmly awoke, then suddenly, I heard your soft walking footsteps!

Carol, you walked through the kitchen, into the hallway and into our bedroom. I knew it was you, Carol, right away. I know the sound of your walk, your cadence, your stride.

It was YOU!

I felt light.

You stared at me as I lay motionless in bed.

I felt a huge smile on my own face.

I did not see you physically, but I felt overwhelming peace and love! How blessed I am to know that you are always with me.

Mom, you were also there with Carol and Jesus.

My Prayer Journal Entry: August 19th, 2022, 9:25 p.m.

Hi Jesus, how are you? Been busy? Thank goodness that you have God and the Holy Spirit to help you out!

Me, too, I'm glad I have all three of you.

Jesus, am I writing the book the way you want it? The way Carol would want it? Jesus, what do you want me to write?

"Tell more stories," Jesus said. **"Your love will shine through better."**

"Oh, OK, I will!"

I pray my heart can speak Your words, Your words, Jesus. Let me be Your fingers, hands and voice!

My Prayer Journal Entry: March 22, 2022

Everything is NEW! Bless my sleep and my dreams; be loving and kind for what's ahead.

I'm so thankful for the hundreds of pictures I have of Carol! Her life was bigger than a book, bigger than a movie.

Jesus, you, too! The Bible is just a glimpse of Your greatness.

While I looked out the front window, the birds were feasting on the wild black berries. I held the "I speak fluent whale" blue coffee mug that Carol had picked out for me just six months before. My heart was curious, but oh so happy that she was in a better place, a place of heavenly freedom and grace.

"How's heaven, Carol?" I enthusiastically asked her aloud as I prayed in our holy prayer corner of the living room, gazing out the large window at a new day of blue sky and wispy white clouds.

Almost instantly, my ears heard her soft gentle voice, distinguished by her giggle and joy, say, **"Joanie, you'll be blown away. Wait 'til you see it! It's AMAZING!"**

Night-night, love! Night-night, Jesus! Xxooxxo

Journal Entry: Lipstick on My Cheek

I awoke this morning, November 22, 2022, with a vivid, colorful, happy dream. I am in a large, brightly lit, multi-colored conference room with lots of laughter, joy, people dressed in colorful clothes—like a party scene, and I hear a mish-mash of adult voices.

My right index finger and long finger are vigorously rubbing my right cheek. My fingers are sliding through slick, gooey, slippery elements of what I think is lipstick. I rubbed my soft fingers slowly over my cheek in circles, over and over, the circles getting bigger and bigger. The tacky substance makes me wonder, "What do I have on my cheek?" It gets caught between my fingers. There's no fragrance and it feels so strange.

A gentle voice says, "When a deceased person is thinking of you, they kiss you." Aha! That must be what is on my cheek! I quickly open my eyes, and I see Carol's glowing face. Her lips—oh my gosh! Her smile loaded with bright, cherry lipstick smeared all over her lips. Really, all over her lips! She looks like a little kid who got into the makeup container. What a mess! I giggle, then I burst into laughter.

I immediately knew she, my deceased but living Carol, had been kissing my cheeks a zillion times. She was thinking of me lots! I laid in bed, not wanting to wake up. I wanted to stay in that moment of red lipstick slobber forever. Then I realized this happens every day around the world to anyone who has lost a loved one. Thank you for this dream, which is really God, alive and well.

I think of you, too, Carol. I know my air kisses reach you as well.

Jesus hold you.
God bless you.

CHAPTER 24
Please Come and Sit With Me

Please come sit and be quiet with me in the garden in June, July, August and September with oodles of rose flowers blooming in all colors, styles and shapes!

Sit here with me on the Hawaiian print padded bench facing the rock creek, staring at the blue metal heron, watching the flowers come to life. Petal by petal, opening from their buds, slow motion, a *National Geographic Special.*

Butchart Gardens in British Columbia, watch out!

Absolutely beautiful! Breathtaking glory, don't you think? Can you see the variety? The plants have hundreds of leaves: dark green, reddish, bright green, pale green and small like a baby's toe and large ones like a teenager's palm.

Sit quietly, watch and feel the gentle breeze move the leaves. Listen to their silence. Listen to them be alive in solitude and peace.

C'mon over here and sit and visit.

Here we are, kicking back in green plastic chairs on the cement patio that is decorated around the edges with Carol's pretty stained-glass pieces.

Soak in the sunshine on your face and shoulders, observe the honeybees buzzing around, flying from one area to the next with their black and yellow bodies with translucent wings and furry heads. Watch the doves land on the ground and *swoosh* when they fly off. You and the roses have Mother Nature's view of it all. Add the bright blue sky to your view.

Oh, look at Stars and Stripes, a rose marbled with pinks and whites. Ahhh, be quiet and look, wow, Daring Spirit, cherry red and a real beauty, and ohhh, lavender Angel Face. Superb! Do you see the Gold Medal Yellow Rose? Astonishing huge blossoms like a big dessert plate! How fun!

Wowie, check out the Rio Samba, bright golden yellow with red edges and some flowers on the same plant that turns pinkish orangish. Delightful! Do you like this one?

Peace and quiet, be still, smell the Alfred Sisley, Double KnockOut, Double Delight, Simply Magnificent, Perfume Delight, Joseph's Coat and the orange rose that smells like a blooming orange orchard. Oh golly, it's like being in an aromatic kitchen. So glad that we have the gift of scent!

This is heavenly sitting here with you.

Thank you for taking the time to sit and be with me.

I hope you are enjoying this lovely afternoon garden.

I love you!

How about you go home with some flowers? One single? A bouquet?

Would you like to give roses to someone?

Reds, yellows, pinks, lavender, white, multi-colored, and FRAGRANT!

Here are the clippers, walk among them and choose.

May the splashing joys of heaven on earth radiate your life.

I have a feeling that your day in heaven will be as beautiful to your loved ones.

Thank you, God, for friends, my favorite things, colors and roses.

Jesus hold you.

God bless you.

ADDENDUM A
Carol's Favorite Recipes, Poetry and Story

CAROL'S FAVORITE RECIPES

Joe's Sour Cream Breakfast Cake

1 ½ cup sugar
2 eggs
1 cup butter or margarine
1 cup sour cream
1 tsp vanilla
2 cups sifted flour
1 tsp baking powder
½ tsp soda

In place of flour, baking powder and soda, use one box yellow cake mix.

Topping:
½ cup finely chopped nuts
½ or 1 tsp cinnamon or nutmeg for Joanie
2 tbs sugar

Cream butter, sugar, add eggs, sour cream, vanilla, baking powder & baking soda. Mix well. Then add sifted flour gradually & mix well. Place dough in angel food pan. Bake at 350 for one hour. Apply topping after baked cake is removed from the pan.

Crepes by Joe Tierheimer, Carol's dad.

Use electric mixer and combine in bowl:
2 cups flour
4 eggs
¼ cup oil

¼ tsp salt
1 tsp sugar
Add 2 cups milk
Heat pan, cover bottom and swirl, use spatula to loosen and flip.
Fill with fresh fruit or fruit spread, squeeze lemon and dust with powdered sugar.

Pork Roast by Carol Tierheimer
1 large onion, sliced

In a bowl mix 1 cup hot water, ¼ white sugar, 3 tbsp red wine vinegar, 1 tbsp ketchup, 2 tbsp soy sauce, ½ tsp salt, ¼ tsp garlic powder, 1 dash hot pepper sauce, ½ tsp ground black pepper, ½ tsp chili powder, 2 tbsp brown sugar.
Rub the mixture on the roast, place onion slices on top of it, then slow-cook for six hours.

Divinity Cookies by Carol Tierheimer
A Christmas treat.

1 cup chocolate chips
¾ cup chopped nuts
3 egg whites
1 cup sugar
½ tsp vanilla
Dash of salt

Break egg whites in top of a double boiler, put sugar, vanilla and salt in the egg whites and beat for 5 minutes. Take off heat. Add nuts and chocolate chips, mix chips but do not stir too much.

Drop on well-greased cookie sheet bake at 250 for 30 minutes.

Cool, put in airtight container and freeze up to 3 months.

You are a very precious person.
Lovely in the Lord Jesus.

ADDENDUM A

CAROL'S ORIGINAL SHORT STORY & POETRY

Downtown

Take the yellow city bus to L.A. downtown.
Get off at Broadway and just walk all around
the streets and stay attuned to all the different sights.
Don't be in any hurry, there's something you might
Miss—people selling salvation near the corner.
The weather-ugly structures all sweating summer
heat, those ancient, relentless sweet sales ladies
pushing merchandise that piles, "How 'bout green daisies.
All woven in a rug," magazine stands cluttered.
Constant flows of depressed, broken people, battered
beyond repair, walk tightly amid solitude
cramming pizza, licking ice cream. Do not exclude
the shuffle, rustle, groans or the aimless chatter
recognizable from the human sea, later
you take the L.A. city bus away from town
waging war on thoughts you never would have found
unless you had taken the yellow city bus to . . .

The Rainbow Dance

Last week the rainbow
danced in the meadows
while the applause of the
Forest trees brought
The mountains to their feet.

ADDENDUM B
Our Joy

It was so much JOY when WE . . . Carol and Joanie . . .

. . . played guitar at mass . . . baked Joe's sour cream cake
. . . had friends come over to play Hand and Foot Card game
. . . went clothes shopping . . . played Rummy Tiles with just us
. . . shared a big hamburger and fries . . . painted our kitchen orange
. . . watched *Jeopardy* and got one correct . . . fell asleep
. . . hosted the neighborhood Christmas gatherings . . . solved problems
. . . missed each other in the middle of the day . . . sang before meals
. . . dyed your hair . . . the phone rang and it was you . . . held hands
. . . laughed so hard our jaws hurt . . . cut each other's hair . . . took drives
. . . danced in the kitchen . . . sang solos to each other . . . wrote love notes
. . . baked chocolate chip cookies . . . smiled at each other
. . . went to medical appointments . . . washed cars...
. . . cried in each other's arms . . . visited family . . . read scripture
. . . had races to the swimming pool . . . went for walks in our neighborhood
. . . sat in silence and tranquility . . . massages to your feet and my shoulders
. . . giggled so as to not be heard . . . saw each other enjoying friends
. . . moved furniture for a new look . . . wrote cards together . . . slept in
. . . stared at Mother Nature . . . fished . . . bought our house . . .
. . . did dishes . . . disagreed but listened to another point of view
. . . kissed and hugged . . . shared laundry and folded each other's clothes

... shared a margarita with two straws ... were spontaneous
... went on cruise ships ... trusted one another to make a decision
... gently embraced ... trusted God and all was wonderful
... wore umbrella hats in the hot tub ... promises came true from God
... shared meals ... went to concerts, plays and sports games
... played Mexican Train game with friends ... hugged a redwood tree ...
... decorated for Christmas ... went to mass together ... planted bulbs
... went out to dinner and ordered dessert first ... ate dim sum ... BBQ'd
... moved to Brookings ... showered ... picked apples
... took and posed for pictures ... talked to the ducks ... flew on airplanes
... complimented each other ... relied on each other ... played tennis
... sat in the sun ... got lost and had to make u turns ... met face to face
... burst into song ... thought the same thing at the same time
... told each other "I love you."....deep kissed ... helped others
... rode ATV's in the sand dunes ... bought and learned a computer
... test drove cars ... explored roads ... paid bills ... thought big
... patiently waited in lines ... testified in court ... visited jails
... visited other churches ... spoke up for people
... did the honest and right thing ... believed in goodness
... ate fajitas and shrimp cocktails ... won at the horse races
... caught fish ... caught crab ... caught clams ... ate them
... encouraged others to be their best ... didn't burn bridges
... made delicious soups to share ... invited people over
... prayed ... cuddled ... hoped
... rode a subway ... met people ... woke up every day ...
... made lots of phone calls to family and friends ... picked flowers
... screwed up and said, "I'm sorry."....forgave each other

. . . went grocery shopping together . . . wore our commitment wedding rings
. . . traveled on vacations . . . carved pumpkins . . . made rocky road candy
. . . got married and said "I do" . . . celebrated other people's wedding days . . .
. . . treated others with kindness . . . listened and lifted friends up
. . . walked and talked with Jesus everyday . . . showed you "I love you"
. . . lived life to the max, smiled big and wore bright colors.

Jesus hold you.
God bless you.

Big hugs and love,

Joanie

About the Authors

JOANIE LINDENMEYER

Joanie Lindenmeyer is a former Catholic nun and retired teacher and coach who enjoys playing and watching sports, traveling, fishing, gardening, playing guitar, listening to music, hiking and walking, baking treats and hanging out with family and friends.

Filled with joy and hope, she believes Jesus is her best friend.

In 1982, she met Carol Tierheimer and they married on August 5, 2020.

Raised in San Diego, California, she taught Physical Education and Health in public high school for 25 years, after teaching Religion and P.E. for four years in Catholic elementary schools. She retired in 2018.

She coached boys and girls sports teams for 20 years.

Joanie worked at two nonprofits and a county Department of Health in areas of community health, addictions, teen pregnancy, sexuality, child abuse prevention, HIV/AIDS prevention, STI testing and counseling, and wellness.

A San Diego State University graduate, she was a member of the university volleyball team and has a California teaching credential.

She was a Catholic Sister of St. Joseph of Carondelet, ministering in many ways.

Her dedication shines to people of all ages, making their lives brighter, happier and healthier. She was committed to her one and only, lifetime lover and spouse of 40 years and is a recent widow.

Joanie and Carol Tierheimer began writing *Nun Better: An AMAZING Love Story* together in the Brookings, Oregon home they shared for 31 years.

CAROL TIERHEIMER

Carol Tierheimer was a former Catholic nun who devoted her life's work to spreading the joy and peace of Jesus while dedicating her heart and soul to her 40-year lovefest with Joanie Lindenmeyer.

Carol loved the majestic beauty of Mother Nature, as well as wearing bright clothes, singing, dancing and embarking on adventures, near and far, with Joanie.

Raised in Los Angeles, California, Carol graduated from St. Mary's Academy as a "blue tie" and entered the Sisters of St. Joseph of Carondelet (CSJ), Los Angeles Providence. Then Sister Veronica Joseph (Carol) enthusiastically began ministry in elementary education.

With her love of music and exceptional talent, she learned and taught guitar plus she developed youth folk groups in parishes and schools including Del Mar, Sonoma, and the Valley. Missioned to Lewiston, Idaho, St. Stanislaus Parish, she provided Adult Ed, RCIA, home-bound visitations, liturgy planning and marriage annulments, and served as the "parish Sister" where she did everything but say the Mass. Hand in hand with the Jesuit priests, she made a huge impact for all.

She moved to Aberdeen, Washington as a parish sister and then Portland, Oregon, where she was the Jesuit Volunteer Regional Director for Alaska. In Brookings, she worked at South Coast Employment Center.

Carol earned her Master's Degree from Fairfield University in Psychology, Counseling and Spirituality, her true gifts. She visited and cared for people in all kinds of situations, needs and circumstances. She was never too busy for a friend and everyone was her friend. Joy, confidence, and love were her daily devotions to all, from bishops to beggars.

Carol loved and encouraged everyone to be their best. In 1982, she met Joanie Lindenmeyer and they married on August 5, 2020. Together they grew more in love with each other and life.

Throughout Carol's life, she devoted herself to helping people to be their "very best self" through her kindness, compassion and joy. This devotion was evident in her actions, jobs and the myriad of organizations she was a part of. People witnessed her humility, wisdom and intuition through her personal relationship with God, Jesus and the Holy Spirit. Carol lived by Proverbs 3:5: "Trust in the Lord with all your heart."

After Carol went to heaven on January 30, 2022, a rose garden was planted and continues to bloom in memory of her joyous, happy spirit in the front yard of the home she shared with Joanie for 31 years.

CPSIA information can be obtained
at www.ICGtesting.com
Printed in the USA
JSHW030143080323
38621JS00001B/1